2,000 years of Christianity

Published in Great Britain in 1999 by
Society for Promoting Christian Knowledge,
Holy Trinity Church,
Marylebone Road,
London NW1 4DU.

First published in the UK by The Daily Telegraph.
Copyright © 1999 Telegraph Group Limited.

British Library Cataloguing-in-Publication Data

A catalogue record for this book is available from
the British Library.

ISBN 0-281-05287-5

Printed and bound in Spain by Book Print, SL,
Barcelona.

The Daily Telegraph

AD

2,000 years of Christianity

Edited by Christopher Howse

Early Christian graffiti from the catacombs of St Callistus in Rome, showing the Chi-Rho (right) and the fish or *ichthus*, opposite. (Photograph by Haydn Denman)

Hollywood called it "The Greatest Story Ever Told", and it was not wrong. The history of Christianity contains the elements of everything that ever sold a newspaper or made a reader turn a page. When we serialised this book for readers in the spring of 1999, their response was unprecedented. Here is war and peace, love and hate, courage and weakness. Here are extremes of tenderness and self-sacrifice, and extremes of brutality and barbarism, so much that is noble and beautiful, so much that is squalid and sad.

As Jesus himself foretold, people will always disagree about the religion which bears his name. But none can deny its extraordinary importance. In most of the world, we measure our years from the (notional) date of his birth. As we enter the 2000th year, we naturally ask why. This book helps give the bones of an answer.

The story means different things to different people. For some, it is the tale of our whole civilisation, the historical DNA which contains the structure of why we, in the West, are as we are. For others, it is a journey of the mind and spirit, an encounter with the most interesting things that have been known and thought in the world. For others still, it is a vast human and aesthetic drama. For all those who call themselves Christians, it is the story of how men and women have tried to deal with the promise of the Way, the Truth, the Life.

For everyone, as the Third Millennium dawns, this is the tale of our time.

Charles Moore
Editor, The Daily Telegraph

Contents

2,000 Years of Christianity

On special occasions such as a wedding or a funeral Christianity features naturally in British life. It is so familiar that it is easy to overlook. We are surrounded by Christian cultural history yet we often do not know why it is there

Christianity today

REUTERS

AD is how we date our newspapers: 1999, 2000, 2001. We take *Anno Domini* – the year of the Lord – for granted. In the same way, the Christian origins of much of British culture are invisible to us because they are so familiar. More than 32 million people in Britain watched the funeral of Diana Princess of Wales in Westminster Abbey live on television – far more than the numbers going regularly to church. They heard the BBC Singers singing *Requiem aeternam dona eis Domine*. As in the photograph opposite they saw things that seemed familiar but remained unexplained. Why do the clergymen wear long, coloured robes (copes)? Why is the nave where the coffin-bearers are standing separated from the altar by a stone screen? On a pillar on the left is a picture of the Virgin Mary and the child Jesus, with candles each side – where did that tradition start? Why is it called an abbey in the first place?

There are about 1,760 million people in the world who adhere to Christianity. In Britain 54 per cent of the population "practically never" go to church. But more than six million people regard themselves as members of one of the main churches, compared to 580,000 who regard themselves as Muslims or 94,000 who regard themselves as Jews.

Yet anyone who visits an art gallery, listens to classical music, reads old books, likes English architecture or the shapes of our old towns finds himself understanding things within the cultural framework of Christianity. Christianity has been around in Britain for a long time. Christians must have come when the Roman legions were still here. The history of the intervening Christian centuries around the world is an extraordinary one.

More than half the nation watched the funeral of Diana Princess of Wales live on television. Apart from *Candle in the Wind*, much of the service seemed vaguely familiar, yet never thoroughly explained. What was that piece by John Tavener that the choir sung? What about *Bread of Heaven*, familiar from rugby matches? The peal of bells was muffled, but why are there bells at the Abbey at all? If it comes to that, who built the Abbey and why?

CHAPTER ONE

AD 1-400

The starting point

The starting point of Christianity is the resurrection of Jesus Christ. That is the event to which his 12 Apostles and disciples acted as witnesses. Their account of his life, crucifixion and resurrection from the dead preceded the compilation of the Gospels and the other writings in Greek that we now call the New Testament.

But an example of how a follower of Jesus might put things is given in the report of a speech by Peter, the chief of the Apostles. This is included in the book called the Acts of the Apostles, seemingly written by Luke the author of his own gospel. In the English translation dating from 1611 given in the King James Bible the speech begins:

"Jesus of Nazareth, a man approved of God among you by miracles and wonders and signs, which God did by him in the midst of you, as ye yourselves also know; him, being delivered by the determinate counsel and foreknowledge of God, ye have taken, and by wicked hands have crucified and slain: Whom God hath raised up, having loosed the pains of death; because it was not possible that he be holden of it. For David speaketh concerning him, I foresaw the Lord always before my face, for he is on my right hand, that I should not be moved: therefore did my heart rejoice and my tongue be glad; moreover also my flesh shall rest in hope: because thou wilt not leave my soul in hell, neither wilt to suffer thy Holy One to see corruption."

The archaic English sounds good but does not make things too clear, particularly in the passage about not being moved. But three things are obvious in Peter's approach. First he claims that Jesus is risen from the dead, and he, Peter, is a witness of it. Secondly that Jesus proved himself the chosen one of God by miracles and signs. Thirdly that Jesus fulfills prophecies in holy scripture (here the Psalms) about the coming of the Messiah. ("Christ" is merely the Greek version of the Hebrew "Messiah", meaning "anointed".)

It is not the purpose of this historical book, *AD*, to prove the truth of the Gospels. But the contents of the Gospels, and the beliefs of those who contributed to them, may be taken as underlying the history of Christianity. The speech of Peter quoted above is recorded as taking place on Pentecost morning. Pentecost takes its name from a Jewish feast that occurred 50 days after Passover. It was, therefore, about 50 days after the resurrection of Jesus. Since then, Peter testified, Jesus had risen, and eaten and drunk with them. Now he had been taken up to heaven.

The Apostles were, they were convinced, the 12 men chosen by Jesus as his special disciples; the word Apostle is from the Greek for "messenger". The Apostles were conscious of the status; after the defection of Judas, who had hanged himself after betraying Jesus, they cast lots to choose a replacement. After the ascension of Jesus to heaven (40 days after his resurrection) they had spent their time in prayer, along with Mary the mother of Jesus and the other women followers.

On this Pentecost day the Apostles experienced the sound of a mighty rushing wind and what looked like tongues of fire coming down upon them. This, Peter told the crowd immediately afterwards, was the coming of the Holy Spirit foretold in scripture.

Soon after Pentecost, Peter and John, having gone to the Temple to pray, heal a lame man in the name of Jesus. In a speech to the astonished crowd outside the Temple, Peter stresses that the miracle is not done by his own power, but by God in order to demonstrate the divine stature of Jesus.

"The God of Abraham, and of Isaac, and of Jacob, the God of our fathers hath glorified his Son Jesus; whom ye delivered up, and denied him in the presence of Pilate," Peter says. He admits that his audience and their rulers acted out of ignorance, but now Jesus has risen, they must repent "that your sins may be blotted out". As Jews, God has chosen them to witness the fulfilment of old prophecies, "according to the covenant which God made with our fathers, saying unto Abraham, And in thy seed shall all the kindreds of the earth be blessed". But these words merely enrage the guardians of the Temple, and Peter and John are brought before the council (where they assert that Jesus, the saviour of all mankind, is the stone rejected by the builders who has become the corner stone) and are imprisoned. They escape by a providential intervention.

This is a pattern for events in the first years of Christianity: preaching, miraculous healing, arguments with the religious establishment, imprisonment, and, sooner or later, martyrdom. Meanwhile the number of followers grows.

Christ in Majesty from the apse of Sant Climent de Taüll in a valley of the Pyrenees, northeastern Spain. The figure of the resurrected Christ, the cornerstone of Christian religion, was the powerful focal point of early church decoration. This painting is in the Romanesque collection of the Museum of Catalan Art in Barcelona.

Enter Paul

The other Apostles hardly knew what had hit them when this persecutor of Jesus's followers joined them and told them they must change

The entry, like a whirlwind, of the energetic personality of Paul transformed the shape of Christianity. It would be impossible to imagine Christianity without him. Yet, unlike the other Apostles, he never knew Jesus during his life in Palestine. His own conversion from a leading persecutor of the early followers of Jesus Christ to an essential shaper of the Church is one of the most remarkable stories in history.

Paul did not invent Christianity, but he was the first to give it a theology. The centre of his thought is Christology, for it draws out the implications of the person and work of Jesus. He calls Jesus "Lord" at least 250 times, more than any other title. "Who art thou, Lord?" he asks when blinded on the road to Damascus.

Paul explains his understanding of Jesus, the Son of God, succinctly in his letter to the Church at Philippi (in northern Greece). Christ Jesus, he says, though he possessed the form of God, did not hold on to his equality with God, but took on the form of a servant, as a man. He humbled himself further, becoming obedient unto death, even to death on a cross. So God the Father has exalted him, so that at the name of Jesus every knee should bend. Therefore we should work out salvation with fear and trembling, for it is God who works in us.

There is, of course, more to Paul's theology than that. And apart from thinking, he acted. He was convinced he had been sent to bring to the Gentiles the possibility of Christ living mystically in them. He is always using the phrase "through Christ Jesus", as a sort of touchstone for the right way of acting. To build up a Church composed of people who accepted the new teaching, he undertook journeys totalling more than 8,000 miles. They were amazingly successful. When he told people about Jesus, hundreds became his followers. If these new communities got into difficulties, Paul stepped in with undoubting authority and sorted them out, in person or by letter.

Paul contrasted the freedom brought by Jesus with the slavery and futility of living under the old law of Judaic practice. That is obvious. But he was also challenging the pretensions of the Roman Imperial cult. In the world of his time everyone was enjoined to celebrate the Emperor's birthday or the anniversary of his accession; this was spoken of as his "epiphany" as a god manifest. The god-emperor was expected to bring *charis* (favour) and *soteria* (salvation). Paul looks for favour (or grace) and salvation only from Jesus, the Messiah.

On the road in wild lands

Paul started out as a scholar who could earn a living by making tents. He ended up travelling for years, thousands of miles round the Mediterranean, imposing his own vision of what Christianity should be

F.H.C. BIRCH/SONIA HALLIDAY PICTURES

Paul would have had to go through this narrow pass in the Taurus mountains (above), called the Cilician Gates, as he travelled through Asia Minor. His home city of Tarsus owed some of its importance to its strategic position to the south of this pass. But it was a notorious haunt for bandits, who would prey on merchants or isolated travellers. This may have been in Paul's mind when he wrote in his second letter to Corinth of being "in perils of robbers, in perils of my own countrymen, in perils by the heathen, in perils in the city, in perils in the wilderness"

There is much that remains unknown about Paul's life – just like the lives of many of his secular contemporaries. How the evidence, chiefly in the Acts of the Apostles and the letters of Paul, is interpreted has often depended on sectarian prejudices.

We know he was born in Tarsus, in the first decade of the Christian era. Tarsus was the prosperous capital of the Roman Province of Cilicia, now south-eastern Turkey; it was where Cleopatra was rowed in her barge like a burnished throne. Saul, as he was called, was the son of a highly religious Jewish family, speaking Aramaic at home and Greek outside. As a youth he was sent to Jerusalem to become a master of the Law. In conformity with the Talmud, the Jewish code of lving, he also learnt a trade, as a tent-maker. As an adult he became one of the most zealous persecutors of the first Christians, who were viewed by the Jewish establishment as heretics or worse.

While on the road to Damascus, where he intended to bring Christians to trial, he experienced a blinding light, fell to the ground and heard the voice of Jesus saying: "Saul, Saul, why do you persecute me?"

The change that came over him was profound and absolute. His immediate reaction, however, was to spend a long period of isolation in Arabia. He then felt able to work on his own account in Damascus.

After three years there he fell foul of the local ruler and, escaping over the walls in a basket, went to Jerusalem, where he sought out Peter, the leader of Jesus's first followers, and James, who was a close relation of Jesus's and the head of the Christian community in Jerusalem. Despite the fear and suspicion that his reputation as a persecutor provoked,

there was a Jewish community, and a synagogue where Paul would often begin his preaching.

There were three main tours made by Paul. To many nowadays who have learnt about them at school they remain a tangled skein of dotted lines on a map sown with unfamiliar names. The journey to Greece, known as the second missionary journey, is shown on the map on the next page.

The first journey, with Barnabas, took them both to Cyprus and then to a number of towns in what is now southern Turkey. Paul returned to Antioch where he had an enormous row with Peter and "withstood him to the face". Though Peter had already recognised the validity of inviting Gentiles to become Christians, now, while staying in Antioch, he refused on ritual grounds, under pressure from supporters of James, to eat with Christians who were not of Jewish descent. Paul considered this refusal to be utterly wrong. He felt it went against a central point of Christ's teachings, namely that salvation was for all.

Paul continued his relentless travelling. After the second missionary journey, he made a third tour, returning to the churches of Asia Minor, Macedonia and Greece. He was much preoccupied during this tour with the bad news from the Church at Corinth, where there were three main problems: sexual morality, the ritual behaviour proper to a Gentile, and the partisan spirit of followers of church leaders.

By this time, the Jews in Jerusalem had grown to loathe Paul and if it had not been for his arrest by Roman soldiers, he would probably have been lynched in the streets. His Roman citizenship guaranteed him official protection, and with rumours circulating of a plot to murder him, the Roman authorities decided to put him out of harm's way in Caesarea.

He was kept in prison in Caesarea for two years, until in 60 the procurator of Caesarea decided to send him back to Jerusalem for trial. Paul avoided this by appealing to Caesar and a trial in Rome. His journey to Rome was interrupted by a shipwreck off Malta. The ship ran aground, its stern was smashed by high seas. A centurion saved Paul and the other prisoners by ordering the soldiers not to kill them. They got ashore on broken timber from the ship. There, gathering sticks for a fire, Paul was bitten by a viper; the barbarians saw this as a sure sign he was a wicked man, but when he came to no harm they took him for a god. At last in Rome, where the account of the Acts of the Apostles breaks off, he lived at his own expense under house arrest for two years and was able to write further letters to Christian communities.

he was accepted as a genuine Apostle of Jesus. Paul withdrew again from the Church in Jerusalem and began to spread his doctrine about Jesus in his native Cilicia, and then, with Barnabas, made his headquarters Antioch, in Syria. It was in Antioch that the followers of Jesus first became known as Christians, and it was there that large numbers of non-Jewish followers were recruited. Paul took Barnabas with him when, in AD49, he went to Jerusalem to attempt to heal, by consulting the Church leaders there, serious divisions about how far followers of Jesus need conform to Judaic practices.

He left the consultation, later known as the Council of Jerusalem, with a clear mandate from James, Peter and John to preach among the non-Jewish heathen, the Gentiles. For the next decade, until his arrest in 58, Paul travelled ceaselessly throughout the eastern Mediterranean, from Antioch to Greece, setting up Christian communities and then revisiting them. By sea and through mountainous territory he travelled for years, in danger from bandits in the wilds and from religious opponents in the cities. Two things made his travels possible at all. First, the Pax Romana held sway; throughout the Roman Empire there were established highways. Paul was proud to be a Roman citizen. Secondly, ever since Alexander the Great (356-323BC) had first encouraged Jewish traders to settle in his new Hellenic towns, the Jewish diaspora had grown swiftly. In every large town of the Empire

Paul visits Peter in prison in the fresco detail above by the Filippino Lippi (c1457-1504). The double portrait reflects the status of the two men as Apostles, but the incident is entirely without historical foundation, deriving from the immensely popular medieval collection of saints' stories called the *Golden Legend*. According to this story, Peter was imprisoned by Theophilus, Prefect of Antioch, until Paul rescued him by telling Theophilus that the prisoner could raise his son from the dead. This he did.

Paul is shown being bitten by a viper in a wall-painting (*right*) in St Anselm's chapel in Canterbury. This story is in the historically reliable Acts of the Apostles. The snake had been hiding in twigs that Paul had gathered to make a fire after a shipwreck. When the bite caused no harm he was taken for a god by his companions

Paul's journey to Europe

The most important of Paul's four epic missions was the second, illustrated here, undertaken around AD51 and lasting four years. Travelling up through Asia to Greece (then the Roman provinces of Macedonia and Achaea), he brought Christianity to Europe. He was accompanied by Silas, a leading member of the church of Jerusalem, and Timothy, whom they met on the way. Paul's missionary strategy was systematic. He would target the larger towns, hoping to set up Christian communities from which his teaching would trickle into outlying areas. He used the local synagogue to make his first stand, preaching to any Jews who would listen. Eventually he would be thrown out of the synagogue for his heretical preaching, at which point he would found a new church with his latest converts making up the first congregations. He would remain in the city, building up the congregation, until the orthodox Jews drove him away.

In Greece there were not always synagogues, so Paul sometimes preached to the gentiles in the open. Athens was no exception. Philosophers in this cosmopolitan and relatively open-minded city invited him to speak before them so that they could consider what he had to say. Their reaction was not, on the whole, favourable. Afterwards he settled for nearly two years in Corinth, teaching and writing.

The journey is recorded in the New Testament in the Acts of The Apostles.

6 Philippi
Paul, Silas and Timothy arrive in Europe at Philippi, the city founded by Philip of Macedon (359-336bc), father of Alexander the Great. They cause such a stir that they are flogged and imprisoned, but an earthquake bursts open the prison doors.
(Acts 16: 11-14)

7 Thessalonica
Paul preaches in the synagogue at Thessalonica but a mob hired by some Jews "set all the city on an uproar "and they are forced to flee in secret.
(Acts 17: 1-9)

8 Berea
At Berea they receive better treatment, but word reaches Thessalonica. Jews arrive and stir up dissent. Paul sets for Athens, leaving Silas and Timothy behind.
(Acts 17: 10-15)

9 Athens
Paul arrives in Athens, converses with some Stoic and Epicurean philosophers and is taken to the Areopagus below the Acropolis. Paul speaks about Jesus and the resurrection of the dead, an idea many laugh at, but "certain men clave unto him and believed".
(Acts 17: 16-34)

Roman towns and provinces in the eastern Mediterranean at the time of Paul's journeys

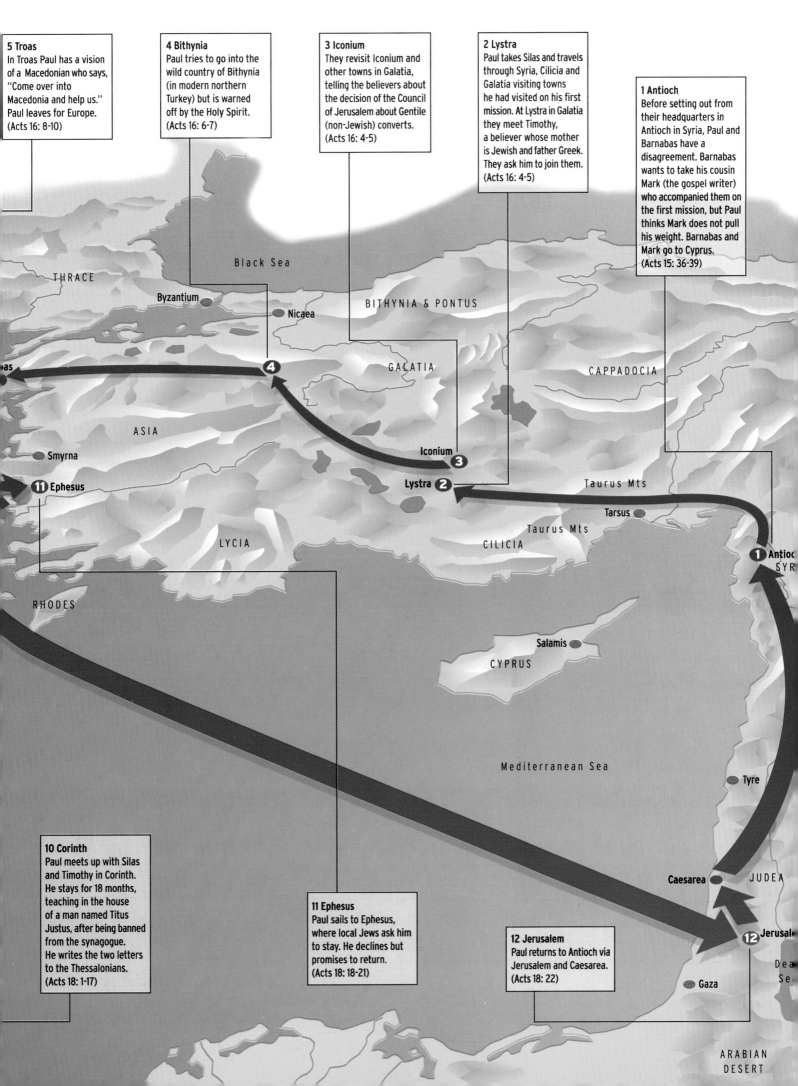

5 Troas
In Troas Paul has a vision of a Macedonian who says, "Come over into Macedonia and help us." Paul leaves for Europe. (Acts 16: 8-10)

4 Bithynia
Paul tries to go into the wild country of Bithynia (in modern northern Turkey) but is warned off by the Holy Spirit. (Acts 16: 6-7)

3 Iconium
They revisit Iconium and other towns in Galatia, telling the believers about the decision of the Council of Jerusalem about Gentile (non-Jewish) converts. (Acts 16: 4-5)

2 Lystra
Paul takes Silas and travels through Syria, Cilicia and Galatia visiting towns he had visited on his first mission. At Lystra in Galatia they meet Timothy, a believer whose mother is Jewish and father Greek. They ask him to join them. (Acts 16: 4-5)

1 Antioch
Before setting out from their headquarters in Antioch in Syria, Paul and Barnabas have a disagreement. Barnabas wants to take his cousin Mark (the gospel writer) who accompanied them on the first mission, but Paul thinks Mark does not pull his weight. Barnabas and Mark go to Cyprus. (Acts 15: 36-39)

10 Corinth
Paul meets up with Silas and Timothy in Corinth. He stays for 18 months, teaching in the house of a man named Titus Justus, after being banned from the synagogue. He writes the two letters to the Thessalonians. (Acts 18: 1-17)

11 Ephesus
Paul sails to Ephesus, where local Jews ask him to stay. He declines but promises to return. (Acts 18: 18-21)

12 Jerusalem
Paul returns to Antioch via Jerusalem and Caesarea. (Acts 18: 22)

Jerusalem and Rome

Jesus and his followers were all Jews, and Jerusalem was the natural centre for early Christians.
But growing frictions and an unlooked-for catastrophe moved the focus to Rome

Jerusalem was taken for granted as the centre for the followers of Jesus in the years after the first Pentecost. This was the ancient home of the Jewish religion. King David had made his capital here around the 10th century BC. Here too the Ark of the Covenant containing the tablets of the Law, which had been carried around while the Jews were nomadic people, had found its resting place. They were not to know that it would be utterly destroyed by troops of the Emperor Titus in AD70.

By Paul's day the city was a flourishing commercial and administrative centre, as well as being the headquarters and place of pilgrimage for Judaism, a religion that had fanned out across the Empire through its large population in diaspora. The Temple had been rebuilt by King Herod by 63 on such a lavish scale that it became one of the extraordinary architectural attractions of the whole Roman Empire.

The Temple was a city within a city. It employed thousands of staff from priests and guards to scribes and dogsbodies, and every day, within its gigantic, smoky sacrificial enclosure, countless cattle were ritually slaughtered. The Temple and its fearsome God were concerned with no one but the Jews.

But of course Jesus was a Jew, as were his disciples. Paul was a Jew in the Pharisaic tradition, but it was his belief that Jesus's message of salvation was for all people that provoked trouble quite quickly. In AD49, after 16 years of preaching in the Jordan valley and the region around Antioch in Syria, Paul travelled to the holy city to meet Jesus's remaining disciples and take part in what later became known as the Council of Jerusalem.

The question was: did new Christians have to undergo circumcision and follow the Jewish law? Some people had come down to Antioch from Jerusalem insisting that the converts of Paul and Barnabas should be circumcised, as in the law of Moses. Peter had already had plenty of trouble himself with the Sadducee party who protected the interests of the Temple against his novel teachings. And Peter had already accepted (as represented in his dream at Joppa of animals, clean and unclean, let down in a sheet) that such provisions as clean and unclean meat did not bind Christians.

Paul, in his letter to the Galatians, records the result of his conference with the leaders of the Church in Jerusalem: "When James, Cephas [Peter], and John, who seemed to be pillars, perceived the grace that was given unto me, they gave me and Barnabas the right hands of fellowship; that we should go unto the heathen, and they unto the circumcision."

James was the leader of the Church in Jerusalem by virtue of his family relationship with Jesus; Peter was consulted by Paul as the rock on which Jesus said he would build the Church; and John, "the Beloved Disciple" who became the author of a Gospel, was clearly respected as an Apostle of great standing. Some have tried to represent Paul as a champion of a Gentile point of view, opposed by the Judaeo-Christians of Jerusalem. But Paul remained a Jew, and the Church in Jerusalem resisted the pressure of un-named Judaisers for an extension of Jewish law to Gentile Christians. They imposed no more obligation on Gentile converts than to abstain from food sacrificed to idols, from the meat of strangled animals and from "fornication" (possibly a provision about marriage between close relatives, rather than the common meaning). What Paul insisted on preserving was "our liberty which we have in Jesus Christ". For his part, as a practical gesture of unity, Paul undertook to collect money from the Gentile communities to support the Church in Jerusalem.

But for anyone who still identified himself as a practising Jew, the refusal of Gentile Christians to accept circumcision, and everything that went with it, inevitably meant separation. Gentiles were not allowed beyond their own court in the Temple compound, for example. Paul had been seen in the city of Jerusalem with Trophimus, a Greek-speaking Ephesian. When Paul was spotted later in the Temple it was assumed that Trophimus was still with him. This accusation against Paul that he had tried covertly to introduce a Gentile into the Temple caused him continuing trouble.

The Church in Jerusalem remained in status and influence by far the most important church. In AD66, the Jewish war began. The brave but hopeless revolt against Roman rule culminated in 70 with the destruction of Jerusalem, the desecration of the Temple, the massacre of thousands and the practical end of the Christian Church in Jerusalem. Christianity would have to grow in new ground. The political centrality of Rome, vitally reinforced by the founding energies of Peter and Paul, who had ended their lives there, ensured that the city replaced Jerusalem as the focus of Christianity.

In this painting of the stoning of Stephen by Gentile da Fabriano (c1370-1427), the martyr is wearing the traditional vestment of a deacon derived from Roman dress. Stephen was the first of the Seven Deacons appointed by the Apostles. Little is known of the other six, except that all had Greek names

BELOW, FROM LEFT: HAYDN DENMAN, BRIDGEMAN ART LIBRARY, BRIDGEMAN ART LIBRARY, SONIA HALLIDAY

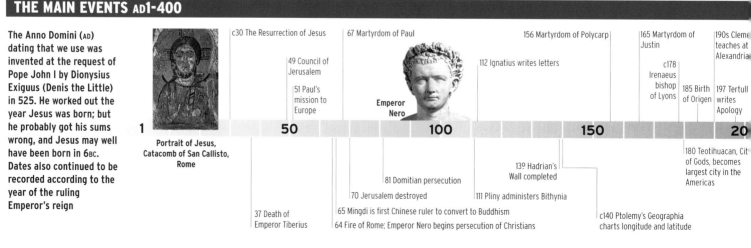

THE MAIN EVENTS AD1-400

The Anno Domini (AD) dating that we use was invented at the request of Pope John I by Dionysius Exiguus (Denis the Little) in 525. He worked out the year Jesus was born; but he probably got his sums wrong, and Jesus may well have been born in 6BC. Dates also continued to be recorded according to the year of the ruling Emperor's reign

Portrait of Jesus, Catacomb of San Callisto, Rome

Emperor Nero

c30 The Resurrection of Jesus

49 Council of Jerusalem

51 Paul's mission to Europe

67 Martyrdom of Paul

112 Ignatius writes letters

156 Martyrdom of Polycarp

165 Martyrdom of Justin

c178 Irenaeus bishop of Lyons

185 Birth of Origen

190s Clement teaches at Alexandria

197 Tertull writes Apology

1   50   100   150   20

37 Death of Emperor Tiberius

81 Domitian persecution

70 Jerusalem destroyed

65 Mingdi is first Chinese ruler to convert to Buddhism

64 Fire of Rome; Emperor Nero begins persecution of Christians

111 Pliny administers Bithynia

139 Hadrian's Wall completed

c140 Ptolemy's Geographia charts longitude and latitude

180 Teotihuacan, Cit of Gods, becomes largest city in the Americas

Peter and Paul die in Rome

In the eyes of future generations of Christians, the tensions between Peter and Paul were reconciled by their common martyrdom, on the model of Stephen's.

Paul, we know, was sent to Rome for trial. Rome was badly damaged by fire in AD64, under Nero. Paul was probably executed in 67 in the Neronian persecution. Peter's name was from the earliest times linked with Paul's as the founding martyrs of the Church in Rome. In about 180 Irenaeus writes that "the universally known church was founded and organised at Rome by the two most glorious Apostles, Peter and Paul."

When state persecution waned and a public church could be built on the site reputed as Peter's grave, the great basilica constructed by the Emperor Constantine was dug into the hillside to ensure its closeness to the holy spot associated with the cult of Peter. In the 1940s early Christian graffiti was found in the remains of a pagan cemetery under the high altar of St Peter's, the grand church that in the 16th century replaced Constantine's. The graffiti are on a red wall behind which Peter's tomb must lie. St Paul had his own basilica outside the walls.

Stephen becomes the first Christian martyr

Stephen was the first Christian martyr. As a witness to Jesus ready to die for his beliefs he became a model for a whole way of Christian thinking in the succeeding centuries. The account of his trial and death is given in the Acts of the Apostles.

Stephen had been chosen by the Apostles as one of the "seven men of honest report" given the job of distributing alms or food. These Seven Deacons all have Greek names, like Stephen's. They were appointed after complaints from the Greek-speaking Jews with whom champions of the Temple cult found such bitter fault. These Hellenists said that their dependants had been neglected in the distribution of alms in favour of the Hebrews. It is clear that among early followers of Jesus some followed Jewish law scrupulously; others stressed the new dispensation to Gentiles as well as Jews. Stephen's Hellenism made the charge brought against him more plausible – that he used "blasphemous words against this holy place [the Temple] and the law".

Stephen certainly held, as Paul was to, that the teaching of Jesus went beyond the Jewish law. Stephen's own view of the place of Jesus in Jewish history is given in the speech at his trial in the Acts of the Apostles. This speech itself was found blasphemous, and Stephen was stoned to death. Paul, still under the name Saul, makes his first appearance in the Bible at Stephen's martyrdom. Jewish law dictated that anyone who bore witness against a criminal was obliged to throw the first stones. Cloaks of those who stepped forward to cast the first stones were guarded by "a young man named Saul".

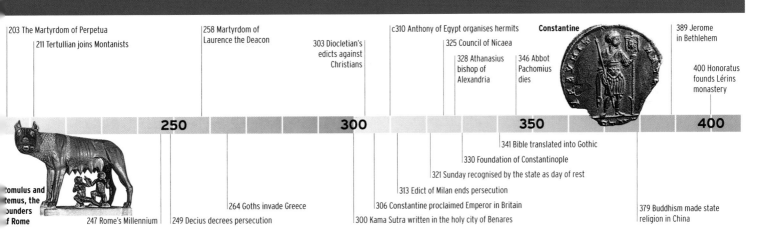

203 The Martyrdom of Perpetua

211 Tertullian joins Montanists

258 Martyrdom of Laurence the Deacon

303 Diocletian's edicts against Christians

c310 Anthony of Egypt organises hermits

325 Council of Nicaea

Constantine

328 Athanasius bishop of Alexandria

346 Abbot Pachomius dies

389 Jerome in Bethlehem

400 Honoratus founds Lérins monastery

250 **300** **350** **400**

341 Bible translated into Gothic

330 Foundation of Constantinople

321 Sunday recognised by the state as day of rest

313 Edict of Milan ends persecution

306 Constantine proclaimed Emperor in Britain

300 Kama Sutra written in the holy city of Benares

Romulus and Remus, the founders of Rome

247 Rome's Millennium

249 Decius decrees persecution

264 Goths invade Greece

379 Buddhism made state religion in China

Persecutio

Martyrdom was an accepted fate of Christians though persecutions depended on the Roman ruler of the day. Deaths were savage, but most went willingly into the lions' jaws or the flames

The stars of Nero's circus

In AD64 much of Rome was destroyed by a fire. The Emperor Nero, who was suspected of contributing to the conflagration, turned to the Christians as scapegoats. Here the Roman historian Tacitus describes the martyrs' fate

All the endeavours of men, all the Emperor's largesse and the propitiations of the gods did not suffice to allay the scandal, or banish the belief that the fire had been ordered.

And so, to get rid of this rumour, Nero set up as the culprits and punished with the utmost refinement of cruelty a class hated for their abominations, who are commonly called Christians. Christus from whom their name is derived, was executed at the hands of the procurator Pontius Pilate in the reign of Tiberius. Checked for the moment, this pernicious superstition again broke out, not only in Judaea, the source of the evil, but even in Rome, that receptacle for everything that is sordid and degrading from every quarter of the globe, which there finds a following.

Accordingly, arrest was first made of those who confessed [to being Christians]; then, on their evidence, an immense multitude was convicted, not so much on the charge of arson, as because of hatred of the human race. Besides being put to death they were made to serve as objects of amusement. They were clad in the hides of beasts and torn to death by dogs; others were crucified, others set on fire to serve to illuminate the night when daylight failed. Nero had thrown open his grounds for the display, and was putting on a show in the circus, where he mingled with the people in the dress of a charioteer or drove about in his chariot.

All this gave rise to a feeling of pity, even towards men whose guilt merited the most exemplary punishment; for it was felt that they were being destroyed not for the public good but to gratify the cruelty of one man.

The Emperor Nero's persecution of Christians beginning in the year AD64 was the first of many such campaigns over the next 250 years. The genuine records of the last days of faithful Christians show a constant theme: that the man or woman is happy to die, despite the fiercest torments, for not only is the suffering temporary and heaven to come eternal, but by suffering they are sharing in the sacrifice of Jesus Christ that won them new life. To be put to death for refusing to deny Christ was seen as the very height of faithfulness to God.

The word *martyr* means witness. For generations the only kind of saint that sprang to mind was the martyr who had given his life. Sometimes Christians seemed unnecessarily keen to undergo martyrdom. Even the widely revered Ignatius, Bishop of Antioch in Syria, sometimes gives the impression of eagerness to jump down the lions' throats. In a series of letters on his way to martyrdom in Rome in 112 he says: "May I have joy of the beasts that are prepared for me. I pray too that they may prove prompt with me. I will entice them to devour me quickly... Let there come on me fire and cross and conflicts with wild beasts, wrenching of bones, mangling of limbs, crushing of the whole body, grievous torments of the devil, if only I reach Jesus Christ."

But the Church at Smyrna (modern Izmir) in its circular letter describing the martyrdom of its bishop, Polycarp, in 156 (*see opposite*), mentions the case of a contemporary, Quintus, who rashly put himself forward as a Christian, yet, when he saw the wild beast prepared to kill him, became so frightened that he was prevailed upon by the Proconsul to offer incense to the Roman gods. "Therefore, brethren," the elders of Smyrna write, "we do not commend those who surrender themselves, for such is not the teaching of the Gospel."

Pliny the Younger, an imperial Roman administrator in Bithynia (just south of the Black Sea in Turkey) had written in about 112 to the Emperor Trajan outlining his practice in dealing with prisoners suspected of Christianity. "I ask them if they are Christians," he says. "If they admit it I repeat the question a second and third time, threatening capital punishment; if they persist, I sentence them to death. Certainly, whatever kind of crime it is to which they have confessed, their stubbornness and inflexible obstinacy should be punished." Some, if they were Roman citizens (as in the case of Paul 40 years earlier), he sent for trial in Rome.

Trajan in reply puts forward a more moderate policy than some of his successors. "They are not to be sought out," he wrote. "If they are informed against, and the charge is proved, they are to be punished, with this reservation: that if anyone denies that he is a Christian, and proves it in practice by worshipping our gods, he shall be pardoned." A few years later, the Emperor Hadrian is following a similar policy, stipulating that if an accuser merely slanders a Christian by denouncing him to the authorities, the accuser is to be penalised.

At the end of the second century, Tertullian, ▶ *p.20*

'Donkey worshippers'

The persecution of Christians worked on many levels. This drawing scratched in the 2nd century on the wall of the Domus Gelotiana in Rome was clearly intended as a mocking reference to the crucifixion of Jesus. Below the drawing of a crucified donkey can be discerned Greek letters reading: "Alexamenos adores God." The derisive charge against Christians of donkey-worship is referred to by the 2nd-century Christian writer Tertullian in his *Apology*: "You imagine the head of an ass to be our God." It was a slur to which the Jews had been subject earlier. Tacitus in his *Histories* records that Jews were accused of worshipping a *caput asinum*, an ass's head.

n and martyrs

How the Bishop of Smyrna burned like gold

Polycarp was Bishop of Smyrna on the west coast of Asia Minor, in what is now Turkey. When he was martyred in about AD156, Polycarp was an old man of 86. St Irenaeus (*c*130-200) remembered meeting him in his youth and asserts that the old man had known the first Apostles. After Polycarp's martyrdom, the people of his local church at Smyrna sent round a letter to other churches giving an account of his last hours. He was arrested in a cottage in the country

So he was brought before the Proconsul, who asked him if he were Polycarp. He said "Yes," and the Proconsul tried to persuade him to deny his faith (urging, "Have respect to your old age," and the rest of it), according to the customary form, "Swear by the genius of Caesar; change your mind; say, 'Away with the Atheists!' [*a pagan nickname for the Christians*]."

Then Polycarp looked with a stern countenance on the multitude of lawless heathen gathered in the stadium, and waved his hands at them, and looked up to heaven with a groan, and said, "Away with the Atheists."

The Proconsul continued insisting and saying, "Swear, and I release you; curse Christ."

And Polycarp said, "Eighty-six years have I served him, and he has done me no wrong: how then can I blaspheme my king who saved me?"

The Proconsul continued to persist and to say, "Swear by the genius of Caesar."

He answered, "If you vainly imagine that I would 'swear by the genius of Caesar', as you say, pretending that you are ignorant of who I am, hear plainly that I am a Christian. And if you are willing to learn the doctrine of Christianity, appoint a day, and listen."

The Proconsul said, "Persuade the people."

Polycarp then said, "You, indeed, I should have deemed worthy of argument, for we have been taught to render, to authorities and powers ordained by God, honour as is meet so long as it does us no harm, but as for those, I do not think them worthy of my making my defence to them."

The Proconsul said, "I have wild beasts; if you will not change your mind I will throw you to them." Then he said, "Bid them be brought: change of mind from better to worse is not a change that we are allowed; but to change from wrong to right is good." Then again said the Proconsul to him, "If you despise the beasts, unless you change your mind I shall have you burnt."

But Polycarp said: "You threaten the fire that burns for an hour, and after a little while is quenched; for you are ignorant of the fire of the judgment to come, and of everlasting punishment reserved for the ungodly. But why delay? Do what you wish."

He put his hands behind him and was bound, like a goodly ram out of a great flock for an offering, a whole burnt offering made ready and acceptable to God. Then he looked up to heaven and said, "O Lord God Almighty, Father of thy beloved and blessed son Jesus Christ, through whom we have received our knowledge of thee, God of Angels and Powers and of all creation and of the whole race of the righteous who live before thy face, I bless thee in that thou hast deemed me worthy of this day and hour; that I might take a portion among the martyrs in the cup of Christ, to the resurrection of eternal life both of soul and body in the incorruption of the Holy Spirit."

When he had offered up his Amen and completed his prayer, those in charge kindled the fire. A great flame flashed out, and we to whom the sight was granted saw a marvel; and we moreover were preserved so that we might tell to the rest what came to pass. The fire made the appearance of a vaulted roof, like a ship's sail filling out with the wind, and it walled about the body of the martyr in a ring. There was it in the midst, not like flesh burning but like a loaf baking or like gold and silver being refined in a furnace. Moreover we caught a fragrance as of the breath of frankincense or some other precious spice.

In the end, when the lawless mob had seen that his body could not be consumed by the fire they commanded an executioner to go stab him with a dagger.

So we afterwards took up his bones, more valuable than precious stones and finer than gold, and laid them where it was fitting. There the Lord will permit us, as we can, to assemble ourselves together in joy and gladness, and to celebrate the birthday of his martyrdom, alike in memory of them that have fought before, and for the training and preparation of them that are to fight hereafter.

The death of the early martyrs was not depicted in the first places of Christian worship. But the three youths in the fiery furnace (in the Book of Daniel in the Old Testament) were a popular image intended to represent heavenly triumph over transient torments. This wall painting is from the catacomb of Priscilla in Rome

who was to join the hard-line Montanist sect that broke away from the main Church, complains that Christians are not allowed to make a proper defence in court to accusations. At the same time he asserts that Christians loyally pray for the Emperor even when he persecutes them. "We call upon God for the safety of the Emperor, upon God the eternal, God the true, the living God whose favour beyond all others the Emperor desires." Tertullian explicitly derives this teaching from an epistle of St Paul, quoting the sentence: "Pray for kings, and princes and powers, that all may be peace for you."

It was a hard-line attitude similar to Tertullian's that provoked a bishop called Novatian into setting himself up in 251 as the first anti-Pope, in opposition to Cornelius (Pope of Rome, 251-253: by this time the Bishop of Rome had become known by the title of Pope, from a Greek word meaning father). Novatian refused to countenance the forgiving of Christians who had denied Christ during persecution. This hard-heartedness drew the wrath of the formidable Cyprian, Bishop of Carthage, the centre of the powerful Church in North Africa.

"Novatian caused a division in the Church," Cyprian wrote, "and drew away some of the brethren to impieties and blasphemies, and introduced as well most profane teaching about God, and falsely accuses our most compassionate Lord Jesus Christ of being without mercy." How dare Novatian banish repentant sinners, Cyprian asks, when Christ is willing to return to help them?

But Novatian collected a following. And the right level of discipline was not easy to settle upon. For, though Cyprian backed Cornelius, Bishop of Rome, in his teaching on reconciliation of the lapsed, he fell out with a successor of Cornelius, Pope Stephen. Cyprian accused Stephen of being too lenient to failed martyrs. By a quirk of history, both Cyprian and Stephen's own successor Sixtus met a heroic martyr's death within weeks of each other in 258; thus reconciled in death, both came to be mentioned in the central prayer of the Roman Eucharist.

Emperors continued to see-saw between toleration and bouts of fierce bloodletting. The later years of Valerian's reign (253-260) saw punishment of "bishops, priests and deacons" and the forfeit of the property of any official found to be a Christian; if they persevered they would lose their heads. Valerian's successor Gallienus issued an edict restoring basilicas and cemeteries to the bishops, and making Christianity a "licit religion".

But the fiercest and most totalitarian persecution, at the beginning of the fourth century, was yet to come.

Certificate of sacrifice

This certificate has survived from the reign of Decius, in AD250. It declares that one Aurelia Demos has sacrificed to the gods. It was written out by her husband, since she was illiterate. The certificate is written on papyrus, a kind of paper made of reeds. Like all the so-called *libelli* that have come down to us, this example comes from Egypt. Many of the *libelli* exist only in fragments, but palaeographers have been able to reconstruct from them an almost standard form of declaration demanded by the Roman authorities. The officials who administered the persecution under Decius were so thoroughgoing in their work that even obvious pagans who were under no suspicion of being Christians were required to have their declarations of sacrifice recorded by the state officials.

Forgiving the failed martyrs

The Roman authorities offered martyrs dishonest ways of escaping death. Christians who denied their religion would seek reconciliation by unusual means

Under the Emperor Decius, in the years AD249-251, there was a campaign to make Christians sacrifice to the gods and the "Genius of the Emperor". Those who did were issued with a certificate, known as a *libellus* (like the one pictured below left). One such, dated June 26 250, was found in 1893 by archaeologists at Fayoum in Egypt.

"To the Commissioners for Sacrifices in the village of Alexander's Island," it read. "From Aurelius Diogenes, son of Satabous, aged 72. Scar on right eyebrow.

"I have always sacrificed to the gods, and now in your presence, in accordance with the terms of the edict, I have done sacrifice and poured libations and tasted the sacrifices, and I request you to certify this. *Vale*.

"Presented by: Aurelius Diogenes

"I certify that I witnessed his sacrifice, [signed] Aurelius Syrus.

"Dated: First year of the Emperor Caesar Gaius Messius Quintus Trajanus Decius, Pius, Felix, Augustus, the 2nd of Epiph."

Many Christians died rather than sacrifice. But to save them from death, officials would often provide certificates either directly to Christians or to their pagan friends, declaring that they had sacrificed to the gods when they had not. Perhaps to many Christians this did not seem such a bad thing to do. But it soon enough became clear that the Church condemned such shifts. Anyone who bought a *libellus* was counted as a *lapsus* – someone who had fallen away, who had lapsed from the Christian religion.

The Church was then left with the problem of what to do about people who had lapsed under pressure but wanted to be readmitted to participation again in the sacred mysteries, as the Eucharist was called.

Outside orthodox Christianity, there were rigid fanatics who insisted that *lapsi* who had denied Christ could never be forgiven. But among mainstream Christians a practice had soon grown up that could ensure forgiveness to *lapsi*. They would commend themselves to prospective martyrs. It was assumed that as soon as the martyr was in heaven he would win forgiveness for the weak *lapsus*, who could take his place again among the worshipping Church.

A martyr on his way to death would even sign a little note called a *libellus pacis* to certify that they were praying for the *lapsus*. Confessors too – those who stood up for the faith and may have been tortured or imprisoned – had the privilege of gaining readmittance for *lapsi*. Before long Church authorities were being presented with hundreds of *libelli pacis*.

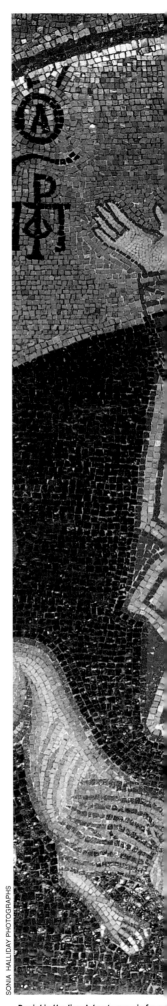

SONIA HALLIDAY PHOTOGRAPHS

Daniel in the lions' den (a mosaic from Daniel, the hero is thrown to the lions

rch of Hosios Lukas in Greece) was a popular way of representing the victory of the just man over evil persecution. In the Book of king of Babylon; early Christians saw martyrs killed by lions in the circuses of Rome, the new Babylon

So happy to die

Perpetua, a married woman of around 22 with a babe in arms, was martyred about AD203. This is her account of her last days

After a few days there was a report that we were to be examined. Moreover my father arrived from the city, worn with anxiety, and he came up the hill that he might overthrow my resolution. He said: "Daughter, pity my white hairs! Pity your father, if I am worthy to be called father by you. I have brought you up to this your prime of life; I have loved you more than your brothers. Do not shame me before the world! Think of your mother and her sister. Think of your baby son, who cannot survive if you are gone. Forget your pride, do not ruin us all. None of us will ever be able to hold up our heads in public again if anything happens to you."

As my father spoke of his love for me, he kissed my hands and threw himself down at my feet. He wept and did not address me by the name of daughter, but used the reverential title "lady". I was very sorry for my father's sake, because he alone of all my family would not have joy at my martyrdom. I comforted him, saying: "It shall happen on that scaffold as God wills, for we certainly cannot rely on our own power, but are in God's hands." My father went away very upset.

The next day we were taken to the forum. The news soon spread and a vast crowd gathered in the forum. We were placed on a sort of platform before the judge. This was Hilarian, the procurator of the province.

The others, who were questioned before me, confessed their faith. When it came to my turn, my father appeared with my baby. He beckoned me down the steps and pleaded: "Have pity on your child." The judge Hilarian joined with my father and said: "Spare the tender years of your child. Offer a sacrifice for the prosperity of the Emperors."

I replied: "No."

"Are you a Christian?" he asked.

"Yes, I am."

My father tried to pull me from the scaffold, but Hilarian commanded that he should be beaten off, and he was struck with a rod. This I felt as much as if I had been hit myself. Then the judge passed sentence on us all and condemned us to the wild beasts. In great joy we returned to our prison.

Christians were meant to love God and their neighbours, but pagans wondered what they got up to behind closed doors. Their most holy mysteries were nothing less than a sharing in the flesh and blood of Jesus

The holy mysteries

The most important event for an early Christian was the gathering on the first day of the week (not the Sabbath, the last day of the week) to celebrate the resurrection. They did so by "breaking bread". This was not an informal picnic round a kitchen table, but was recognised as a consciously formal re-enactment of the sacred rites handed from Jesus via the Apostles. It is interesting to note that even the phrase "breaking bread" (*klao ton arton*) was not a common expression for taking a meal.

The development from a meal like the Last Supper, possibly on the lines of a Jewish Passover meal, must have taken place rapidly. There are few accounts to rely on, but the celebration of the mysteries was soon easily distinguishable from an *agape* – a charitable community meal shared by rich and poor, probably in the evening, not in the early morning.

Ignatius, writing in about AD112, when people still had personal memories of the Apostles, said: "Let that be considered a valid Eucharist over which the bishop presides, or one to whom he commits it." The earliest documents agree in describing a solemn blessing and thanksgiving being uttered over bread and wine as a memorial of the death and resurrection of Jesus.

In 1875 an ancient manuscript was discovered in Constantinople, called the *Didache* or *The Teaching of the Twelve Apostles*. It dates probably from just after the year 100. "Concerning the Eucharist," it says, "give thanks in this way: First for the cup; 'We give thanks to thee, our Father, for the holy vine of David thy servant, which thou madest known to us through thy servant Jesus. To thee be glory for ever.'

"And for the broken bread: 'We give thanks to thee, our Father, for the life and knowledge which thou madest known to us through thy servant Jesus. To thee be the glory for ever. As this broken bread was scattered upon the hills, and was gathered together and made one, so let thy Church be gathered together into thy kingdom from the ends of the earth; for thine is the glory and the power through Christ Jesus for ever.'

"Let none eat or drink of your Eucharist, save such as are baptised into the name of the Lord. For concerning this the Lord hath said: 'Give not that which is holy to dogs.'"

This admonishment not to regard the Eucharist as just any bread is repeated by Justin (*see page 27*) in about the year 150: "This food is called the Eucharist, and of it no one is allowed to partake but he who believes that our teachings are true, and has been washed with the washing for remission of sins and unto regeneration, and who also lives as Christ directed. For we do not receive them as ordinary food or ordinary drink. But, just as, by the word of God, Jesus Christ our Saviour took flesh and blood for our salvation, so also (we are taught) the food blessed by the prayer of the word which we received from him (by which through its transformation our blood and flesh is nourished) – this food is the flesh and and blood of Jesus who was made flesh."

One of the reasons there are few detailed descriptions of the precise rituals of the Eucharist is that the Christians were wary of pagan persecutors. They regarded their sacred books as things that would be defiled by unbelievers. It was regarded as a terrible crime to hand them over. Indeed there was a strict discipline that forbade Christians from making the sacred mysteries known to unbelievers.

Their wariness was not decreased by the slanders spread around, about how Christians were cannibals or slayers of babies. Even those receiving instruction in Christian beliefs left the building before the solemn celebration of the Eucharist. Only after the "awe-inspiring rites of baptism" were they trusted with the secrets.

It was second nature for the Christians to express their beliefs by way of metaphor, even in graphic art. The vine with its grapes stood for the Eucharistic wine. Ears of wheat were depicted in mosaics to signify the Eucharistic bread. Or a basket of loaves might be shown. A favourite wall-decoration was a picture of the sacrifice of Melchizedek, the mysterious priest in the Old Testament who offered up bread and wine – a sacrifice quite unlike slaughtered cattle or sheep. He was taken as an archetype of the sacrifice of the Eucharist. Another was Abel, whose acceptable sacrifice of a lamb was seen as a prefiguring of the sacrifice of the Lamb of God, Jesus.

Despite the wariness of Christians and the attempts of persecutors to destroy the holy books, we do have an ▶

The Eucharist is symbolised in this 6th-century mosaic from the wall of St Vitale, Ravenna. Abel offers up the acceptable sacrifice of a lamb, foreshadowing Jesus, the Lamb of God. Melchizedek, the priest-king, offers up bread (marked with a cross) while on the doubly-hung altar stands a chalice of wine. The hand of God, signifying his transforming power, is seen coming from a cloud.

SONIA HALLIDAY PHOTOGRAPHS

MELCHISE

extraordinary document surviving from about AD225. It used to be known as the Egyptian Church Order, for it gives prayers used by Christians in Egypt. Even more surprisingly, perhaps, it records Eucharistic prayers still in use in Ethiopia today. But most scholars connect it primarily with the name Hippolytus, a well known presbyter in Rome in the early 3rd century.

The text as we have it is not supposed to be a definitive formula for celebrating the Eucharist. At that time bishops and presbyters would extemporise or vary prayers on an established framework. Yet the introductory exchange of prayers between the bishop and the people is familiar to anyone who goes to an Anglican or Catholic church in England today: *Dominus vobiscum. Et cum spiritu tuo. Sursum corda. Habemus ad Dominum. Gratias agamus Domino. Dignum et iustum est.* (The Lord be with you. And also with your spirit. Lift up your hearts. We have raised them up to the Lord. Let us give thanks to the Lord. It is right and fitting.)

There follows a prayer of thanks to God, recalling the saving life of Jesus Christ, leading up to a repetition of the words of the Last Supper when the Apostles were commanded to perform just such a Eucharistic rite – "He took bread and gave thanks to thee and said: 'Take eat: This is my body which is broken for you.' Likewise also the cup, saying: 'This is my blood which is shed for you. As often as you do this you shall do it in remembrance of me.'" After this, prayers are said to the Holy Spirit, asking that the Holy Spirit might make this offering by the Church an acceptable one.

In a spirit of antiquarianism, or more likely in an attempt to bring Christian worship back to its roots, both the Roman Catholics and other churches have in the past few years included this ancient prayer recorded by Hippolytus among those that may be chosen to be said at the Eucharist today.

Love and wine

This typical 3rd-century Christian wall painting from a catacomb in Rome shows figures at a table eating and drinking. Above them are inscriptions in capital letters IRENE DA CALDA and AGAPE MISCEM. Some would interpret this as a metaphorical invocation of Peace (*irene*) and Love (*agape*) at the celestial banquet of the Eucharist where the people of God are signified by water. *Calda* = warm water, which the ancients mixed, *miscem*, with their wine. Newly baptised Christians learnt how, at the Eucharist, water is mixed with wine before the ceremony just as, when Christ was crucified, blood and water flowed from his side when it was pierced by a lance. It has to be admitted, though, that some commentators regard such wall-paintings not as metaphorical delineations of the sacred rites but as realistic daubs showing meals that are nothing more than the *agape* run riot – of the kind against which St Paul complained to the Corinthians. In this interpretation Irene and Agape in the pictures are merely serving girls impatiently summoned by the diners to bring more wine.

Jonah and the fish

An engaging or inventive sculpture or painting often held a hidden meaning for the early Christians

This lively sculpture dates from the 3rd century and was made in the eastern Mediterranean. It depicts Jonah swallowed by a sea beast (in the King James translation of the Book of Jonah the creature is called "a great fish").

"Jonah was in the belly of the fish three days and three nights." To the metaphorically minded early Christians this sentence was enough to remind them of the period, a part of three days, spent by Jesus in the tomb before his resurrection. In the story of Jonah, the prophet is recorded as praying to God from the belly of the fish, and God, hearing him, saves his life.

This interpretation is confirmed in the Gospel of Matthew, where these words of Jesus are given: "An evil and adulterous generation seeketh after a sign; and there shall no sign be given it, but the sign of the prophet Jonas. For as Jonas was three days and three nights in the whale's belly; so shall the Son of man be three days and three nights in the heart of the earth."

All this would automatically come to the mind of ordinary Christians of the first centuries. They were used to hearing such interpretations of scripture from the teaching bishops and presbyters.

A fish – usually the scaly, dish-sized, edible kind – features very frequently in early Christian wall paintings and mosaics. It was a symbol for Christ, for the letters of the Greek word ichthus making up the initials of his title: Iesous Christos Theou Uios Soter (Jesus Christ, of God the Son, Saviour).

Moreover the Christian would be reminded of the fish miraculously multiplied in the feeding of the five thousand (itself a metaphor for the Eucharist), and of the fish cooked by Jesus on the shore for the Apostles' breakfast after his resurrection.

"Let our emblems be either a dove, a fish, a ship scudding before the wind, a musical lyre or a ship's anchor," wrote Clement of Alexandria in the 3rd century.

The anchor stood for hope, and sometimes had a cross incorporated in it, as did the very common sign of the Chi-Rho. This takes its name from the first two letters of Christ's name and looks more or less like X and P superimposed.

Celebrating a new birthday

A widespread custom of pagan times survived in the first three centuries or so of Christianity. This was the *refrigerium* or "refreshment". After the death of a member of the family, relations would gather at the grave (and later on his birthday), have a picnic and drink some wine. Some of this would be poured out – in pagan times as a libation to the gods in charge of the dead. In some way the dead was thought to take part in this meal; wine might even be poured into a hole leading to the grave.

Christians would mark the anniversary of death – the new birthday or *dies natalis*. An obvious replacement for pagan memorial rites was the celebration of the Eucharist at the site of the grave. There is written evidence from as early as AD170 in Asia Minor of such rites on the third day after death. We read, towards the end of the 4th century, of Monica, the mother of Augustine of Hippo, on first visiting Milan innocently taking along a basket containing some porridge and a little flask of wine to a church where she intended to celebrate a simple ceremony in the African tradition at the tombs of the saints. The porter stopped her and told her such rites were forbidden by the bishop. The bishop happened to be the great Ambrose, who had imposed the ban because of its resemblance to pagan rites, and to prevent drunkenness among those less conscientious than Monica. Nevertheless the custom of *refrigerium* encouraged devotion to saints on the very spot of their burial or martyrdom. Sometimes almost all that is still known of a martyr is the place of his or her martyrdom.

This is the case with St Emeterius and St Celedonius, who are revered at Calahorra in Spain. They probably died in the persecution under Diocletian in 303. A cathedral was built around their relics, not like the rest of the city on a hill, but at the site of their martyrdom by the river.

These extraordinary gold heads with neat red wounds on the necks were made in the 16th century to hold the relics of the 4th-century Saints Emeterius and Celedonius. They are kept beneath the high altar of Calahorra cathedral in Spain and annually carried in procession

The good shepherd

The Lord is my shepherd

The Lord is my shepherd; I shall not want.

He maketh me lie down in green pastures: he leadeth me beside the still waters.

He restoreth my soul: he leadeth me in the paths of righteousness for his name's sake.

Yea, though I walk through the valley of the shadow of death, I will fear no evil: for thou art with me; thy rod and thy staff they comfort me.

Thou preparest a table before me in the presence of mine enemies: thou anointest my head with oil; my cup runneth over.

Surely goodness and mercy shall follow me all the days of my life: and I will dwell in the house of the Lord for ever.

— Psalm 23

I lay down my life for the sheep

I am the good shepherd: the good shepherd giveth his life for the sheep.

But he that is an hireling, and not the shepherd, whose own the sheep are not, seeth the wolf coming, and leaveth the sheep, and fleeth: and the wolf catcheth them, and scattereth the sheep.

The hireling fleeth, because he is an hireling, and careth not for the sheep.

I am the good shepherd, and know my sheep, and am known of mine.

As the father knoweth me, even so knoweth I the Father: and I lay down my life for the sheep.

And other sheep I have, which are not of this fold: and them also I must bring, and they shall hear my voice; and there shall be one fold, and one shepherd.

Therefore doth my Father love me, because I lay down my life, that I may take it again.

No man taketh it from me, but I lay it down myself. I have power to lay it down, and I have power to take it again.

— St John's Gospel, chapter 10

This 3rd-century wall painting of Christ as the Good Shepherd is from the catacomb of Priscilla and is one of several found in catacombs in Rome. The Good Shepherd was an image familiar from pre-Christian pagan art. But to early Christians the pictures had different and familiar meanings. One was from the Psalms, the ancient Jewish collection of sacred poetry. The Psalms were at first the only hymns regularly used in Christian worship. In them, foreshadowing of the life of Jesus was detected. The other image of the Shepherd, as Christ himself, came from the Gospel of St John, where Jesus contrasts the fickle hireling with his own self-sacrificing care

First rites: the ceremony of initiation

Before taking a full part in the sacred mysteries, a convert had to undergo initiation – baptism, a ritual washing in water. This could be very simple. A eunuch from the court of the Queen of Ethiopia is described in the Acts of the Apostles riding in his chariot and discussing the teachings of Christianity with Philip, a deacon. As they bowl along the highway, they come across some water and the eunuch is baptised.

Soon, preparation became more arduous. "Those who promise to live in this way," writes Justin in about AD160 "are taught to pray and, while fasting, to implore God to forgive their sins." Candidates learnt by heart formulas summing up the faith, like the so-called Apostles' Creed. Baptism, preceded by a fast, was by immersion. Going down was a dying with Christ; coming up a share in his Resurrection. Spring water was often used, for the word for running water meant "living water", and baptism meant a new life as a Christian. This essential rite was accompanied by solemn ceremonies, such as anointing with oil, signing with the cross, putting on a white robe. All this is recorded from the second century. Baptisms were usually on Easter night. Afterwards the new Christian would partake for the first time in the Eucharist.

Making sense of beliefs

What was an early Christian to tell his pagan friends to justify his own behaviour and beliefs? How did the Gospel teachings stand up to philosophical enquiry? Here is how five thinkers first dealt with these important questions

Justin (cAD100-165), a professional philosopher and a convert to Christianity, was born in Samaria. He was to be executed as a martyr in Rome. His philosophical turn of mind was noted by his contemporary Irenaeus: "Justin well says, 'I would not have announced any other God than he who is our Framer, Maker and Nourisher.'"

It was Justin who made the celebrated pronouncement: "Whatever has been uttered aright by any men in any place belongs to us Christians; for, next to God, we worship and love the reason [Word] which is from the unbegotten and ineffable God."

Tertullian (c160-230) was not having anything of that. This fierce writer preferred to denounce the errors of philosophy. "Wretched Aristotle! He taught argument, that art of building up and demolishing, so protean in statement, so far-fetched in conjecture, so unyielding in controversy, so productive of disputes; self-stultifying, ever handling questions, but never settling anything. . . . What is there in common between Athens and Jerusalem? What between the Academy and the Church?"

Tertullian, living in Carthage, in North Africa, a thoroughly Latin culture, was surrounded by warring factions, most of which he denounced. By about 211 he had it seems joined the Montanists, a schismatic group defined principally by their harsh judgment on backsliders. Tertullian said that the Church *could* forgive sins, such as fornication, committed after baptism, but priests *ought not* to, lest the sinner repeat them.

The Montanists condemned running away from persecution. They recognised a "spiritual" church, ruled by the Holy Spirit, in distinction from the visible Church. Tertullian, because of his reputed falling away from the Church, has never been called "saint".

Irenaeus (c130-200) said that he had heard Polycarp, Bishop of Smyrna, preach. So he was probably himself from that city (in what is now Turkey, opposite Greece). But he became Bishop of Lyons (in modern-day France) where he died. He attempted to explain doctrines clearly and convince heretics of their errors. These heretics were mainly of the Gnostic variety, fond of secret interpretations of Christian teaching, mixed with pickings from Mediterranean cults.

For Irenaeus, Christ is the recapitulation of all true things: he redeems the nature of mankind and in him is taken up the historical plan that God has for man. As a guarantee of the truth of his teaching, Irenaeus appeals to the succession from the Apostles Peter and Paul, and lists the Bishops of Rome to his own time. "For with this church, because of its position of leadership and authority, must agree every church, that is, the faithful every-

where." In the Church, the Apostles lodged the truth, as in a bank; "all the rest are thieves and robbers".

Irenaeus had heard from Polycarp an anecdote about John the Apostle. In Ephesus he had gone to the baths, but rushed out, having spotted Cerinthus, a man of false teaching: "Let us flee, before the baths fall in, for Cerinthus the enemy of the truth is inside!"

Clement of Alexandria (c150-215), a true philosopher, ran the renowned catechetical school at Alexandria, near the mouth of the Nile. He excelled in fusing the teaching of the Gospel with Greek culture. He also follows Philo, an exponent of Alexandrian Judaism, who had interpreted episodes in the Old Testament as allegories. Clement applied the method to Old Testament prefiguration of the actions of Christ.

Clement follows Philo too in applying secular techniques of learning to theology. He uses grammar, etymology and logic to unravel the meaning of Scripture. Philosophy can enable us to move from common sense to scientific knowledge. Through research and logical argument it is possible to reach sure knowledge. Clement calls this certain knowledge *gnosis*, thus making a conscious effort to make respectable a term used by the heretical Gnostics. In this he did not really succeed.

Clement was certain that ancient cultures had received revelations from God. Curiously, he sought equivalents in Homer for episodes in the Bible; 1,700 years later this became a hobby of the British prime minister, William Gladstone.

Origen (c185-255) took over the school at Alexandria from Clement. He wrote more than 2,000 works in Greek. "He was the first man who urged me to study the philosophy of the Greeks," wrote Gregory Thaumaturgus (c210-260). "And he persuaded me by his own moral example to hear and to practise the teaching of morals."

During a stay in Palestine, Origen was ordained a priest by the Bishop of Caesaria. The bishop of Alexandria objected, and Origen was dismissed from the Church in Alexandria. Origen entertained surprising speculations. He seemed to think that at the end·of time Satan would be reconciled to God. He also had the unexpected idea that stars were not only ruled by living beings, but also that Christ died to redeem them from sin. Though Origen suffered torture during the persecution of Decius, he was never proclaimed a saint, not because of his fizzing theology but, it was thought, lest others should imitate his memorable, if not certainly historical, self-castration, provoked by misunderstanding a sentence in the Gospel of Matthew: "There be eunuchs which have made themselves eunuchs for the kingdom of heaven's sake."

A font designed for the total immersion of a candidate for Christian membership, at Sbeitla in Tunisia, dating from the 4th century. At each side are the steps by which the candidate would descend into the waters of symbolic death and resurrection. Also visible are the stumps of the pillars which would have supported a dome decorated with mosaics

Bishops, priests and deacons

The Twelve Apostles were clearly in charge. But what happened when they were absent or after their deaths? Within 100 years a triple division was established, setting out the demarcation of the different ministries

By the middle of the 15th century when Fra Angelico executed this portrayal of St Laurence, he was seen as the very model of a deacon. Laurence was one of the Seven Deacons of Rome and was martyred in the year 258, as tradition has it by being roasted on a gridiron. Tradition also tells that, on being ordered by a Roman official to turn over all the treasures of the Church, he gathered together the lame and blind and sick and declared: "Here is the treasure of the Church."

What connection, though, is there between the deacons, priests and bishops of the Renaissance Church, or today, and the ministers of the Apostles' time? It would be simple if the Deacons mentioned in the Acts of the Apostles were exactly the same as deacons in the Church today. But they seem not to have been.

Sometimes in the New Testament the people in charge of local communities of Christians founded by the Apostles are just referred to generally as "leaders" (*hêgoumenoi* in Greek) or as "presidents in the Lord"(*proistamenoi en tô Kuriô*). It is not always clear from the text alone what function these leaders filled.

Sometimes, though, they are called by more specific titles: *episkopoi* – "overseers", the origin of our word bishop; *presbuteroi* "elders" or "presbyters"; and *diakonoi* or "deacons". But the categories often seem to overlap.

A partial parallel for presbyters may be found in the elders of the Jewish synagogue. And in some of the Dead Sea Scrolls, dating from around the time of Jesus, we find the Hebrew word *mebaqqêr*, referring to a supervisor or overseer of a local community; perhaps this is an origin

St Laurence Distributing Alms by Fra Angelico (*c*1387-1455) is part of a cycle of his life from the Chapel of Nicholas V in the Vatican. Laurence was often depicted as a deacon wearing a dalmatic (a deacon's vestment) and carrying a purse, as he is here. He was entrusted with with the Sacred Books by Pope Sixtus II, and he became the patron saint of librarians. Fra Angelico was renowned for his pictorial insight into sacred subjects and for the holiness of his own life

of the concept of *episkopoi*, the bishops of New Testament times.

In communities where one of the original Apostles was still around, there was no doubt who was in charge. But where there is no Apostle there appears to have been a number of elders, and not all of them were *episkopoi*. Paul writes to "all the saints in Christ Jesus that are at Philippi, with their *episkopoi* and *diakonoi*".

Very soon in the early Church it was recognised as important that the *episkopoi* should derive their role from an apostolic commission. Clement, Bishop of Rome, writing about the year 95, explains how he sees the passing on of this commission: "Now the gospel was given to the Apostles for us by the Lord Jesus Christ; and Jesus Christ was sent from God. That is to say, Christ received his commission from God and the Apostles theirs from Christ. The order of these two events was in accordance with the will of God. So thereafter, when the Apostles had been given their instructions, and all their doubts had been set at rest by the resurrection of our Lord Jesus Christ from the dead, they set out in the full assurance of the Holy Spirit to proclaim the coming of God's kingdom. And as they went through the country and towns preaching, they appointed their first converts – after testing them by the Spirit – to be bishops and deacons for the believers of the future."

It is clear that in Clement's eyes the job of the bishops was, like that of the Apostles, not just to act as priests, presiding during worship, but also to teach and to rule the whole of the bishop's territory or diocese from day to day. As elsewhere, *episkopoi*, bishops, are identified as a kind of elder with responsibility for oversight of the whole community.

There is an attempt at formulating the distinctions within Holy Orders in the compilation of church rules called The Apostolic Constitutions. This was put together in the late 4th century, but a good part of it reflects much earlier practice. "A presbyter blesses," it says. "He lays on hands, but he does not ordain." A deacon, it says, does not bless. "He also does not baptise, and does not offer the Eucharist. However, when a bishop or presbyter has offered, the deacon distributes to the people. He does this, not as a priest, but as one who ministers to the priests."

So it is clear that both bishop and presbyter (priest) perform the sacraments. The term sacraments, or mysteries, applied most obviously to the Eucharist, but also to baptism. Presbyters also had power to absolve from sins, a matter of some urgency on occasion in the dangerous persecutions of the mid-3rd century. Deacons were not expected to preside at the Eucharist or ordinarily to administer baptism. They retained the role indicated in the Acts of the Apostles of looking after material needs. But the ministry of a deacon did not have joined on to it the further powers of a presbyter or bishop.

Presbyters had a task of teaching: to proclaim the Gospel and give sound doctrine. To them was handed down the sacred teaching of the Apostles. In this they emulated the bishop, whose *cathedra*, the chairs of teaching, was to give the name to the cathedral of the diocese. The presbyters also gave spiritual advice to individuals. And they shared in the bishop's responsibility for public discipline, as a shepherd.

"The improvement of the body," writes Clement of Alexandria in about 195, "is the object of the medical art; the improvement of the mind is the object of philosophy. Ministerial service is rendered to parents by children, to rulers by subjects. Similarly, in the Church, the presbyters attend to the ministry that has improvement of the flock for its object; the deacons attend to the physical things."

The understanding of the triple distinction of bishop, presbyter (rendered in English from Saxon times as priest) and deacon was, through the centuries, subject to much development. But it lies behind the Holy Orders visible in the Church today.

The persecution h

The last great wave of persecutions against the Christians was under Diocletian, a reforming Emperor who wanted to impose totalitarian government values. Its effects were long lasting – particularly on apostates who later wanted to return to the Church

An efficient Emperor, Diocletian (reigned AD284-305), was to bring a more thorough-going persecution than ever. It was like a Stalinist secret police sweep. In 297 the emperor issued an edict against the Manichaeans, a non-Christian sect felt to be dangerous because of its supposed criminal activity, and, worse, its Iranian origins. The argument that was used against Manichaeans could be used against the Christians, too: that it "is criminal to throw doubts on what has been established from ancient times". To D iocletian, Christians were atheists.

Twenty years into Diocletian's reign Christians were barred from the active list in the army. Edicts passed in the year 303 provided for the destruction of churches, the confiscation of books and sacred vessels, and then the arrest of "leaders of churches" – interpreted as any clergyman. The next step was to offer liberty to anybody who offered sacrifice (such as burning incense) to the image of the emperor or the Roman gods. The alternative was a cruel death by beheading, drowning, being thrown from cliffs or being given to wild animals in the arena. Or there might be deportation to the mines, which was a guaranteed death sooner rather than later in a manner reminiscent of the forced labour camps of Nazism or Stalinism.

What motive Diocletian had is not clear. In effect, defiance of the Emperor's totalitarian dictates reinforced his determination to prevent it being defied. The dialogue reproduced on the opposite page between the magistrate and the Christians being searched in the year 303 at Cirta, in North Africa, show how the state officials set Christians against each other if they could. "If there has been any omission," the magistrate says, "the responsibility is yours."

The persecution lasted longest – for 10 years – in the East. In Britain, which came under the control of Constantius, the father of the future Emperor Constantine, only the edict against churches, books and vessels came into effect, and was not always enforced. In Rome, Christian practice was so disrupted that it was impossible for four years to elect a successor to Pope Marcellinus.

The reaction of Christians varied. Some courted prosecution by calling at the governor's office with a copy of the Gospels (as in the case of the martyr Euplius in Sicily). This looked too close to suicide or, almost as bad, to a heretical tendency reminiscent of the Montanists. These rigorists disapproved even of running away from the police. At the lax end of things there were various dodges. The crafty Bishop Mensurius of Carthage handed over books written by heretics. Others, particularly in Syria, Egypt and Asia Minor, where the persecution went on and on, obtained fraudulent certificates declaring they had sacrificed to Roman gods, when they had not. Then there were plain apostates who saved their skins by turning their backs on Christianity. And there were many martyrs.

Though martyrdom was regarded as the seed-bed of the Church, the local churches in the short term were in

ots up

places destroyed by the deaths of martyrs and the loss of apostates.

In the years after the establishment of peace under Emperor Constantine, the question remained of what to do with apostates who wanted to return to Christianity. Then there were the *traditores*, who had handed over sacred books, and those who had bought their lives with forged certificates of sacrifice. In North Africa the question split the Church. A schismatic sect grew up known as the Donatists. They repudiated any bishop who had been a *traditor*; they refused to be in communion with anybody in communion with the backsliders. They took their name from Donatus, the successor of a bishop elected in the place of a *traditor*. His organisational genius guaranteed the sect's survival.

The Donatists became more extreme. They declared that those who had denied Christ should be re-baptised. They asserted that any sacrament – the Eucharist, Penance, Baptism itself – was invalid if it was performed by members of local churches in communion, or on friendly terms, with the sinners.

The Donatists in effect made themself a Church of the perfect. They persisted in rejecting the authority and even the sacred powers of the successors of the bishops that they had rejected. For the first time, the Church saw two parallel traditions of Christianity being practised in the same towns for a period of several lifetimes.

Some of the most extreme supporters of the Donatists came from the poorer stratum of North African society, the Berber or Carthaginian underclass that had no stake in Roman colonialism. Violent bands of landless Donatists known as Circumcellions roamed the countryside, feared for their habit of blinding victims with lime. They sometimes attacked rich men with no apparent religious motive. But their lawlessness was a gift to orthodox Christian apologists.

Efforts by Constantine to put down the Donatists led to dissension and gave the schismatics martyrs of their own. In 361 the neo-pagan Emperor Julian the Apostate favoured the Donatists; his successor tried to confiscate their churches. People born children of Donatists knew nothing of any doctrinal differences with Catholics; they merely stayed loyal to inherited traditions.

The Donatist schism and heresy made the Catholic Church consider what it was that made valid the holy mysteries, the sacraments. It became clear that it was not the worthiness of the minister that counted, but the performance of the act in the name of the Church. It also made Christians think about what the creed meant by one, holy and catholic (universal) Church.

A priority of the North African, St Augustine of Hippo, was to vanquish the Donatists, at the beginning of the fifth century. As it happened the victory did not endure; from 429, the year before Augustine's death, the conquest of the Roman territories by the Vandals put paid for ever to the influential Latin-speaking Church in Africa north of the Sahara. Rome had already, in 410, been sacked by the Goths, but Rome had survived. The Vandals broke African Latin-speaking civilisation to pieces and paved the way for later Islamic invasions.

A mosaic in the 5th-century Mausoleum of Galla Placidia, Ravenna, shows the gospels of Mark, Luke, Matthew and John carefully stored in a cupboard fitted with doors. They were not to be given up to unbelievers or persecutors

An unexpected visit from the security police

In the reign of Diocletian (pictured on the coin, below) when a magistrate came calling, he would demand Christians to hand over their valuables, their scriptures and the names of their friends

In the eighth and seventh consulships of Diocletian and Maximian, [*May 19 303*], from the records of Munatius Felix, high priest of the province for life, magistrate of the colony of Cirta [*later Constantine or Qa-Centina, Algeria*]. Arrived at the house where the Christians used to meet, the magistrate said to Paul the bishop: "Bring out the writings of the law and anything else you have here, according to the order, so that you may obey the command."

Bishop: The readers [*minor church officials who had the care of books*] have the scriptures, but we will give what we have here.

Magistrate: Point out the readers or send for them.

Bishop: You all know them.

Magistrate: We do not know them.

Bishop: The municipal office knows them, that is, the clerks Edusius and Junius.

Magistrate: Leaving over the matter of the readers, whom the office will point out, produce what you have.

[*There follows an inventory of the church plate and other property, including large stores of men's and women's clothes and shoes, produced in the presence of the clergy, who include three priests, two deacons and four sub-deacons, all named.*]

Magistrate: Bring what you have.

Silvanus and Carosus [*sub-deacons*]: We have thrown out everything that was here.

Magistrate: Your answer is entered on the record.

[*After some empty cupboards had been found in the library, Silvanus produced a silver box and a silver lamp, which he said he had found behind a barrel.*]

Victor [*the magistrate's clerk*]: You would have been a dead man if you hadn't found them.

Magistrate: Look more carefully, in case there is anything left here.

Silvanus: There is nothing left. We have thrown everything out.

When the dining-room was opened, there were found there four bins and six barrels.

Magistrate: Bring out the scriptures that you have so that we can obey the orders and command of the emperor.

Catullinus [*another sub-deacon*] produced one very large volume.

Magistrate: Why have you given one volume only? Produce the scriptures that you have.

Marculius and Catullinus: [*sub-deacons*]: We haven't any more, because the readers have the books.

Magistrate: Show me the readers.

Marculius and Catullinus: We don't know where they live.

Magistrate: Tell me their names.

Marculius and Catullinus: We are not traitors: here we are, order us to be killed.

Magistrate: Put them under arrest.

[*They apparently weakened so far as to reveal one reader, for the magistrate now moved on to the house of Eugenius, who produced four books. The magistrate now turned on the other two subdeacons, Silvanus and Carosus.*]

Magistrate: Show me the other readers.

Silvanus and Carosus: The bishop has already said that Edusius and Junius the clerks know them all. They will show you the way to their houses.

Edusius and Junius: We will show them, sir.

The magistrate went on to visit the six remaining readers. Four+ produced their books. One declared he had none, and the magistrate was content with entering his statement. The last was out, but his wife produced his books; the magistrate had the house searched by the public slave to make sure that none had been overlooked. This task over, he addressed the subdeacons: "If there has been any omission, the responsibility is yours."

Constantine

The Emperor Constantine turned the world upside down by recognising Christianity instead of persecuting it like his predecessors. It meant freedom of worship and a church-building boom, but it also set a trend for emperors to interfere with church decisions, from the inside

Early in the 4th century the two richest seams in what was to become Western civilisation – the Roman imperium and the Christian religion – came together for the first time and to their mutual and lasting benefit, if not without complications for both. The architect of this fusion, which was to end the sporadic persecution of the rapidly spreading religion, and would eventually perpetuate Roman influence through its extenuated decline to its eventual renaissance, was the Emperor Constantine (c274-337).

Son of the Emperor Constantius, he was proclaimed Caesar by the legions at York on his father's death in AD306; but for many years he was just one of several claimants to the imperial purple. While much of his 30-year reign was taken up with eliminating his rivals first in the West, then in the East, at some point he opted for Christianity as the new state religion – with momentous consequences.

Legend has it that he experienced an almost Pauline conversion in 312 before the battle of the Milvian Bridge, near Rome, where he defeated the pagans under Maxentius. According to his biographer Eusebius he saw the figure of a Cross accompanied by the words "By this sign you shall conquer"; a second vision instructed him to emblazon his army's shields with the Christian symbol.

Exactly when and how Constantine himself embraced the new religion is much disputed. He was baptised only shortly before his death, and his espousal of Christianity did not deter him from killing several members of his own family, including his second wife and eldest son. What is certain, and much more relevant, is that official policy towards Christianity was transformed after the Milvian Bridge victory.

From 313, under the so-called Edict of Milan, all Christians were given complete freedom of worship, and there was an immediate restitution of goods which had been confiscated under the Diocletian persecutions of 10 years earlier. This was soon followed by tax and property concessions to the clergy of the "very holy Catholic Church". The first Christian symbols appeared on the coinage in 315 while the last pagan ones disappeared in 323. The judgments of episcopal courts, even in purely civil cases, were recognised by the state, and churches were allowed to benefit from legacies. Christians quickly began to take up the highest offices of state, such as the consulship and the prefectures of Rome and the Praetorium.

In 321 Sunday was recognised. "All judges, city-people and craftsmen shall rest on the venerable day of the Sun. But countrymen may without hindrance attend to agriculture, since it often happens that this is the most suitable day for sowing grain or planting vines."

There was a boom in church building to accommodate the flood of new converts. The basilica – a rectangular building divided into naves by rows of columns, with a curved apse at the end – became commonplace, with Rome alone having more than 40, and there were dozens of others in Jerusalem, Bethlehem and Byzantium (Constantinople). And of course there was intense theological debate. The spread of Christianity demanded more complex structures to maintain discipline and preserve doctrinal purity. The organisational structure mirrored that of the state; bishops based in the chief cities met in synod in the provincial capitals. Though conflicts over papal supremacy were still in the future, the bishopric of Rome, the see of St Peter, had an honoured status along with those of Antioch, Alexandria and, later, Jerusalem and Constantinople.

But with such heady freedom came opposition and division. From its beginnings Christianity, like Judaism, had attracted suspicion, even persecution, because of its refusal to compromise with other religions (especially the official emperor-worship). While Christianity was up against persecution, heretical beliefs did not necessarily seem like the worst enemy of the future existence of the Church. But with such sudden legitimacy, followed so rapidly by establishment, schism and heresy took on new, much darker colours.

The first such heresy to trouble the legitimised Church was the continuing popularity of the Libyan theologian Arius (c250-336), who taught that the Son was not co-equal and co-essential with the Father but merely the chief of his creations; that the two persons were substantially similar (*homoiousion*) rather than the same (*homoousion*).

In an attempt to settle this long-running dispute, Constantine in 325 called and presided over the first of the great Church councils at Nicaea in Bithynia (in modern Turkey). The judgment of the 300 or so assembled bishops survives in the words of the Nicene Creed (*see right*). In the repetitious language and the concomitant anathemas one still detects the high passions that the controversy aroused.

Arianism aside, Nicaea formed a blueprint for the way the Church was to formulate doctrine. It established the practice whereby articles of faith and aspects of moral behaviour could be worked out by reasoned debate that went far beyond simply interpreting Scripture.

The sudden transformation of their semi-outlawed cult to the established state religion must have been as much of a shock, albeit a pleasant one, to Christians of the day, as the collapse of communism was to the West in the 1980s. Like Gorbachev in 1988, Constantine's supreme achievement was to see that an idea's time had come.

Constantine changed the face of Christianity. With the sponsorship of Christianity as a religion fit for the Empire, he gave to the religion the peace it needed to grow. Some dangers were obvious – insincerity on the part of new converts, the compromise of principles with the new administration of money. More insidious was the arrogation by the Emperor of control of the Church. That would challenge the Church throughout the coming centuries and the Church was sometimes to come up with surprising responses.

A gigantic head of the Emperor Constantine in Rome. He restored stolen property to the Church, but wanted it run his way

The creed of Nicaea

The Emperor Constantine was annoyed in AD324 to find the Christians in the eastern part of his Empire in an uproar of argument. He deputed his expert in church affairs, Bishop Hosius of Córdoba, to find out what was the matter.

Fortunately Hosius was a clever man with a nose for the true line of doctrinal development, because the row he was expected to untangle was a knotty one. It was all to do with Jesus Christ. He was a man, and God too. But how was he different, as God, from God the Father? This was not just of academic interest, because Christians believed that they had been saved from sin and damnation by Jesus; if he was less than God the Father, could he really reconcile God and mankind?

Soon Egypt was at the throat of Palestine, Bithynia raging against Galatia. Populous regions that we now know only as attractive ruins were torn by bishops anathematising bishops, mobs set against mobs. So Constantine called a grand council – the first universal or ecumenical council. The Emperor allowed bishops the privilege of using the Imperial postal service to arrange it. Three hundred bishops met at Nicaea, in Asia Minor, conveniently near Constantinople, the imperial capital. More than 100 of the bishops were from Asia Minor, less than 20 from Palestine and Egypt, hardly any from the Latin-speaking West. Pope Sylvester was represented by two priests, accidentally setting a precedent for popes to send legates to future councils.

Under pressure from Constantine agreement was speedily arrived at. Only two bishops dissented from the new formula of belief. For the first time a term not found in scripture – *homoousion* "of one substance" – was proposed as an expression of essential Christian belief. Constantine was pleased at having put down dissent, but the conflict was only beginning.

The wording of the creed settled upon at the Council of Nicaea, AD325

We believe in one God the Father Almighty, maker of all things visible and invisible;

And in one Lord Jesus Christ, the Son of God begotten of the Father, only begotten, that is, of the substance of the Father, God from God, Light from Light, true God from true God, begotten not made, of one substance [homoousion] with the Father, through whom all things were made, things in heaven and things on the earth; who for us men and our salvation came down and was made flesh, and became man, suffered, and rose on the third day, ascended into the heavens, is coming to judge living and dead.

And in the Holy Spirit.

And those who say "There was when he was not" and, "Before he was begotten he was not," and that, "he came into being from nothingness," or those that allege that the son of God is: "of another substance or essence" or "created" or "changeable" or "alterable" these the Catholic and Apostolic Church anathematises.

Desert monks

The idea of monastic life, of a lone, isolated existence, began in the deserts of Egypt. Here, in the hostile wilderness, early Christians lived as hermits, having visions and resisting all temptations

Christians in Egypt began in the late 3rd century to leave their villages and towns to live as hermits in the desert. This trend profoundly affected the future history of the Church. Within a century there were hundreds of monasteries in Egypt, and others growing up in Syria and Palestine. Those who answered the call of the desert looked to earlier models, such as Elijah and John the Baptist, who spent periods of their lives in secluded prayer, and above all to Jesus. The desert dwellers hoped to imitate the story of Israel's liberation from captivity in Egypt, out into the freedom of the desert. They were heeding the psalmist:

"Oh that I had wings like a dove! For then would I fly away, and be at rest. Lo, then would I wander far off, and remain in the wilderness." (Psalm 55)

Accounts of the early hermits are extravagant and full of marvels. The spiritual insights and humility of these men are obscured by sensational stories of their fasting and self-mortification, of demons and angels. Those who lived on pillars, the stylites of the next century, were the most extreme, and we might wonder if some were not disturbed person alities who simply caught at imaginative elements in popular religion.

The early hermits had no canonical status or agreed rule of life. A hermit would only be ordained to the priesthood to ensure that the others might have access to the sacraments. Their lives were thus stripped as bare as the desert in which they lived.

The words monastic and monk come from the Greek *monos*, "alone". The psychological pressures they confronted would have been immense. They did not come from nomad stock and their natural attitudes to the desert would have been of distaste, hatred and certainly deep fear. By reputation the desert was the soundless place of death and burial.

Anthony of Egypt, born about AD250 in Memphis, on the Nile, was among those who set up as a hermit in lower Egypt. His violent temptations were the subject of extravagant portrayal in paintings 1,000 years later. He realised that work as well as prayer were needful for a monk. From about 310 Anthony sought greater seclusion in a cave at Mount Kolzim, north-west of the Red Sea. He was constantly sought out by Christians seeking his advice. The great Athanasius, exiled in the Egyptian desert in the late 4th century, wrote an influential life of Anthony. By 390, 50,000 monks were said to have gathered together to celebrate Easter.

Anthony had overseen loosely knit communities of desert monks. Pachomius (*c*290-346), founder of several monasteries in Egypt, provided a written rule for his monks. Not unreasonably, Pachomius made it clear that a communal life was likely to be holier and more stable than life as a solitary hermit. Pachomius also organised some monasteries for women, communities of whom had already been established. Macrina, the elder sister of Saints Basil and Gregory of Nyssa, headed a convent of nuns in Asia Minor. She died in about 327.

The example of the desert hermits and monks was transported to Gaul by John Cassian (*c*360-435). He spent years asking desert fathers for counsel and then set up a monastery for men and another for women near Marseilles. His writings were permanently influential on monastic life. John Cassian had also visited the island monastery off the coast of Gaul (near Cannes) founded in about 400 by Honoratus. This monastery of Lérins remained a living influence until its suppression in 1791.

The hermits of the Egyptian desert as imagined in this detail of a stylised painting by Gherardo Starnina (1354-1413). If his hermitages owe more to the spirit of St Francis of Assisi and the recluses of medieval Italy, the artist is right in showing the respect with which long-separated holy men greeted one another

Athanasius against the world

The Emperor knew what he wanted people to believe. So did the bishops at his court. But Athansius stuck by the orthodox creed, and was exiled five times for his pains

Athanasius is seen here in a mosaic at Monreale Cathedral, Sicily. He holds a scroll with the first words of the Athanasian Creed still found in the Book of Common Prayer

Athanasius pulled off an almost impossible feat – being right when everyone else of importance was wrong. A phrase about him became proverbial: Athanasius contra mundum – Athanasius against the world. Athanasius was a small, wiry, energetic man, prematurely balding, with a long beard. He was Bishop of Alexandria, the capital of Egypt, when the city was a bustling metropolis with a tradition of theological excellence. His troubles came partly through the precedent set by the Emperor Constantine in calling the council at Nicaea in AD325 to decide church doctrine. It made his successors want to rule the Church.

The bishops at Nicaea had set out what were the orthodox beliefs about Jesus Christ as the Son of God. In future it was not to be so easy. Even Constantine was surrounded by ecclesiastics who defied the teaching of Nicaea – they included the cleric who belatedly baptised him, Eusebius. These rebels were called Arians, after Arius, a priest of Alexandria and a master of public relations. He even got labourers to sing songs championing his cause.

The strong public feeling was not misplaced. Although differences between the Arians and orthodox Christians have been mocked as quibbles over one letter, one letter can make all the difference: rats are not cats. Catholic Christians believed that God the Father and God the Son were of the same – homoousion – substance. Arians said they were merely similar – homoiousion. The orthodox side responded that, taken to its conclusion, this meant that Jesus was not fully God. If Jesus was not God, then mankind had not been saved from its sins. Athanasius stuck to the orthodox, and it earned him exile five times.

He had been born in 295. As a deacon he had gone with his bishop to the Council of Nicaea. Three years later, in 328, he was made Bishop of Alexandria. Within two years

the Arians had accused him of murdering a man called Arsenius and using his body for magic – an absurd charge. But in 335 they had better luck. Constantine wanted a Church at peace, and Athanasius's enemies represented the bishop as the troublemaker. The Arian dirty tricks department claimed Athanasius would try to cut off essential Egyptian grain supplies to Constantinople. Athanasius was exiled to Augusta Treverorum in Gaul (now Trier in Germany).

On Constantine's death in 337 his empire split. One son, Constantius, ruled the East and was an Arian; the other, Constans, was orthodox and ruled in the West. Constans was supported by the Pope, but that worked both ways, for many Eastern churchmen were jealous of the Roman claim to primacy. Though Athanasius had been allowed to return to Alexandria in 337, he was exiled again two years later. His refuge was Rome itself, and he could not return for seven years.

The other exiles may be summarised: third exile, under Constantius, from 356 to 362, in the Egyptian desert. Fourth, under Julian the Apostate (who tried to reintroduce paganism) from October 362 to September 363, also in the desert. Fifth, under Valens, who favoured the Arians, from October 365 to January 366, in the desert. The Egyptian desert was a very good place to hide from emperors, and was also the home of the austere monks who enthusiastically supported Athanasius.

Before his death in 373, Athanasius wrote more than one exploration of doctrine on the Trinitarian God – Father, Son and Holy Spirit. Theologians in recent years have found these books useful to revisit; he showed a rare ability to get beneath the surface of a creed. In exile he also wrote a biography of Anthony of Egypt, which had a huge influence on the development of monasticism.

He was called by John Henry Newman, 1,500 years later, "a principal instrument after the Apostles by which the sacred truths of Christianity have been conveyed and secured to the world".

CHAPTER TWO

AD 400-800

Converting the barbarians

Christianity had gained new freedom from the edicts of the Emperor Constantine from AD313 onwards. Emperors began interfering in church affairs, but then, if a policy of persecution had continued, could Christianity have survived?

No sooner had Christians started to construct foundations, than the unthinkable happened: the sack and eventual fall of Rome. Thus the most influential theologian in Christian history – Augustine – and the man who established a stable text for the Bible – Jerome – both worked with barbarians at the gate.

When the barbarians won and a king with an outlandish German name sat in Rome, the world did not end. Rather, Christians set out to convert these warlike people to the orthodox faith, within the framework of their cultures. Clovis became the Christian king of what had once been Roman Gaul; Patrick implanted Christianity in the hard, rocky and cold territory of Ireland; even the Germanic tribes settled in Britannia succumbed to the persuasion of Augustine of Canterbury.

Meanwhile Benedict was adapting the monastic life in a way that would change the face of Western civilisation.

Right: *Vision of St Augustine* by the Venetian Vittore Carpaccio (*c*1460-*c*1525). Augustine of Hippo was one of the four Latin Doctors of the Church, along with Jerome, Ambrose and Gregory. Here he is shown caught in contemplation in an idealised study, his mitre on a sacristy table in the niche, his bishop's crozier leaning beside it

New ideas, new

After the collapse of the Roman Empire at the start of the 5th century n and this was the task of Jerome, while Augustine of Hippo, pictured he

beginnings

ndations were needed if Christianity was to be a world force. A readable Bible was essential,

ovided a theology which could survive the centuries. His life and times are analysed on the next pages

We know more about the life and character of Augustine (AD354-430) than of any other person in the ancient world. He was fascinated by the working of his own mind. In his autobiographical *Confessions*, for example, he psychologically dissects a youthful incident when he and his companions steal pears from an orchard. He did not want the pears to eat them – he threw them away after the theft. Why then did he steal them? Was the attraction the illicitness of the act itself? And so on.

This sort of insight into motive is unparalleled among writers of his time. And when Augustine has changed his life and become the ideal bishop, we are able to hear today even his throwaway lines during his sermons – his apology for keeping his audience standing, or his admission that he has tired himself out. These come down to us with the exact words he used, because shorthand writers, trained in the best practice of Roman court reporting, wrote down what he said. It is these transcripts that have survived, not just his own sermon notes.

Augustine was born into a prosperous household on November 13 354 at Tagaste in the part of North Africa then called Numidia, now Algeria and Tunisia. It was a thriving Roman province, its culture more thoroughly Latin than in Italy itself, where Greek was spoken in parts. Tagaste was one of more than 500 cities in North Africa that had a bishop.

Augustine's father Patricius was not a Christian; his mother Monica was. The boy was not baptised (though when he was sick he had asked to be). As was not uncommon at that time, he was enrolled as a catechumen, a candidate for eventual baptism. When he was 17 his father died. Augustine was to have been a lawyer, and although his education was paid for by a friend of his father's, he became fascinated by rhetoric and then philosophy and

never took to the law. If he had, we should know no more of him than of Romanianus, his father's friend.

In 370 Augustine went to Carthage, and threw himself into its exciting intellectual life and more immediately attractive sexual opportunities. When Augustine whispered that half-prayer "Lord make me chaste, but not yet" he was still a teenager. He was living fairly stably (they stayed together 14 years) with a woman who bore him a son, Adeodatus, by the time he was 18.

When he was 19, Augustine fell for the attractions of the Manichaean religion. This was not a Christian heresy, but an oriental religion with some similarities to Zoroastrianism, and some to the much later Catharism or Albigensianism of the Pyrenean area. Among other things it proposed an evil deity as the one who has put bad things in the world. It also offered philosophical answers to questions that fascinated Augustine. "Wait till Faustus is here," his Manichaean friends would tell him, "he will explain everything." This was the celebrated Faustus of Mileve, an intellectual champion of Manichaeanism. But when Faustus did come, Augustine was disappointed. He knew no more than Augustine himself.

By then Augustine was 29. He moved to Italy and after a while took up a professorship at Milan. In that city he met Ambrose, the bishop, who impressed him. (Augustine later recalled how he was taken by the way Ambrose read to himself without mouthing the words.) Augustine began reading more philosophy. The Platonists set him looking for the ultimate truth. One day in 386 in a garden in Milan, he was struck while reading Paul's letter to the Romans (13, 12)

Augustine, the model theologian

Augustine set a pattern that was followed for hundreds of years. He was the ideal bishop; methods of preaching were copied from his published sermons; above all he set the topics that theologians have have continued to develop up to today

Augustine was Bishop of Hippo for 34 years, until his death in AD430. For later generations his behaviour demonstrated exactly what a bishop should be. Augustine saw his chief role as that of a shepherd to his church – the people of Hippo. He instructed them weekly, sometimes daily. He decided on disputed cases – sometimes he was so crowded by litigants that he complained that they should go to civil magistrates. He reconciled sinners to the Church. In Augustine's time there was a lengthy process of public penance for public sinners to go through. But for sinners who came to him privately he had a surprisingly maternal tenderness.

As a bishop Augustine was driven to combat false teaching. He repeatedly held public debates with the leaders of the heretical Donatists, who set up rival churches

to the Catholic ones. He did not hesitate to persuade the civil authorities to take action against Donatist dissent.

In the bishop's house where Augustine lived he set up a community like that of a monastery. He spent much time writing books or dictating letters. There was a library to which he could refer. But Augustine did not have possessions of his own; he dressed in a dull robe and lived a hard life. He was often sick and he hated travelling. In his last two decades, the great men and women of the day came to see him.

For later centuries he was celebrated as the Doctor of Grace. All that means is that he was convinced that the grace of God, through Jesus Christ the man and God, was the only thing that could save him. Sometimes Augustine is blamed for holding in a strong form some marginal Christian teaching, when all he is doing is shining a strong light on the common doctrine that he found in the Church around him.

The key themes

Augustine's characteristic themes are the Fall (mankind sinning), the Atonement (Jesus Christ reconciling mankind with God), Grace (the application of God's love and his life to individual people) and Predestination (God's foreknowledge of people's response to his grace).

There is no doubt that Augustine was convinced that it was easy to be damned. He saw damnation as a reflection of God's justice – for in justice no one deserves heaven. He did not think that damnation militated against God's love and mercy. He taught that the people who reach heaven are predestined to that salvation; he did not make clear what it is about predestination that leaves the damned in hell. He recognised the freedom of human beings, and certainly did not think God cruelly creates them just to people hell.

A respect for science

Augustine is also without rival in his theology of the Church. The Church for him is the mystical Body of Christ. In his day when the *disciplina arcana* still prohibited for Christians the public discussion of the mysteries of the Eucharist he explained the presence of Christ in the Eucharist as a unifying participation in the Body of Christ, living in the Church.

Augustine was not a neatly systematic thinker. In his treatises on the Trinitarian God or in his commentaries on scripture he works round subjects in a way that would have annoyed a late medieval theologian trained in a logical method. Because of this technique, Augustine is easy to take out of context. He builds up a picture, and when it is a big book such as *The City of God*, the argument fills a very large canvas. *The City of God* sets out to show that the fall of Rome in 410 was not caused by the by the answer: Jesus Christ was the way to truth, and salvation. With his son Adeodatus, his mother Monica, and some friends of his own age he withdrew to a country villa to work things out. At Easter in 387, with Adeodatus, now aged 15, he was baptised by Ambrose along with the other candidates in the cathedral at Milan. Monica, who had been praying for her son all the while, died before the year was out.

This year remade Augustine anew. And on this occasion the change lasted. He returned to Africa and gave away his possessions to the poor. Though it was not his idea, he was persuaded in 391 to become a priest by the enthusiastic urgings of the Christians at Hippo. Five years later he was ordained as Bishop of Hippo, a rather busier and more cosmopolitan city than backwater Tagaste.

Augustine was Bishop of Hippo till his death 34 years later. And what did he do? Principally he preached: he taught his people, Sunday after Sunday, commenting on the scriptures. He also wrote a great deal; we still have 113 of his books. He was a more penetrating theologian than had yet lived. He wrote the *Confessions*, one of the world's classic autobiographies. He wrote *The City of God*, which has been read ever since.

By any standards Augustine was an amazing figure. Perhaps he was frightening, though there are many suggestions of a compassionate side. In any event he left an indelible mark on the life and thought of Christianity. He died in Hippo on August 28 430 as the Vandals were besieging the city.

St Augustine of Hippo preaching to his people, from a 12th-century Anglo-Saxon manuscript of *De Civitate Dei*, The City of God

The Roman province of Numidia, in what is now Algeria and Tunisia, was a thriving centre of Latin culture. Country dwellers spoke Punic. Augustine was born at Tagaste and in 396 he became bishop of the seaport of Hippo, dying on the eve of the Vandal invasion

abandonment of pagan religion. But that great theme takes in many digressions. In his commentaries on scripture modern readers may find his allegorical interpretations fanciful. He has a baffling habit of using numerology, though this made sense to his contemporaries. Below the allegory, Augustine is convinced that the literal meaning of the Bible should first be determined. It is this hermeneutic (method of interpretation) that is sound: "We must be on our guard against giving interpretations that are hazardous or opposed to science, and so exposing the word of God to the ridicule of unbelievers," he wrote in a commentary on the Book of Genesis.

A genius when one was needed
In the mid 19th century it was fashionable to claim that Augustine was the father of evangelical Protestantism and his opponent Pelagius (c360-420) was the father of Catholicism. From about 1870 the coin was tossed the other way.

"Where, in the history of the West, is there to be found a man who, in point of influence, can be compared with him?" asked the Protestant theologian Adolf von Harnack (1851-1930). "In the 5th century, at the hour that the Church inherited the Roman Empire, she had within her a man of extraordinarily deep and powerful genius: from him she took her ideas, and to this present hour she has been unable to break away from them."

That is still true.

'Where is thy God?'

Augustine would preach to a crowd of dusty, hot people standing in the basilica-like church in Hippo. Some of them would be country folk for whom Punic was their first language. Most were city dwellers in Hippo Regius ("Regius" because of its popularity with the old kings of Numidia). Hippo was a tough seaport and there were temptations from the amphitheatre and its lewd dramas. Sunday after Sunday Augustine followed a course of instruction for his people. He was worth listening to. In Latin-speaking society rhetoric was prized, and Augustine was a master. But his approach was popular. He responded to his audience; if time ran out or they were tired he simply stopped. Here he preaches on a phrase from Psalm 42: "Where is thy God?"

One who truly loves the invisible God says, as he sighs for the love of him: "My tears have been my bread day and night, while it is said to me daily: Where is thy God?"

Why should the tears and sighs of one who loves like that not become his bread? Why should they not be food to him and satisfy his hunger? Why should he not gladly weep until such time as he actually has sight of what he loves, while he still hears daily said to him: "Where is thy God?"

If I ask a heathen, "Where is thy God?" then he shows me his statues. If I break his statues to pieces, then he shows me a mountain, a tree, an ordinary stone from a riverbed. One that he picks up from among a number of stones, sets in a place of honour and then bows down low and worships – that is his god. If then I laugh at his stone and take it and break it or contemptuously throw it away, he points with his finger to the sun or the moon, he shows me this star or that, calling one Saturn, another Mercury.

Of something that happens to come into his mind, of something that he can point to with his finger, he says to me, "That is my god". Since I see the sun before me and cannot break it in pieces, and since I cannot fetch down the stars, he thinks he has very much got the better of me, for he can indicate things which are visible and point with his finger at all kinds of things and say, "This is my god", and then he turns to me and says, "Where is thy God?"

When I hear this, when I hear him say, "Where is thy God?", then I have nothing which I can show to the eye.

You say, "Show me your God." I say, "Show me your soul!" Why can you not do this? Because it is invisible. For all that, it is the best thing within you.

Now you say that you know your soul from your works, and you say this rightly. Well, in exactly the same way, I know my God, for he who has created all that you can admire when it is within yourself – he is my God.

Jerome's new Latin Bible

By the 5th century the Church had decided which books from the Old Testament and which writings from after the time of Jesus should make up the canonical text of the Bible. The trouble was that translations into Latin were so varied that no two seemed to agree. Since Latin was replacing Greek as a lingua franca, Jerome was given the urgent task of producing a reliable, consistent version. His so-called Vulgate version set a standard for the King James version in English 1,200 years later

Jerome was the most learned man of his day. His great achievement was the translation of the Bible into Latin, still used internationally and a large influence on the English versions we know today. But even without that, his fierce temperament and razor intellect would have won him notice. Jerome was called in Latin Eusebius Hieronymus and was born at Strido in Dalmatia (now in Croatia) in about the year AD342. Like many of his contemporaries he was brought up a Christian, but was not baptised till he was an adult, when he was 18.

By then he had studied in Rome for eight years under a leading grammarian, Donatus, whose learned accomplishments went far beyond what we mean by grammar today. Like his Eastern contemporary Chrysostom (*see page 42*), Jerome went to live among the desert hermits, in the wilds near Antioch in Syria. He learnt Hebrew from a Jewish rabbi, and then went to study under Gregory Nazianzus, one of the holiest and deepest of the theologians of Cappadocia (in modern central Turkey).

Though he was ordained a priest at Antioch, Jerome was convinced his vocation did not lie in that office, which he refused to exercise. But between 382 and 385 he served as secretary to Pope Damasus I, a saintly and learned man energetic in reforms. In Rome, Jerome became the leader of a group of pious and high-born women. At the same time he fell out with many good men, for his letters were astonishingly acerbic and contentious and his judgment was of a rigorist bent.

Enmities forced him to return to the East after the death of Pope Damasus, and he lived from 386 at Bethlehem. The building of a sort of holy academy there, with a communal house for men and another for women, was paid for by one of his women followers, Paula. She was the widow of a Roman senator and had five children. She had learnt Greek from her father and now learnt Hebrew, so that she might sing the Psalms in the language of their composition.

At her foundation at Bethlehem, pilgrims were offered hospitality and the local children were taught by Jerome free of charge. He had the good sense to see that Paula possessed the calm efficiency and tact he lacked, though he criticised her excessive penances and financial generosity. This indeed left her daughter with debts when Paula died in 404, movingly mourned in letters by her teacher and protégé Jerome.

All the while Jerome kept up a controversial correspondence. His views on celibacy vied in their trenchancy with his stance on the heresy of Pelagianism (*see page 46*). He even quarrelled with his friend from childhood, Rufinus. This is a typical Jerome row, and it is one that is not easy to follow at this distance. Rufinus had translated works by the theologian Origen (*c*185-255) quite faithfully into Latin. Jerome had used Origen too, not only his edition of parallel translations of the Bible – the *Hexapla* – but also his doctrinal works. Jerome complained that Rufinus, a convinced follower of Origen, was heretical. Rufinus responded energetically, pointing out that Jerome himself had quoted without disapproval supposedly suspect passages from Origen. It seems the truth of the matter was that Jerome did not entirely understand Origen but had orthodox intentions; Rufinus did understand Origen but was not always honest.

But Jerome's main work was the translation of the Bible. The labours of this work might be some excuse for his bad temper, though the source of that must perhaps be sought in the man's angular character. He once dreamt he was being scourged by angels for being fonder of Cicero, the Latin stylist, than of Christ.

The translation was finished by about 404, and not a moment too soon, for with the influx of warlike barbarians Jerome's world soon became dangerously upset. Refugees from the sack of Rome in 410 flocked to Bethlehem. Huns and Isaurians made raids uncomfortably near. Houses of learning he had founded were destroyed by religious separatists. He lived on till 420, his crankiness forgiven, his reputation hammered into one for holiness.

Later pictures show him with an attendant lion, from whose paw of course he had removed a thorn, and with a wide, red, tasselled cardinal's hat, though he was not a cardinal in the later sense, for no such post had yet been invented. Sometimes renaissance paintings show him wearing spectacles at his desk. The pictures of him beating his breast with a stone as he fasts in the desert are nearer the mark. He is one of the four Latin Doctors – great founding theologians – of the Church, with Augustine, Ambrose and Gregory. Since the 16th century further Doctors have been added to the Western Church.

The popular image of St Jerome in the wilderness about to take the thorn from a lion's paw is here painted by the Venetian Giovanni Bellini (*c*1440). Like the 2nd-century legend of Androcles, in this story the lion is tamed, to become his companion. Other painters depict the lion asleep at Jerome's feet

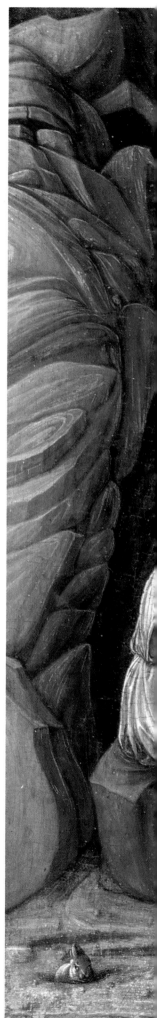

A book for everyone

The committee that translated the Bible into English in 1611 (the so-called King James version, *see page 134*) had great praise for the labours of Jerome, who was "moved to undertake the translating of the Old Testament out of the very fountains themselves; which he performed with that evidence of great learning, judgment, industry, and faithfulness, that he hath for ever bound the Church unto him in a debt of special remembrance and thankfulness".

Jerome's achievement was breathtaking. To accomplish it he improved his mastery of Greek and went off to learn Aramaic and Hebrew in Palestine. Some parts he translated quickly — the book of Tobit, which he did not regard as of the central canon, in one day, out of the Chaldee. The rest of the Old Testament took him 15 years.

Greek was the lingua franca of the first two centuries AD. Even in Rome the educated classes spoke Greek, and the Church in Rome recited its Eucharistic prayers in Greek. North Africa was the heartland of Latin-speaking culture. When Jerome came to the Bible, it had already been translated into the so-called Old Latin version, but, as he complained to Pope St Damasus who had commissioned him to revise it, hardly any two manuscripts agreed in their readings. Jerome's finished work became known as the Vulgate (a reference to its being in the common tongue). This is what he did with six different parts of the Bible:

1 Old Latin version of the books of Baruch, Wisdom, Maccabees and Ecclesiasticus. These Jerome did not touch.

2 Old Latin version of Acts, the Epistles and Revelation. These he revised, leaving much uncorrected.

3 The Chaldee versions of Tobit and Ruth. These he translated freely and rapidly.

4 The Psalms translated from the so-called Septuagint version, in Greek (dating from the 3rd century BC). This version is carried by the Vulgate Bible. Jerome later made a separate translation from the original Hebrew.

5 The Old Latin version of the four Gospels. This he revised and partially corrected, making reference to the best manuscripts of the original Greek.

6 The rest of the Old Testament. Jerome's was the first independent translation from the original Hebrew ever made.

IHOVANES BELINVS

The last page of Matthew from the Lichfield Gospels (AD 720-730) in the Vulgate version Jerome had corrected using the original Greek

SONIA HALLIDAY PHOTOGRAPHS

Eastern approaches

John Chrysostom is honoured as a saint in the West and as the holy founder of a whole tradition in the East.
But during his life he became the catalyst for fierce arguments between the Eastern Emperor and the Pope in Rome.
It was an early sign of differences to come

St John Chrysostom, the Golden Mouth that condemned riches. This 15th-century mural comes from the church of the Holy Cross in Platanistasa, Cyprus

It was an argument over the figure of John Chrysostom that caused a breach between the Eastern Emperor (in alliance with the great see of Alexandria, in Egypt) and Rome, the see of the successor of Peter. Chrysostom had been appointed Archbishop of Constantinople in AD397 by Arcadius, Emperor of the East. The quarrel began after Chrysostom was deposed in 403. His cause continued to be championed by the Pope, who remained in conflict with the Eastern Emperor even after Chrysostom's death. Relations were broken off, and for 11 years (404-415) there was no communion between Rome and Constantinople. It was a foreshadowing of trouble in centuries ahead.

John Chrysostom is counted as one of the four Doctors of the Eastern Church (along with Basil, Gregory Nazianzus and Athanasius). The chief liturgy of medieval Byzantium was also named after him. The name Chrysostom, "golden-mouth", was a later tribute to his oratorical skills. He has a just claim to be called the most accessible of the early Church fathers: he was interested in everything that passed before him in the world and used examples to enliven his sermons. Among the works by John Chrysostom read today is his series of commentaries on the Bible, particularly on the Epistles of St Paul.

John Chrysostom was born in Antioch in 347, the son of an army officer. He was brought up by his widowed mother, a Christian, though he was baptised only in adulthood. He studied oratory under a renowned pagan master, Libanius, but then went to live in the mountain wilderness. After six years ill health forced him to return to Antioch. There he worked for the bishop Flavian and gained a reputation for his preaching.

His appointment by the Emperor as Archbishop of Constantinople entailed his serving as court chaplain. John's ascetic background and intransigent character ill-fitted him for court intrigue. On his arrival in Constantinople, he gave to charity the money his predecessors had spent on lavish hospitality, and he sacked many clergy, saying they were unfit for holy orders.

Such behaviour did not endear him to the establishment. He also attracted the jealousy of Theophilus, the Archbishop of Alexandria, who soon clashed with him over his treatment of some desert monks he had expelled from Eygpt. From then on Theophilus sought to end John's career, a cause made very much easier by John's ability to infuriate the rich among his congregation. He was popular with the poor, but John's reservations about the use of private property – a result, he said, of the fall of Adam – horrified the wealthy. Worst of all he upset the Empress Eudoxia; she never forgot a pointed reference to Jezebel, the scarlet woman of the Old Testament, in one of his sermons.

Theophilus then gathered a council outside Constantinople and deposed John, on slender grounds. The decision would have been ineffectual had the imperial family not been angry with him. He was sent into exile, only to be recalled the next day when an earth tremor struck the city; the Empress had seen it as a bad omen. But a few months later, he fell into imperial disfavour again by explicitly comparing Eudoxia to Herodias, who had the head of John the Baptist served to her on a platter.

This time, he refused to leave the city. There was bloodshed when the Emperor sent troops to drive the faithful out of church on Easter Saturday. John complained to Pope Innocent I, who exhorted Theophilus to appear before a council. But two months later John was ordered into exile in Armenia. The Pope then sent five bishops to Constantinople to arrange a council, but they were imprisoned in Thrace. The Emperor, meanwhile, irritated by the popular support for John which had turned his place of exile into a resort for pilgrims, ordered him to move on to the eastern edge of the Black Sea. During the gruelling journey, John died at Comana in Cappadocia on September 14 407.

The Alexandrian church, having added a feud with Rome to its clash with John Chrysostom, refused to add his name to its diptychs (the lists of names read during the Eucharistic liturgy). In 428 a feast in honour of John was instituted at Constantinople.

EYEWITNESS

First sight of the Holy Land

Etheria, who came from northwest Spain or southwest France, made a pilgrimage to Jerusalem in about AD400. On the way she visited Mount Nebo, from the summit of which Moses had seen the Promised Land

We arrived at the foot of Mount Nebo, which was very high; but we were able to climb most of it on donkeys, though a little bit was steeper and had to be climbed laboriously on foot. But we made it. We arrived at the top of the mountain, where there is now a fairly small church. So we said some prayers, and did the things one does in such places. We were just going out of the church when the people who knew the place – the priests and holy monks – told us: "If you want to see the places mentioned in the books of Moses, come outside the door, and from that side of the summit have a look and we will tell you what each place is that you can see." We were delighted at this and hurried out.

From the door we could see where the Jordan runs into the Dead Sea. On the opposite side we saw not only Livias, but also Jericho, on the other side of the Jordan. The place where we were standing, outside the door, was very high. We could see right over Palestine, the Promised Land and the whole land of Jordan, as far as the eye could see.

From the left-hand side we could see all the country of the Sodomites, and Segor, the only one of the five cities [destroyed by God for their sinfulness] that exists today. There is a memorial, but there is nothing left to see of the other cities, apart from a heap of ruins, as they were after being turned into ashes. We were shown the place where there was an inscription about Lot's wife [turned into a pillar of salt for having looked back towards Sodom]. Believe me, dear ladies, the pillar cannot be seen; only its site. The pillar itself is said to have been covered by the Dead Sea.

Pilgrim power

The discovery of the True Cross in Jerusalem brought Christians from all over Europe

The journey to Jerusalem in about AD400 recounted by Etheria (left) bore familiar likenesses to a pilgrim's package tour today: the guides eager to make money out of the pilgrims, the clergy eager to show off sometimes unconvincing relics, but also the kindness of Christian strangers. If pilgrimage was a pre-Christian appetite in many cultures, it gained an impetus in the 4th century from the discovery by Helena, the mother of the Emperor Constantine, of a cross – the True Cross on which Jesus suffered, she was convinced – buried in Jerusalem, at the spot where the church of the Holy Sepulchre now stands.

Pilgrim routes became established and news was exchanged between settlers in the Holy Land, such as Jerome (see page 40) and people back home in Rome, or much less well connected places. Ordinary lay people, women not excluded, made journeys of hundreds of miles by sea, if they could, or by land, to visit the places connected with the life of Jesus in Palestine, or of the Apostles and martyrs in Rome.

Yet, as Jerome pointed out, it was not the fact of being in Jerusalem, but living virtuously there that counted. "Et de Hierusolymis et de Britannia aequaliter patet aula coelestis" – even places at the ends of the earth like Britain are as near to heaven as Jerusalem.

The appetite for pilgrimage was to play its part hundreds of years later, at the end of the 11th century, in the crusades (see page 86). Nevertheless, John Chrysostom would eagerly have travelled to Rome to see the shrines of St Peter and St Paul if his duties as bishop had not tied him to his see. "If I were free from my labours and my body were in sound health," he wrote, "I would eagerly make a pilgrimage merely to see the chains that held Paul captive and the prison where he lay."

Above: a 6th-century mosaic map of Jerusalem from the Greek Orthodox church of St George in Madaba, Jordan. Jerusalem had never really recovered from its destruction in AD 70. But it was transformed by the Emperor Constantine after his mother believed she had discovered the True Cross buried there. The Church of the Holy Sepulchre, built on the spot, was the first of many fine buildings reflecting its new status as a centre of pilgrimage

A new light on Jesus

That Jesus was both God and man had been defined at Nicaea in AD325. But new theories threatened to undermine the accepted teaching. Another universal council of bishops was needed

The twin powers of Church and Emperor were both well pleased that a universal council of bishops at Nicaea had in AD325 reached a peaceable resolution of a violent controversy about who and what Jesus was (*see page 33*). But just over a century later, new and more dangerous differences threatened the stability of the Empire. The Emperor was Theodosius II; the champions of the two sides were Nestorius, the Archbishop of the Emperor's capital, Constantinople, and Cyril, the Patriarch of Alexandria. It was a clash of personalities as well as a political hot potato. The Emperor pretended to be neutral, but at every move betrayed his sympathy for the Archbishop of Constantinople. Cyril was an unbending defender of the orthodox Catholic position, but he used terminology that annoyed Nestorius, who belonged to a different and venerable school of theology. In 428 Nestorius denounced Cyril as a heretic for exaggerating orthodox teaching and so falling into error on the opposite side.

What was all the fuss about? It concerned Jesus, the very matter of Christian belief. He was God and he was man; so much the Council of Nicaea and all Christendom declared. But what could you say about him *as God* or *as*

A catalogue of errors

At the heart of the debate at the Council of Ephesus were the propositions known as the Anathemas of Cyril of Alexandria. He appended them to a letter to Constantinople condemning the teaching of Nestorius, who had objected to the title Theotokos being given to Mary the mother of Jesus. The Anathemas were approved by the Council of Ephesus in 431.

If any one does not acknowledge that Emmanuel is in truth God, and that the holy Virgin is, in consequence, "Theotokos", for she brought forth after the flesh the Word of God who has become flesh, let him be anathema.

If any one does not acknowledge that the Word which is from God the Father was personally united with flesh, and with his own flesh is one Christ, that is, one and the same God and man together, let him be anathema.

If any one presumes to call Christ a "God-bearing man", let him be anathema.

If any one says that Jesus as man was operated by God the Word, and that the "glory of the only-begotten" was attached to him, as something existing apart from himself, let him be anathema.

If anyone presumes to say that "the man who was assumed is to be worshipped together with the Divine Word", let him be anathema.

If any one does not confess that the Word of God suffered in the flesh and was crucified in the flesh, let him be anathema.

man? Cyril drew up a list of sometimes surprising propositions (*see box, left*) about Jesus, such as "If anyone presumes to call Christ a 'God-bearing man' let him be anathema." (The anathema was the formalised curse with which false teachers were reprobated.) But what Nestorius objected to was calling Jesus's mother, Mary, by the title "Theotokos" – the Bearer of God, or the Mother of God. "We must not say that God is two or three months old," said Nestorius. Perhaps not, but Jesus had once been a baby, and he, as Nicaea had taught, was God. Jesus was a person, and mothers are mothers of persons, not of abstract natures.

What happened next was furious and complicated. Cyril, with the authority of the Pope, Celestine I, condemned Nestorius's teaching (which suggested Jesus was two persons) and deposed him from his bishopric of Constantinople. In 431 the Emperor decided to call a universal council of bishops, to which everyone agreed. (He invited Augustine of Hippo, not having heard he had died in the siege of Hippo by the Vandals the year before, so disrupted were communications by the barbarian incursions.) The bishops gathered at Ephesus, a city on a marshy and unhealthy plain near Smyrna in Asia Minor. A contingent of bishops from the Middle East presumed sympathetic to Nestorius hung back, and the others deliberated without them. The Pope sent legates to represent him and report back.

The bishops, about 200 of them, meeting in the cathedral, declared against Nestorius and confirmed his deposition from his bishopric. The council specifically referred to the teaching (read out to the delegates in a letter) of the Pope as Bishop of Rome and successor to Peter. The people of Ephesus enthusiastically showed their support for the majority in the council. The Emperor was still not so sure. He countenanced the holding of a separate meeting of bishops, mostly the delayed contingent from the Middle East, which denounced Cyril. Meanwhile the majority bishops were kept virtual captives in the sweltering heat of Ephesus; funerals began to be held daily. To avoid murderous supporters of Nestorius they had to smuggle a report of their decision to Constantinople in a hollow stick carried by a messenger disguised as a beggar. When the monks of Constantinople, a formidable party, heard the result they marched in thousands through the city bearing tapers and cheered by the people. When, in addition, Emperor Theodosius heard that the Pope had confirmed the findings of the majority, he turned against Nestorius. Nestorius retired to a monastery and wrote a book of self-justification called *Tragedy*. He died in exile but his teachings lived on, resolutely held by millions, chiefly in the East.

This icon from the Zverin monastery, Novgorod, painted in 1399, shows bishops and people under the protection of the Theotokos (Mother of God). It was that title that precipitated a crisis in AD431

Shock waves at t

The Goths sacked Rome in AD410. It was almost unthinkable that the centre of Western civilisation and its Church should have fallen to barbarian hordes. Why had God allowed the holy city of Peter and Paul to be pillaged? Was it the end of the world? If not, could Rome coexist with the barbarians or even bring them within the fold of orthodox Christianity?

A terrible shock ran through the civilised Western world when in AD410, Alaric and the Goths sacked the city of Rome. The invaders were compared to the Horsemen of the Apocalypse, and the sack to the destruction of Sodom. To Romans, anyone who could not speak Latin or Greek but stuttered in a strange tongue was a barbarian capable of any atrocity. The pagans in the former empire blamed Christianity for the city's downfall, saying the old gods to whom she owed her imperial greatness were angry.

Some Christians asked why Rome's Christian patrons Saints Peter and Paul, whose bones lay in the city, had not protected them from invasion. But Alaric, who was an adherent of Christianity, even if of the heretic Arian variety, did not touch most of the large churches. Those who had sought shelter there were safe.

All the same, the Romans' confidence in the orderly establishment of Christianity and the friendly dispositions of divine providence had been badly shaken. St Augustine of Hippo addressed these doubts in the *City of God*, a monumental apologia for Christianity, written between 413 and 427. He urged the faithful to place their hopes on the kingdom of heaven, which existed forever, regardless of the fate of temporal empire. "The greatest city in the world has fallen in ruin," he wrote, "but the city of God endures forever."

The ritual practices of paganism in Rome had been made illegal. With the loss of imperial support any hankering after the old religion had dwindled, although pagan loyalties remained among a portion of the elite, such as senators, intellectuals and teachers. The new Christians were surrounded by the pagan heritage of empire whose traditions were far from dead. Even at the end of the 5th century, Pope Gelasius (reigned 492-6) had to protest about the public celebration of a pagan feast. Pope Leo the Great (reigned 440-460) rebuked his congregation in the middle of the century for bowing to the sun before entering St Peter's basilica. In the climate of confusion that went with repeated barbarian incursions into the city of Rome, unpredictable and sudden out-

breaks of heretical belief presented themselves for the Church authorities to combat as they might.

The principal heresy to affect Rome in the early years of the century was Pelagianism. This was propagated by a monk called Pelagius, who had come from Britain and while living in Rome built up something of a following. Pelagius held strong views on the difficult question of original sin and free will. He believed that mankind, represented in its first parents, Adam and Eve, had sinned wilfully, but that this sin had not radically damaged the faculties of human nature. In other words Pelagianism suggested that everyone could be good without needing the aid of God's grace.

Oddly enough this interpretation of human nature made Pelagius something of a hard taskmaster. He was shocked by the easygoing morality prevalent amongst the affluent in Rome and he blamed it on Church teaching

This 19th-century aquatint by the German artist Adam Eberle shows Alaric and the Goths sacking Rome. In fact Alaric, like most Germanic barbarians, was an Arian Christian and he left the churches – and those hiding in them – alone

he Sack of Rome

"Great", as his actions showed. He lived up to the claims of the Bishop of Rome, the Pope, reflected by his assumption of the title of Pontifex Maximus (Supreme Priest), a title previously used by the Emperor.

The Church saw the apostles Peter and Paul as the fathers of Christian Rome just as Romulus and Remus had been of the pagan city. Leo made it clear that, whatever he said, whatever he did, he spoke and acted with the voice and authority of Peter. Always in his mind seemed to be the words of Jesus from St Matthew's Gospel: "Thou art Peter, and upon this rock I will build my church; and the gates of hell shall not prevail against it." Leo's mission was to ensure the entire Church followed the teaching and practice of Rome, according to the apostolic tradition. He undertook a vast and continuous correspondence with his fellow bishops, in Italy, Gaul and Africa, shoring up contact between them and the See of Rome – no easy feat while the Western world fell subject to barbarian invasions.

Leo's convictions sometimes fitted ill with the attitude of the Eastern part of the old Roman Empire. Since the sack of Rome in 410, the mantle of civilisation had consciously been assumed by Constantinople, the "New Rome" founded the century before by the Emperor Constantine. It was proud of its ecclesiastical traditions and rights. But in the mid 5th century the Christian world was confronted with yet another heresy concerning the nature of Jesus Christ. Patriarch Flavian of Constantinople presided at a synod of bishops in 448 which condemned Eutyches, a monk who taught an extreme form of Monophysitism – he held that Jesus was not both man and God, but had one nature, dominantly divine.

Pope Leo, at Flavian's invitation, endorsed the findings of the synod. His summary of the orthodox understanding of the incarnation of God as man are contained in his letter of reply, known as the *Tome to Flavian*. Meanwhile, the Eastern Emperor had summoned a council of bishops on his own account, convened on August 8 449. This was later nicknamed *Latrocinium* – the den of thieves – for, not only did it find in favour of Eutyches, but it deposed Flavian as Patriarch of Constantinople. Three days later he was brutally beaten to death by a mob of his opponents.

Leo had to wait for the universal council of Chalcedon in 451 to see the orthodox belief vindicated. In the meantime Attila the Hun had invaded Italy and the Pope decided to go to Mantua to meet him. He succeeded in persuading Attila to turn his army back. But three years later, he could persuade Genseric, the leader of a Vandal horde, only to refrain from setting fire to Rome. The Vandals spent a fortnight looting its riches. The last Roman Emperor of the West was Romulus Augustulus, and he was deposed by Odoacer, the Germanic warrior, who in 476 became the first barbarian king of Rome.

A medallion of Emperor Valentinian III (425-455) with the head of a barbarian beneath his foot. During his reign Vandals invaded North Africa.

about divine grace. He thought people were only too ready to believe that they could do nothing by their own efforts and that they used this as an excuse for lax morals. If only, Pelagius implied, they made the effort, they would be much more godly.

After the Sack of Rome, Pelagius went to Africa, where he clashed with Augustine, the Bishop of Hippo. Two councils were held in Africa to judge Pelagius's teaching. Pope Innocent I (reigned 402-17) condemned Pelagianism and its adherents. But after Innocent's death his successor Pope Zosimus (417-19) was briefly won over by the declarations of orthodoxy made by some of Pelagius's followers. Eventually, the Pelagians were banished from Rome, by imperial edict as a threat to the peace.

Amid the gloomy days of the mid-5th century the figure of Leo the Great (reigned 440-460) raised the reputation and power of Rome. Leo deserved the description

Roman and Ostrogoth

For old-fashioned Romans it was a trial to live under a barbarian king, especially one who was an Arian heretic. Boethius was one such Roman. As chief of the palace he was accused of treason; while awaiting execution he turned to the consolation of philosophy

For the 1,000 years after his death in AD525 Boethius was one of the writers most read and revered by Christians in the West. His masterpiece, *The Consolation of Philosophy*, was translated by both King Alfred the Great and by Queen Elizabeth I. His life spanned the declining splendour of Rome and the new barbarian regimes. Anicius Manlius Severinus Boethius was born in 475 into an aristocratic Roman family which had become Christian some time in the 4th century. Among his ancestors Boethius could number men of wealth, several consuls, two emperors and a pope. As a boy he received an excellent education in the liberal arts. Crucially, he gained a fluency in Greek which opened to him the world of the ancient philosophers.

His public career began at an early age when, for reasons now unknown, the Ostrogoth king Theodoric, ruler of the Western Empire, spotted Boethius and took him into his service. His rise was rapid: by 510 he was consul and soon after that he was made *magister officiorum* – head of the civil service and chief of the palace officials. But there were bound to be tensions between him and Theodoric. The king was an Arian heretic; though he was king, and ruled Rome, he was in theory subject to the Emperor in Constantinople. It was on suspicion of secret dealings with Theodoric's enemies in Constantinople that

Boethius was arrested, imprisoned and cruelly executed.

Despite the success of his public career, the study of philosophy had always been his prime interest; reading the ancient authors was, he said, the chief solace in life. He approached the subject with enormous dedication and wanted to make his life's work the translation of all Aristotle's works and those of Plato from Greek into Latin for a Western readership. Aristotle's methodology was essential to the development of medieval theology.

Boethius's immense scholarship also formed the background for his masterwork, written during his imprisonment before his execution: *The Consolation of Philosophy*. In this work, which alternates between verse and prose, Boethius laments the world he lives in, where evil seems to triumph over good. Philosophy personified

The Three Kings in a 6th-century mosaic in Sant' Apollinare Nuovo, Ravenna. Unlike the Emperor at the time, these barbarian kings wear trousers. Their Phrygian caps were worn by freed Roman slaves, and were in later times adopted by the Jacobins in the French Revolution

THE MAIN EVENTS AD400-800

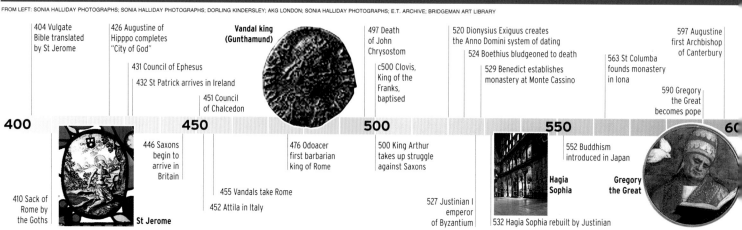

404 Vulgate Bible translated by St Jerome

426 Augustine of Hipppo completes "City of God"

Vandal king (Gunthamund)

497 Death of John Chrysostom

520 Dionysius Exiguus creates the Anno Domini system of dating

524 Boethius bludgeoned to death

597 Augustine first Archbishop of Canterbury

431 Council of Ephesus

432 St Patrick arrives in Ireland

451 Council of Chalcedon

c500 Clovis, King of the Franks, baptised

529 Benedict establishes monastery at Monte Cassino

563 St Columba founds monastery in Iona

590 Gregory the Great becomes pope

400   **450**   **500**   **550**   **60**

446 Saxons begin to arrive in Britain

476 Odoacer first barbarian king of Rome

500 King Arthur takes up struggle against Saxons

552 Buddhism introduced in Japan

Hagia Sophia

Gregory the Great

410 Sack of Rome by the Goths

St Jerome

455 Vandals take Rome

452 Attila in Italy

527 Justinian I emperor of Byzantium

532 Hagia Sophia rebuilt by Justinian

The source and goal of the cosmos

The ninth poem from "The Consolation of Philosophy" by Boethius,
addressed to the cause of all things

O Thou who dost by everlasting reason rule,
Creator of the planets and the sky, who time
From timelessness didst bring, unchanging Mover,
No cause drove Thee to mould unstable matter but
The form benign of highest good within Thee set.
All things Thou bringest forth from Thy high archetype:
Thou, height of beauty, in Thy mind the beauteous world
Dost bear, and in that ideal likeness shaping it,
Dost order perfect parts a perfect whole to frame.
The elements by harmony Thou dost constrain,
That hot to cold and wet to dry are equal made,
That fire grow not too light, or earth too fraught with weight.
The bridge of threefold nature madest Thou soul, which spreads
Through nature's limbs harmonious and all things moves.
The soul once cut, in circles two its motion joins,
Goes round and to it returns encircling mind,
And turns in pattern similar the firmament.
From causes like Thou bringst forth souls and lesser lives,
Which from above in chariots swift Thou dost disperse
Through sky and earth and by Thy law benign they turn
And back to Thee they come through fire that brings them home.
Grant, Father, that our minds Thy august seat may scan,
Grant us the sight of true good's source, and grant us light
That we may fix on Thee our mind's unblended eye.
Disperse the clouds of earthly matter's cloying weight;
Shine out in all Thy glory; for Thou art rest and peace
To those who worship Thee; to see Thee in our end,
Who art our source and maker, lord and path and goal.

BOETHIUS EXTRACT: PENGUIN BOOKS LTD, TRANSLATION BY V.E. WATTS. MAIN PICTURE: SONIA HALLIDAY PHOTOGRAPHS

as a woman appears in his cell and instructs him on how the world and its doings are justly ordered by God.

All worldly gifts, such as fame and money, are in reality worthless and illusory. Human achievements may reflect some aspects of goodness, but humanity would do better to search for true goodness directly, for it is synonymous with God himself. The less a man concerns himself with the day-to-day and the more he focuses on the truly good life, the closer he comes to God.

The resolution to the problem is, on the surface, achieved entirely through Neoplatonic philosophy rather than through theology – the book is titled *The Consolation of Philosophy* not *The Consolation of Religion*. In a parallel case, who would guess from *Utopia* (written 1,000 years later than Boethius) that its author, Thomas

More, was a saintly Christian? Certainly Boethius's *Consolation* is a far cry from, for example, St Augustine of Hippo, for whom man can achieve nothing on his own. For Augustine the only consolation could be the knowledge that Christ had already died for his sins and that God's grace was endless. For Boethius, man can approach God through his own efforts.

This concept is Neoplatonic and pagan. And yet in the *Consolation* Boethius eschews all the apparatus of the Neoplatonic cosmology. He refers explicitly to a single God, not to a supreme essence. Most notably at the end of the *Consolation* he advises prayer. While for some modern readers Boethius's masterpiece is a synthesis of pagan philosophy and Christianity, for the Middle Ages there was no difficulty in seeing its author as a saint.

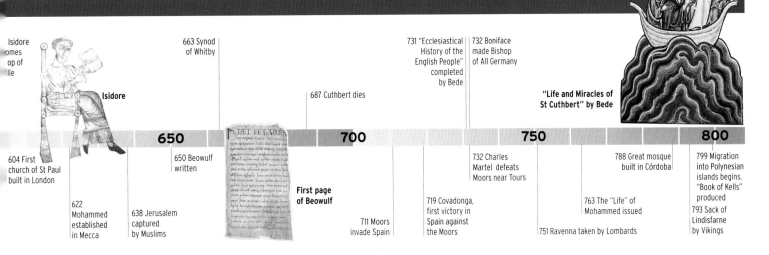

Isidore
[b]omes
[bish]op of
[Sevi]lle

663 Synod
of Whitby

731 "Ecclesiastical
History of the
English People"
completed
by Bede

732 Boniface
made Bishop
of All Germany

Isidore

687 Cuthbert dies

**"Life and Miracles of
St Cuthbert" by Bede**

650

700

750

800

604 First
church of St Paul
built in London

650 Beowulf
written

**First page
of Beowulf**

732 Charles
Martel defeats
Moors near Tours

788 Great mosque
built in Córdoba

799 Migration
into Polynesian
islands begins.
"Book of Kells"
produced

622
Mohammed
established
in Mecca

638 Jerusalem
captured
by Muslims

711 Moors
invade Spain

719 Covadonga,
first victory in
Spain against
the Moors

763 The "Life" of
Mohammed issued

751 Ravenna taken by Lombards

793 Sack of
Lindisfarne
by Vikings

Hagia Sophia: wisdom in stone

Hagia Sophia – the church of the "Holy Wisdom" – in Constantinople is the supreme expression of the Byzantine genius for architecture. A church had stood on the site since the 4th century, but after it was burnt down in riots in AD532, Justinian decided to rebuild it as the showpiece of the empire. Since the plans are said to have been drawn up in six weeks, he had perhaps already been contemplating something that would leave an adequate mark on history – the largest religious building in the world.

The architects were a professor of geometry at the University of Constantinople, Anthemius of Tralles, and Isidore of Miletus. Their designs marked a radical departure from the rectangular basilica (derived from the shape of Roman public buildings) that had hitherto served as the standard shape for churches. Instead Hagia Sophia was to be a square capped by a dome broader and higher than anything attempted before; the church was to reach up to God.

Justinian is said to have set two rival teams of 5,000 men to work on building the church from opposite ends; what is certain is that it was completed in less than six years – in the 17th century St Paul's Cathedral would take 35.

The Byzantines were not concerned with the exterior appearance of the building but with its interior – a vast, dimly lit space that is at once harmonious and elusive; it is hard to see all of it at the same moment. The inside of the church was richly decorated with glass, ivory, silver and silk, and with mosaics that conveyed a feeling of life and movement when candlelight flickered across them. Justinian's court historian Procopius wrote of the interior that "one might imagine that one had chanced upon a meadow in full bloom". And when Justinian himself entered his completed church for the first time he is said to have murmured, "Solomon, I have outdone thee."

ILLUSTRATION: DORLING KINDERSLEY. FLOORPLAN: VIVIAN KENT

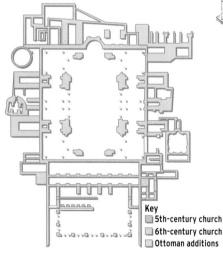

Key
- ☐ 5th-century church
- ☐ 6th-century church
- ☐ Ottoman additions

There are scant remains of the church that burned down in 532. Justinian's rebuilding remains the central core of Byzantium's great church. In the 15th century under the Ottomans it became a mosque, and was enlarged with mausoleums, fountains and minarets

5 IMPERIAL GATE
The door by which the Emperor entered, watched by women from the galleries – only men could worship at ground level, and even then the nave was probably only used on great occasions. It is also the door by which the Ottoman conqueror of Constantinople, Mehmet II, entered Hagia Sophia in 1453. He turned it into a mosque

6 BUTTRESSES
Needed to support the outward thrust of the dome. Even so, the dome collapsed twice and had to be rebuilt

1 THE DOME
107 ft across and reaching 180 ft above the floor, the saucer-shaped dome is pierced by 40 windows. These make it appear as if it is almost floating above the church. Procopius wrote: "It seems not to rest upon solid masonry but to cover the space, as if suspended from heaven by a golden chain"

2 PENDENTIVES
The space above the angle of two walls on which a dome rests, here used on a far greater scale than ever before. They were decorated with mosaic seraphim whose faces were hidden by stars

3 COLONNADE
Anthemius described architecture as "the application of geometry to solid matter", and he skilfully used the screened aisles and galleries of the church to conceal its structural supports. The central columns of the colonnade are of porphyry and green marble requisitioned from the ruins of classical temples

4 THE NAVE
Anthemius's achievement was not just to have satisfied with his engineering the Byzantine passion for mathematical harmony. The great airy central space of the church contrasts with the gloom of the galleries and sets up a play between void and solid, light and dark which gives the church a heightened and unclassical sense of the mystery of God

Justinian, the Christ

Justinian, pictured here on a mosaic made for a church he built in Ravenna, saw himself as every inch the Christian Roman Emperor. Reigning in Constantinople, he expanded his borders, brought peace at home and meddled in Church doctrine

The mosaic above shows the Emperor Justinian as he wanted to be. It was made for the new church of St Vitalis, Ravenna, in AD547. The Emperor, formally attired in Roman dress, holds a golden bowl, ready to take part in the Offertory procession during the divine liturgy. On his left is Bishop Maximian of Ravenna, bearing a cross, and two deacons, one with a jewelled book of the Gospels, the other with a censer. On the Emperor's right stand soldiers; their shield displays the Chi-Rho device, signifying the name of Christ, as it had to Constantine the founder of Constantinople two centuries before.

The figures on the mosaic are symbolic. Justinian never visited Ravenna, and 547 was a difficult year for him. He was at war with the barbarian rulers of northern Italy. His motives were twofold: to re-establish Byzantium's territorial control and to combat the Arian heresy to which the barbarian kings adhered. By 547, Justinian's best army commander, Belisarius, was bogged down in a campaign against the Ostrogoth king Totila. By then in Italy only Otranto, Ancona and Ravenna itself were left in Byzantine hands. Not until 562 was the whole of Italy

under Justinian's control. The exhausted country hardly matched the fine vision of Justinian's mosaic.

Justinian was originally a Latin-speaking Illyrian, being born in 483 probably near Nis in what is now Serbia. His original name was Petrus Sabbatius, but he was renamed after his elderly and childless uncle the Emperor Justin. The young Justinian was educated in Constantinople, though it was said he always spoke badly accented Greek. He was legally adopted by his uncle and in 527, while the old man was alive, was made co-emperor, with the title Augustus. By then he was married to the former actress Theodora, who received the rank Augusta. She had a strong influence over him.

On August 1 527 Justin died and Justinian succeeded him as Emperor. Two tasks immediately presented themselves: conflict with Persia in the east and the restoration to the Byzantine Empire of the barbarian-ruled territories in the west. In 532, with the military success of Belisarius, a peace was concluded with Persia. It cost Justinian five tons of gold which he had to pay the Persians. War dragged on intermittently until a treaty in 561. As well as the Ostrogoth Arians in Italy, North Africa was con-

The strange case of the missing writer Dionysius

Some of the most influential writing in medieval times was attributed to a man who could not have possibly been who everyone thought

Dionysius must be one of the most influential men who never existed. During the so-called Dark Ages some Greek manuscripts began circulating full of speculation about the behaviour of angelic powers. They were supposedly the work of Dionysius the Areopagite, the Athenian mentioned in the Acts of the Apostles who had been convinced by the arguments of St Paul.

Though we know now that these writings are not the work of Dionysius the Areopagite, in the Middle Ages they were taken very seriously indeed. To add to the misunderstandings, in the 9th century, when the books were first translated into Latin by John Scotus Erigena (an Irishman), it was thought that this Dionysius was also Denis, the first Bishop of Paris. None of this was inherently implausible.

Only in Renaissance times was it realised that the author could not be the man he claimed to be, for he drew on the philosopher Proclus, who was active in the 5th century. It seems likely that the pseudo-Dionysius, as scholars call him, wrote around the year 500. He was probably Syrian, and that is all we know. He was not a lying forger, though; conventions of literary property were different from our own.

His writings were studied in the main academic courses of medieval colleges. Another, more accurate, translation was made by John the Saracen (a friend of John of Salisbury, a friend of Thomas Becket's) in about 1165, and this was available to the great Thomas Aquinas in the 13th century (*see page 100*). He is quoted more by Aquinas than any other writer.

Questions of interest to the pseudo-Dionysius in AD500 were still live issues 800 years later. In his book *The Divine Names* Pseudo-Dionysius comes up with a dictum embraced by later philosophers — *bonum est diffusivum sibi* — "good is essentially self-communicative". God lets his goodness spread outwards, to the creatures he has made. In turn they hunger for the goodness in him and can only be fully satisfied by the infinite goodness in God, not by transitory enjoyment. This strand of thought stretches from Plato's *Timaeus*, through Augustine of Hippo, Boethius and Aquinas, to modern philosophy.

It is not now easy to appreciate the liveliness of the interchange of ideas, even between rival cultures, between the time of the pseudo-Dionysius and the dwindling of Latin as a learned language in the 18th century, more than 1,200 years later. Pseudo-Dionysius champions, for instance, the idea of the immateriality of angels — their being pure spirits.

His arguments were later used to counter the 11th-century philosopher known as Avicebron, that is, Solomon Ibn Gabirol, a Jew living in Spain but writing in Arabic. So the thoughts of "Dionysius", an obscure Syrian, were of equal interest to Jewish, Arabic and Christian thinkers from the Atlantic shores of Ireland to the deserts of the East.

Like the Old Testament, Christianity took the existence of angels for granted. Pseudo-Dionysius's concept of angelic beings is a lofty and sophisticated one. Behind medieval paintings of men with wings lay the idea of beings of vast power, able to act at distances millions of miles apart from one second to another, understanding all natural knowledge with burning clarity, and acting as the servants of God's goodness.

Dionysius brought order to the idea of angels, which Christianity took for granted. This mid 14th-century painting, *The Heavenly Host*, is by Guariento di Arpo (c1350)

an builder

trolled by Arian Vandals. In 533 Justinian launched an attack on North Africa. By 534 the whole of North Africa was back in the Imperial fold, as well as Sardinia, Corsica and the Balearic Islands.

At home Justinian set out to be a perfect ruler. He was a gifted administrator, choosing capable ministers. He rooted out corruption and set about collecting and harmonising the laws of the Empire in the *Codex Justinianeus*. Theological order proved to be more problematic to introduce.

The building of Hagia Sophia, in Constantinople (*page 50*), was his most durable religious project. But he was much annoyed by those who denied the orthodox doctrine, agreed in 451 at the Council of Chalcedon, that Christ had two natures, divine and human. Those who held that his humanity was swallowed up in the one divine nature were called Monophysites.

Monophysitism was popular in Syria and Egypt as a rallying point for anti-Byzantine feeling. Rome and the West were strongly opposed to the Monophysites. Justinian's attempts at reconciling the parties only succeeded in angering them all.

Victory in battle persuades Clovis to take the plunge

When Clovis decided to seek baptism, he consciously modelled himself on the Roman Emperor Constantine, according to the 6th-Gregory of Tours, who describes the dramatic ceremony at Rheims cathedral in around AD500

Queen Clotild prayed that her husband might recognise the true God and give up his idol-worship. Nothing could persuade him to accept Christianity. Finally war broke out against the Alamanni and in this conflict he was forced by necessity to accept what he had refused of his own free will. When the two armies met on the battlefield there was great slaughter and the troops of Clovis were rapidly being slaughtered.

Clovis raised his eyes to heaven when he saw this, felt compunction in his heart and was moved to tears. "Jesus Christ," he said, "you who Clotild maintains to be the Son of the living God, you who help those in travail and give victory to those who trust in you, in faith I beg the glory of your help. If you will give me victory over my enemies, and if I may have evidence of that miraculous power which the people dedicated to your name say that they have experienced, then I will believe in you and I will be baptised in your name."

Even as he said this the Alamanni turned their backs and began to run away. As soon as they saw that their King was killed, they submitted to Clovis…

The Queen then ordered Saint Remigius, Bishop of Rheims, to be summoned in secret. She begged him to impart the word of salvation to the King.

The Bishop asked Clovis to meet him in private and began to urge him to believe in the true God, maker of heaven and earth, and to forsake his idols, which were powerless to help him or anyone else.

The King replied: "I have listened to you willingly, holy father. There remains one obstacle. The people under my command will not agree to forsake their gods. I will go and put to them what you have just said to me."

He arranged a meeting with his people, but God in his power had preceded him, and before he could say a word all those present shouted in unison: "We will give up worshipping our mortal gods, pious King, and we are prepared to follow the immortal God about whom Remigius preaches."

This news was reported to the Bishop. He was greatly pleased and he ordered the baptismal pool to be made ready. The public squares were draped with coloured cloths, the

churches were adorned with white hangings, the baptistry was prepared, sticks of incense gave off clouds of perfume, sweet-smelling candles gleamed bright and the holy place of baptism was filled with divine fragrance.

God filled the hearts of all present

with such grace that they imagined themselves to have been transported to some perfumed paradise.

King Clovis asked that he might be baptised by the Bishop first. Like some new Constantine he stepped forward to the baptismal pool, ready to wash away the sores of his old leprosy.

istorian

Gaul becomes France

When Clovis, King of the Franks, was baptised his subjects pretty quickly followed suit. His Christian kingdom formed the basis for Charlemagne's renaissance

Virtually all the leaders of the barbarian tribes from Germany that invaded the decaying Roman Empire from the 5th century onwards were Christians, albeit of a heretical sort. But Clovis, the leader of the Franks, was a pagan for the first 30 years of his life, though he had a Christian wife, Clotild.

A man of considerable ability, and as ruthless and cruel as he was ambitious, Clovis incorporated into his kingdom most of Roman Gaul and Thuringia, in eastern Germany. He was granted victory in a battle after praying to Christ, and some time between AD496 and 508 Clovis was baptised, along with his 3,000-strong army, at a dramatic ceremony in Rheims cathedral. Further victories followed and in a few years his kingdom extended to the Pyrenees. Bishops, as well as former Roman officials, were called on to assist in the administration of the kingdom, and in return the Church was strongly supported by Clovis, and many monasteries were founded. Writing to the king not long after his baptism, the Bishop of Vienne said, "Your faith is our victory."

On the death of Clovis in 511, however, the kingdom broke up and for the next two centuries the territory was beset by civil wars. The life of the Church was inevitably affected by the instability and by the decline of civic life but it made great progress in the vast rural areas. The number of country parishes increased and popular Catholic worship attracted the peasants. Monks kept the orthodox faith alive in the monasteries and led any evangelistic enterprises. The period also bred notable Christian personalities, two of whom are of particular interest.

Radegund (520-587) was the daughter of a prince of Thuringia but was carried off by invading Franks and compelled to marry King Clothair I. He was an appalling character and, when in 550 he murdered her brother, she left the court and persuaded the Bishop of Noyon to permit her to found a nunnery at Poitiers. There she remained for the rest of her life and enjoyed a close friendship with the poet Venantius Fortunatus (530-610). He had been born near Venice, educated at Ravenna and settled in Poitiers in about 567. Having got to know Radegund, he was taken on as steward of the convent and became its chaplain.

His great gift however was the writing of poetry in which he combined the classical style with Christian spirituality, and sometimes erotic mysticism. The gift to the convent of a large fragment of what was claimed to be Christ's cross led him to write two great hymns, *Vexilla regis* and *Pange, lingua gloriosi*, which are still in common use. His poetry is formalised and sometimes conventionally flattering. He preserved the cultivation of an educated Roman while writing a new style of medieval Latin verse. His admiration – was it love? – of Radegund led him to say of her, "Human eloquence is struck almost dumb by the piety, self denial, charity, sweetness, humili-

ty, uprightness, faith and fervour in which she lived." She was eventually declared to be a saint.

The way to the reunion of the sundered parts of the Frankish kingdom was prepared by Charles Martel, who defeated a Muslim army which advanced from Spain in 732. The anointing of his son, Pepin, as King of the Franks by Pope Stephen II in 754 strengthened the growing sense of unity and also led to a very close link with the papacy. This culminated in the crowning of Pepin's son Charles – Charlemagne – as Holy Roman Emperor by the Pope in St Peter's, Rome, on Christmas Day 800. Unity did not long outlive Charlemagne and by 843 the land of the Franks became a separate country – France.

Hymn to the Holy Cross

The poet Venantius Fortunatus wrote Latin verse that is mid-way between classical and medieval models. His Hymn to the Holy Cross is still used by churches in the days before Easter.

Pange, lingua, gloriosi proelium certaminis
et super crucis tropaeo dic triumphum nobilem,
qualiter redemptor orbis immolatus vicerit.

Crux fidelis, inter omnes arbor una nobilis,
nulla talem silva profert flore, fronde, germine,
dulce lignum dulce clavo dulce pondus sustinens.

Flecte ramos, arbor alta, tensa laxa viscera,
et rigor lentescat ille quem dedit nativitas,
ut superni membra regis mite tendas stipite.

Sing, my tongue, the glorious battle,
Sing the ending of the fray;
Now above the Cross, the trophy,
Sound the loud triumphant lay:
Tell how Christ, the world's Redeemer,
As a victim won the day.

Faithful Cross! above all other,
One and only noble tree!
None in foliage, none in blossom,
None in fruit they peer may be.
Dearest wood and dearest iron!
Dearest weight is hung on thee.

Bend your boughs, O Tree of Glory!
Thy relaxing sinews bend;
For awhile the ancient rigour
That thy birth bestowed, suspend;
And the King of heavenly beauty
On thy bosom gently tend.

King Clovis stands in a font as Bishop Remigius of Rheims pours the water of baptism on his head in this 14th-century manuscript illustration from *Grandes Chroniques de France* in the Musée Goya, Castres

A stern faith for Ireland

The peculiar nature of Irish Christianity stemmed from the country's rural isolation and the character of its first founder, the great St Patrick. Even stripped of the later myths attached to his name he appears as a stern but irresistible figure

The life of St Patrick has acquired a heavy accretion of myth as he has grown into the chief symbol of Irish Christianity and Irishness itself. The banishing of snakes from Ireland, the use of the shamrock to explain the doctrine of the holy Trinity and the communing with God or a guardian angel at the summits of various mountains – none of these is historical.

But St Patrick did exist and his importance to Irish Christianity is without parallel. He stands as a monumental figure even without any mythical embellishments. He was born in about AD385, in a town called by his contemporaries Bannavem Taberniae. This was probably on the west coast of what is now England – where exactly we do not know. We know a little about a Romano-British family: his father was a civil official of some sort and that his grandfather had been a priest.

The west coast of Britain was vulnerable to Irish raiders and when Patrick was aged 16 he was captured by a raiding party, taken to Ireland and put to the task of herding cattle. He spent the next six years of his life in captivity in Ireland before making his escape. His whereabouts for the next 15 years or so is also unknown. What is certain is that he must have received training for the priesthood either in Gaul or Britain. But it was probably

EYEWITNESS

Patrick's confessions

In *Confession,* one of only two surviving works written by the saint, Patrick recounts a dream that made him return to Ireland

And next a few years later I was in Britain among my parents who received me for their son and earnestly requested that I should now, after all the troubles which I had experienced, never leave them again. And it was there that I saw in a vision of the night a man coming apparently from Ireland whose name was Victoricus, with an unaccountable number of letters. And he gave me one of them and I read the heading of the letter which ran, "The Cry of the Irish".

And while I was reading aloud the heading of the letter I was imagining that at that very moment I heard the voice of those who were by the wood of Voclut which is near the Western Sea, and this is what they cried, as with one voice: "Holy boy, we are asking you to come and walk among us again." And I was struck deeply to the heart and I was not able to read any further. And at that I woke up.

not until 432 that he returned to Ireland and began his missionary activity. The contemporary evidence for Patrick's work is found in the only two surviving pieces of writing that are certainly by him: the *Confession,* in which he reviews his life, and his *Letter to Coroticus.*

Coroticus was a chieftain of an Irish tribe. In the letter Patrick denounces an attack by Coroticus's men on one of his congregations. Patrick follows the letter-writing protocol of his time by beginning the letter with a passage steeped in humility, confessing his sinfulness.

"I Patrick, a sinner, very badly educated, in Ireland, declare myself to be a bishop. I am quite certain that I have received from God that which I am. Consequently I live among barbarian tribes as an exile and refugee for the love of God; God himself is the witness that this is true." He was right about the bad education; his Latin is peculiarly strained, though part of this impression comes from the character of the late Latin spoken in Britain at the time. But his reference to "barbarian tribes" is more important in understanding St Patrick's life and work.

To an educated person of classical antiquity, Ireland was quite literally at the edge of the earth. It lay further west than any other lands that the Romans knew, and beyond it lay the freezing Atlantic Ocean. As far as St Patrick was concerned, God had chosen him to preach in the last country on earth, on the eve of the Day of Judgment. The beginning of the 5th century could be a terrifying time for a civilised person in the Roman Empire. With the fall of Rome, it could seem as if chaos and darkness were about to engulf the entire world.

A Christian living through these times might well have thought that the last days of the world were drawing in. So Patrick's mission seemed to him all the more urgent. He says in the *Confession* that his return to Ireland would be permanent and that he would never again leave the country's shores. He dwells on his career as a bishop and he mentions that he has converted and baptised thousands of people and ordained many clergy.

He has travelled, he says, throughout the wild and dangerous country, preaching the gospel to people who had never heard it before and suffering much hardship and pain. It is easy to imagine the wild Irish terrain and weather behind his reminiscence.

By 444 Patrick had established his episcopal see at Armagh. By the time his active evangelising was at an end he had left an indelible mark on the history of Christianity by almost single-handedly bringing into being the monastic structure of the Irish church. When and where he died is also unknown to us, though the chief myth is that he was buried at Saul, a village in County Down.

These stone beehive-shaped huts on the side of a rock above the stormy Atlantic off the west coast of Ireland reflect the toughness of early Irish Christianity

Left: St Patrick from a 13th-century manuscript in Huntington Library and Art Gallery, California

A hard sort of monastery in a weather-beaten place

The idiosyncratic nature of Irish monasticism created the country's own peculiar brand of Christianity, even though St Patrick, the main founder of the tradition, had been trained in Britain or continental Europe – we do not know where.

European monasteries of the time were usually made up of men who wished to live a holy life, gathered in a community around a bishop in a city. This was the case with Martin at Tours in about AD370, or with Ambrose at Milan in the same decade. These communities and the island monastery founded by Honoratus at Lérins in 400 consciously borrowed from the tradition of the East – from Pachomius, Basil and Anthony, whose lives were written or translated into Latin for their Western imitators. But the model of a community gathered round a bishop in a city was not one that Ireland could follow. Ireland was still divided along clan lines with no towns worth speaking of. In these circumstances it was the

monastery itself, not the city, that became the focus of Christian life.

Irish ecclesiastical territories came to be ruled by the abbot, or as was sometimes the case the abbess, not the bishops. Moreover the abbot or abbess often came from the clan of the founder of the monastery and the surrounding people. The ordinary function of the bishop in teaching and ruling his diocese came to be subordinated to that of the abbot. The bishop lived among other monks who owed the abbot obedience; his role at times resembled that of the queen bee – he alone had the power to ordain new priests and bishops to succeed him.

Even to look at, Irish monasteries were very different from those in Europe. Instead of the majestic ashlar church and abbey, an Irish monastery would offer a visitor the sight of a group of small huts surrounded by an earth wall. The challenging asceticism of Irish monastic life is vividly seen in the surviving cluster of weather-beaten stone huts at Skellig

Michael on a rocky island pinnacle in the stormy Atlantic. But Irish monasticism was not insular in outlook. It used the Latin liturgy and acknowledged the Pope as the successor of Peter. Irish missionaries soon set off to bring Christianity to the unknown world. Stories exist of Irish monks drifting off into the frozen seas of the Arctic.

In 563 Columba founded a monastery on Iona, off the west of Scotland, which became a powerhouse of scholarship and missionary activity. From there, Christianity was brought to the tribes living in Scotland and Irish ideas diffused throughout northern England.

A monk from Iona, Aidan, founded Lindisfarne in 635; Aidan's pupil, the abbess Hilda, established another famous monastery at Whitby, ruling separate foundations for men and women. In 585 another monk, Columbanus, travelled from his monastery at Bangor in Ireland, to the European mainland to found the monasteries at Luxeuil and St Gall (*see page* 64) and Bobbio in Italy itself.

Taming the English

What to do with the local pagans

From Rome Pope Gregory writes to the mission he had sent to England, led by Augustine, advising them how to deal with newly converted pagans

I have decided after much thought about the English people, that their idol temples should not be destroyed, but only the idols in them. Take holy water and sprinkle it in these shrines, build altars and place relics in them.

For if the shrines are well built, it is essential that they should be converted from the worship of devils to the service of the true God. When this people see their shrines are not destroyed they will be able to banish error from their hearts and be more ready to come to the places with which they are familiar, only now worshipping the true God.

Because they are in the habit of slaughtering animals as sacrifices to devils, some solemn rite ought to be supplied for them as a substitute. So on the day of the dedication of the church or the festivals of the holy martyrs whose relics are deposited there, let them make themselves huts from branches of trees around the churches which have been converted out of shrines, and let them celebrate the solemnity with religious feasts.

Do not let them sacrifice animals to the devil, but let them slaughter animals for their own food, so they may praise God and give thanks to the giver of all things for his generous provision.

Given the 18 July in the 19th year of the reign of our most religious emperor Maurice Tiberius, and in the eighteenth year after his consulship and in the fourth indiction.

[*Maurice Tiberius ruled from 582 to 602, so this letter can be dated to around 600*]

When Pope Gregory sent Augustine to convert the English he turned back once on the way. A second attempt made him the first Archbishop of Canterbury

A ugustine, an Italian monk who became the first Archbishop of Canterbury, was sent to England at the end of the 6th century by Pope Gregory the Great to reintroduce the Christian religion into a country that had lapsed into paganism following the end of Roman rule in AD409. Christianity had come to England during the Roman occupation, but the number of its followers remained small until the early part of the 4th century when the Emperor Constantine made it the official religion of his Empire. But within 100 years, the invasion of pagan Saxons, Angles and Jutes from northern Europe led to the destruction of churches and to the retreat of Christians to Cornwall and Wales.

Aware of this, Gregory – at that time Abbot of St Andrew's monastery in Rome – chanced to see a group of fair-haired boys for sale in the city's slave market and, so the famous story (given by the English historian Bede) goes, enquired who they were. On being told that they were pagan Angles he punned: "That is appropriate, for they have angelic faces, and it is right that they should become fellow-heirs with the angels in heaven." He thereupon planned to lead a mission to England. But the people of Rome would not let him go, and it was not until some 20 years later, after he had become Pope, that he entrusted the mission to Augustine, the Prior of his own monastery.

Augustine set off from Rome in 596 with a party of 40, but while crossing France they got cold feet, having learned that, far from being angelic, the Anglo-Saxons were, in the words of Bede, "barbarous and fierce and spoke another language". Augustine returned to Rome in the hope that Pope Gregory would call off the mission, but he would have none of this. "The greater the labour," he promised, "the greater will be the glory of your eternal reward." They set off again and landed in East Kent in the spring of 597.

It was known that although the King of Kent, Ethelbert, was a pagan, his Queen, Bertha, was a Christian. Kent was also accounted the most powerful kingdom in England, and Ethelbert's jurisdiction as overlord extended as far as the Humber. Gregory knew the importance of influencing the influencers.

Augustine and his party, now including an interpreter recruited in France, were well received. The king left his capital, Canterbury, to meet them in Thanet. The historic encounter took place in the open air, with the missionar-

Augustine is shown as the enthroned Archbishop in this 1190 seal (above) from Canterbury. He was sent to England by Pope Gregory, depicted writing with the Dove of the Holy Spirit at his ear on this 10th-century ivory panel from Reichenau in Germany. Gregory, one of the Four Latin Doctors of the Church, had first wanted to convert England when he was Abbot of St Andrew's monastery in Rome. He had to wait 20 years before he could send another monk of his old abbey to begin the task

ies holding a silver cross as their standard and a painting of the crucified Christ on a board. Ethelbert told them that, while it was impossible for him to abandon what he called "the age-old beliefs of the English nation", he would nonetheless supply them with provisions and leave them free to preach their faith in his country. The two parties then went in procession to Canterbury, where the missionaries were allocated a house and two old churches, one of which later became Augustine's cathedral.

After this promising start, progress was swift. Preaching missions were undertaken throughout east Kent, the holiness of life displayed by the monks created a great impression, and on Christmas Day 597 some 10,000 people were baptised. The king had set an example a few months earlier.

Augustine, meanwhile, had gone to France to be consecrated Bishop of the English and on his return sent a progress report to Rome with a request for advice on problems facing the infant Kentish church. These included intra-family marriage and the punishment of those who rob churches. Before long another delegation was on the way to Rome to seek reinforcements, especially clergy, and among those recruited were two who were to become Archbishops of Canterbury after Augustine and another who became Archbishop of York. The Pope sent Augustine a *pallium* – a cape of lamb's wool – to denote that he had been given jurisdiction over the whole nation. In an accompanying letter Gregory instructed him to consecrate 12 bishops in different places in the south of England, and a bishop for York who would in turn consecrate 12 bishops for the north. London was to have its own bishop, but still under Augustine.

This policy failed to take account of the views of other bishops and abbots on the Western edges of the country who had been ministering long before Augustine's arrival. The Irish monk Columba had also started missionary work in north Britain from the island of Iona, off Scotland. These leaders saw Augustine as an intruder.

Augustine convened a conference with the Western bishops in 603 and courteously invited them to accept Roman customs and to share in the mission to the heathen. But they requested another conference, before which they asked a holy man how to discover whether Augus-

If the Archbishop rose to meet them, this would show his humility and that he was a follower of Christ

tine was a man of God. This holy man said that if the Archbishop rose to meet them this would show his humility and that he was a follower of Christ, but if he remained seated then they could be certain he despised them. Unfortunately, Augustine stayed in his chair. The visitors therefore refused to accept his authority and he responded by prophesying their deaths at the hands of the heathen.

So that was that. Augustine thereafter confined himself to Kent, though he consecrated bishops for West Kent and for the East Saxons. He consecrated Laurentius, a fellow missionary from Rome, as his successor and died on May 26, in a year between 604 and 609 which cannot be determined.

The claim of Canterbury to exercise jurisdiction beyond its own borders went into abeyance for a time, but by 664 the Roman influence won the day at the Synod of Whitby, when Roman customs relating to the date of Easter and the style of the tonsure (a cleric's symbolic haircut) were adopted by the Northumbrians. Soon there would be a unified church subject to a single Catholic authority, but the conversion of the whole of England took longer.

The ruins of St Augustine's monastery lie just to the East of Canterbury's present medieval walls.

England's first historian

Much of our knowledge of post-Roman Britain comes from Bede, the scholar at the heart of the cultural flowering of the north

The Dream of the Rood

The author of this Old English poem, probably a contemporary of Bede, dreams that Christ's Cross speaks to him.

Long ago was it — I still remember it — that I was cut down at the edge of the forest. Men bore me on their shoulders, till they set me on a hill. Then the young Hero — he was God almighty — unflinching, stripped himself; he mounted on the high cross, brave in the sight of many, when he was minded to redeem mankind. Then I trembled when the Hero clasped me.

As a rood was I raised up; I bore aloft the mighty King, the Lord of heaven; I durst not stoop. They pierced me with dark nails; the wounds are still plain to view in me, gaping gashes of malice; I durst not do hurt to any of them. They bemocked us both together. I was all bedewed with blood, shed from the Man's side, after he had sent forth his Spirit.

Cold grew the corpse, fair house of the Soul. Then they began to cut us all down to the earth; that was a dread trial. They buried us in a deep pit. Yet there the followers of the Lord, friends, found me out; (then they raised me from the ground), decked me with gold and silver.

Now, my loved man, thou mayest hear that I have endured bitter anguish, grievous sorrows. On me the Son of God suffered for a space; wherefore now I rise glorious beneath the heavens, and I can heal all who fear me.

Bede was a rounded character as well as a scholar of European renown. He went to great lengths to add to the accuracy of his *History of the English Church and People* (completed in AD731), and is justly regarded as the Father of English History. No dry as dust history here, but a delightful pageant of kings and bishops, priests and monks, saints and sinners. The reader is transported into a different world, but one that is recognisably English.

This was, however, just one of his 40 books, for he wrote several enlightening commentaries on books of the Bible, a number of biographies of saints, primers on Latin and astronomy, and a highly technical book of calculations to determine the date of Easter (in which, for the first time in England, the calendar years were dated from the birth of Christ). Unlike his Spanish counterpart Isidore of Seville a century before, Bede went much further than merely cataloguing scraps of learning.

All of this was achieved by a monk who spent virtually the whole of his life in a monastery at Jarrow, then a remote place on the Northumbrian coast. He was born a few miles south of there at Wearmouth in about 673 and entered the local monastery when he was only seven. Two years later he was transferred to a new foundation at Jarrow, but soon after his arrival all the monks responsible for leading the worship were wiped out by plague, leaving only the abbot and the child Bede to maintain the

A scribe thought to be Bede, from a 12th-century manuscript of his *Life and Miracles of St Cuthbert*. Based in Jarrow, Bede was a scrupulous and lively chronicler of post-Roman Britain, and he has come to be regarded as the "Father of English History"

services. His commitment to a highly disciplined life of prayer is said to date from that experience. He became a deacon at 19 and was ordained priest when he was 30, by which time it was evident that he was called to be a scholar. Apart from brief visits to York and Lindisfarne he remained close to Jarrow's fine monastic library.

His great *History*, written in Latin of the purest style, and first translated, in part, into English by King Alfred in the 9th century, remains wonderfully readable. What is more, it has stood the test of later historical research. Bede gathered his material from reliable sources and even had a monk colleague researching for him in the Pope's archives in Rome. Without Bede our knowledge of the history of England from the time of the Roman occupation until the 8th century would be very sketchy indeed.

In his Bible commentaries, which circulated widely among the monasteries of Europe, Bede used the work of the earliest Christian scholars and added his own understandings of particular passages, which proved to be specially illuminating. His book of tables to calculate the date of Easter was prompted by the decision of the synod held at Whitby in 664 that the English church should adopt the Roman method of determining the date. But few people in any part of Europe understood this system until Bede explained it.

Bede also found time to write a long letter to his pupil, Egbert, who had become Archbishop of York. In this he set out what he believed to be the duties of a bishop, stressing the importance of Confirmation, daily Communion, almsgiving and Masses for the dead. By now his own death was near and there is a moving account of how this came on the eve of Ascension Day in 735, immediately after he had written the final words of his commentary on St John's Gospel.

His contemporaries described him as a loveable man with a simple straightforward nature. He was regarded as a saint, and the adjective Venerable often attached to his name merely expressed the admiration in which he was held. He was buried at Jarrow, but during the 11th century his bones were moved to Durham Cathedral, where a tomb bearing his name is still to be seen.

Taking on the Germans

Boniface came from Crediton in Devon. He ended up converting the Germans after chopping down the Oak of Thor

Boniface has some claim to be the most successful Christian missionary who has ever lived. Not for nothing is he known as the "Apostle of Germany", for though there had been some Christians in that territory from the 3rd century onwards, most of its people remained unconverted and pagan invaders had hampered any efforts to establish the Church.

Boniface, born at Crediton in Devon in about AD675, became a monk at Exeter, then transferred to Nursling, near Southampton, where he was Master of the monastic school. He was ordained priest at the age of 30 and in 716, having heard of missionary work being started in Frisia, near the present border between Germany and the Netherlands, he obtained his abbots permission to join the enterprise. The timing proved unfortunate, for on his arrival in Frisia he found that the country had been laid waste by a neighbouring pagan prince. No progress was possible, so he returned to Nursling, where the monks tried to elect him as their abbot. But he declined and instead went to Rome. There he was warmly welcomed by Pope Gregory II, who commissioned him for missionary work in Germany.

For the next three years Boniface worked with great success from a missionary base in the Low Countries, which had been established by Willibrord, a Northumbrian monk. He then he turned south to the German state of Hesse, which was partly Christian, yet still practised pagan worship. His success there led to his being recalled to Rome, where the Pope made him Bishop for All Germany East of the Rhine.

On his return he courageously felled an oak that was believed to be the abode of Thor – the god of Thunder – and used the timber to build a chapel. The impact of this was considerable, and led to many more conversions to Christianity.

He was now joined by other helpers from Wessex, and such was his ability and drive that by the year 739 he had founded three bishoprics for Hesse and Thuringia and re-founded a bishopric for Bavaria. On the strength of this he was made an Archbishop.

Quite a lot is known about Boniface, not least from the many letters he wrote to the Bishop of Winchester, a surprising number of which have been preserved. These reveal a loveable man, as well as a notable scholar and preacher. He was an efficient organiser, and this enabled him to re-organise the whole of the German church.

Several aspects of his missionary work, besides its scale, are of note. His work was based on minsters – wooden buildings that housed communities of monks and nuns who offered regular worship and prayer and then went out to preach to the pagans in the surrounding district. He presided over a series of Councils designed to reform the life of the church and extend its mission.

This accomplished, he was appointed Archbishop of Mainz, which gave him authority over the Church throughout Germany. Yet after a few years he resigned and, although over 70, went back to the north to resume his work as a missionary bishop. On June 7 754, he and 52 companions were massacred by a band of pagans while awaiting the arrival of Christian converts who were due to meet them on the bank of a river. Robbery rather than religion seems to have been the motive for the attack and, almost accidentally, Boniface became a martyr.

Boniface baptising the Germans (above left) and (right) meeting an untimely end, in a manuscript from the church of St Salvatoris in Fulda, Germany

Spain before the Moors

When the Visigoths replaced the Romans as rulers of Spain they were Arians at odds with their orthodox Catholic subjects. A brief growth of Christian culture was soon overrun by the Muslim invaders

RIGHT: SONIA HALLIDAY PHOTOGRAPHS. MAIN PICTURE: HENRI STIERLIN

The Visigoths, amid the great wave of barbarians that broke over the Roman Empire in the 5th century, swept over the Pyrenees and, though they strove for nearly two centuries with the rival Suevi, dominated Spain until the Muslim invasion in AD711. The native Hispano-Roman population outnumbered the invaders by perhaps 25-1, and the Visigoths gained as much as they gave culturally. Like many barbarians they had picked up an Arian form of Christianity on the way. Arianism, a belief that God the Son was inferior to God the Father, was not just an optional opinion; it cut off its adherents from unity with the rest of orthodox Christendom.

The Visigothic King Leovigild (reigned 568-586), in an attempt to unite his people, removed the ban on intermarriage between Hispano-Romans and Visigoths, but unwisely also tried to impose Arianism on the Hispano-Romans. This only had the effect of provoking a revolt of the southern province of Baetica, led by Leovigild's son Hermenegild, who had become a Catholic.

Another of Leovigild's sons succeeded him to the throne. This was Reccared (reigned 586-601). He too was brought to Catholic orthodoxy by Leander, Archbishop of Seville (Hispalis, in Latin); and where the king led, most of the nobles followed. Thus began a tight alliance between king and bishops. The king assumed the right to appoint bishops; the bishops regularly gathered at councils at Toledo to listen to the king and enact laws. A Roman province that had produced Seneca and Lucan, the Emperors Hadrian and Trajan, had by now sunk into cultural dissolution, but there were bright spots. Visigothic church architecture was dignified (there is a theory that the Moors copied its horseshoe arches) and its carvings energetic. The jewellery of the Visigoths was gorgeous. Of their writers Isidore succeeded best.

Isidore of Seville (560-636) was born at Cartagena (which had been called Carthago Nova – new Carthage – by the Romans). He followed his elder brother Leander as Archbishop of Seville and set about educating the people of the whole nation, newly converted from Arianism. His writing was perhaps pedantic. He wrote a history of the Visigoths, but his masterwork was the *Etymologies*, a vast encyclopedia of ancient learning, from werewolves to astronomy. Hundreds of laboriously copied manuscripts of it survive as witnesses to its popularity and influence. Isidore was at the heart of the standard course of education in Western Europe for 900 years after his death. The nine liberal arts set out by the classical author Varro (116-27BC) had been reduced, by the dropping of architecture and medicine, to seven: grammar, logic, rhetoric, geography, arithmetic, astronomy and music. This made up the *trivium* and *quadrivium* adopted by the influential Martianus Capella, the early 5th-century encyclopedist in whose footsteps Isidore followed. Isidore in turn was edited by the Englishmen Bede and Alcuin.

Around 1300 Dante put Isidore in heaven next to Bede, Ambrose, Boethius and Dionysius the Areopagite.

All this time Visigothic society was constantly torn by political violence. On the death of King Witiza in 710. Roderic, Duke of Baetica was made king and Witiza's family turned to the Muslims of North Africa for help. In 711 Tariq ibn Ziyad, the governor of Tangier, landed at Gibraltar with 7,000 men, mostly Berbers. King Roderic was beaten in battle. For the next three centuries, most of the peninsular was to be under Islamic control. Christianity survived, and in the northern mountains of Asturias, Visigothic leaders plotted the *reconquista* – the reconquest.

That slow process was to underlie much at the core of modern Christian Spain's identity.

Isidore of Seville gives a book to his sister, from a Latin manuscript. He had followed his elder brother Leander as Archbishop of Seville. Leander had converted the Arian Visigothic king of Spain to Catholic orthodoxy; Isidore wrote a history of the Visigoths. The rural basilicas of the Visigoths, such as San Juan de Baños in Palencia (right) are based on early Romano-Christian churches

A monastic rule that lasted

Desert hermits had banded together into monasteries. Irish monks had defied nature with their austerities. Benedict wrote a Rule for a gentler kind of monastery that enabled humanity to grow towards God, through prayer, work and learning. The Rule he wrote has lasted

Benedict (*c*480-*c*547), wrote the Rule which became the accepted guide to leading a monastic life. Born into a Christian family of provincial gentry at Nursia, 70 miles north east of Rome, Benedict was educated at home before being sent to the city, which he found so full of temptations that he abandoned his studies. He settled at a church in Enfide, where he performed his first miracle, mending a sieve broken by his nurse, who had insisted on coming with him. He then fled to be alone to Subiaco. For three years he lived in a cave on the face of a cliff, having food lowered to him by rope.

As Benedict's reputation grew he reluctantly agreed to become abbot of a nearby monastery, but his regime so exasperated its easy-going members that they tried to kill him. The Man of God – as St Gregory the Great calls him in his *Dialogues*, the only direct source for Benedict's life – returned to his cave but soon agreed to become superior of a group of 12 monasteries. Again there was trouble. A jealous priest sent Benedict a poisoned loaf, which was obligingly carried away by a raven, then dispatched dancing girls to seduce the monks.

Accompanied by a few companions Benedict moved to Monte Cassino, 1,700 ft above the road from Rome to Naples, where he built a single monastery which attracted not only noble recruits but a visit by the invading Ostrogoth King Totila in 543. The saint told him to mend his way, and correctly predicted that he would enter Rome but die in 10 years time.

It was at Monte Cassino that Benedict wrote his "little rule for beginners". Unlike the regimes of the desert fathers it was aimed at ordinary men, and prescribed warm clothes, sufficient sleep and adequate nourishment. Benedict would have liked to ban wine, but it was so ingrained in Italian culture that he confined himself to demanding that there should be no drunkenness.

The Rule vests absolute control in an abbot, elected by the whole community. But the abbot is reminded that he represents God, and should consult both old and young. He "must be chaste, sober and merciful, ever preferring mercy to justice... Even in his corrections let him act with prudence and not go too far, lest while he seeketh eagerly to scrape the rust, the vessel be broken." Benedict divides each day into eight liturgical offices (mostly singing Psalms), manual work and spiritual reading. He stipulates a cool welcome for all recruits, suggests what kind of person should be appointed cellarer and confronts the question of what a brother should do if commanded to perform the impossible.

The Rule's influence began to spread when, some 30 years after Benedict's death, a Lombard invasion drove the community out of Monte Cassino to settle in Rome. The Church recognised that the monks' training made them an asset. It duly insisted that they be ordained priests then sent to preach the Gospel in Europe. It is now unclear whether the 40 monks who landed ▶

with St Augustine in Kent in 597 used the Rule exclusively, but their monastic descendants certainly did. As members of a learned and clerical profession Benedictines were not only in the forefront of scholarship (not least by preserving manuscripts) and teaching, they became a key element in the governance of the medieval state.

Although most of the great monasteries were uprooted between the Reformation and the French Revolution, today there are some 8,500 Benedictine monks around the world. Even if they find it impossible to live entirely by the Rule as written, they demonstrate its warmth and continuing practicality after almost 1,500 years.

The Rule of St Benedict

An abbot called John is seen here offering St Benedict a copy of his *Commentary on the Rule of St Benedict*, from which this illustration from Monte Cassino comes. The Rule of St Benedict succinctly lists the virtues monks should have and how they are to spend their days – chiefly in prayer and work. One of the most challenging tasks is to be the abbot.

The Abbot

"The abbot should always remember what he is and what he is called, and should know that to whom more is committed, from him more is required. Let him realise also how difficult and arduous a task he has undertaken, of ruling souls and adapting himself to many dispositions. One he must humour, another rebuke, another persuade, according to each one's disposition and understanding, and thus adapt and accommodate himself to all in such a way, that he may not only suffer no loss in the sheep committed to him, but may even rejoice in the increase of a good flock."

Eating and drinking

"Every man hath his proper gift from God, one after this manner, and another after that. It is therefore with some misgiving that we determine how much others should eat or drink. Nevertheless, keeping in view the needs of weaker brethren, we believe that a hemina [*possibly half a pint*] of wine a day is sufficient for each. But those upon whom God bestows the gift of abstinence, should know that they shall have a special reward.

"But if the circumstances of the place, or their work, or the heat of the summer require more, let the superior be free to grant it. Yet let him always take care that neither surfeit nor drunkenness supervene. We do, indeed, read that wine is no drink for monks; but since nowadays monks cannot be persuaded of this, let us at least agree upon this, to drink temperately and not to satiety: for wine maketh even the wise to fall away."

The model monastery

By the end of the 8th century monasteries could resemble villages, with all their needs met within an enclosure dominated by the abbey church, as in this plan drawn at the beginning of the 9th century

Monasticism had found a stable character just when Europe was convulsed with wars and a breakdown of civilised life. A remarkable plan of the ideal monastery was sent with a letter from Hitro, Bishop of Basle and from AD803 Abbot of Reichenau (on Lake Constance), to his "dearest son Gorbert" who was Abbot of St Gall in Swabia (now Switzerland). Drawn in red and black ink on five pieces of parchment sewn together to make a sheet 44 inches long, it shows the monastery with all its supporting services neatly parcelled out — geese here, medicinal herbs here. The infirmary could be used sometimes for long periods by monks who were aged or weak, for, like the novitiate for new recruits, it has a

chapel with its own entrance. Dominating all, of course, is the monastery church. Around the high altar the monks would assemble in choir to sing their daily offices, chiefly psalms sung as unaccompanied plain chant. Around the aisles are several side chapels, for any monk ordained as a priest would say daily Mass in addition to the conventual Mass attended by the whole community. As well as workshops and storehouses, the monastery has a library of manuscripts to be copied for exchange with other monasteries. It has a school for children from outside, and a guest house for visitors attracted by its learning or worship. In the centre of the orchard is the cemetery for monks whose days have been fulfilled.

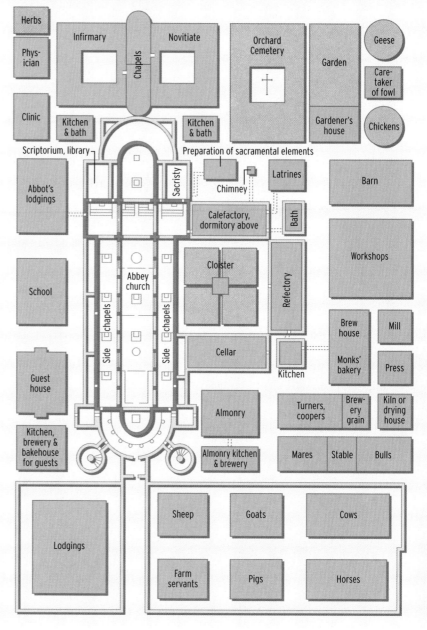

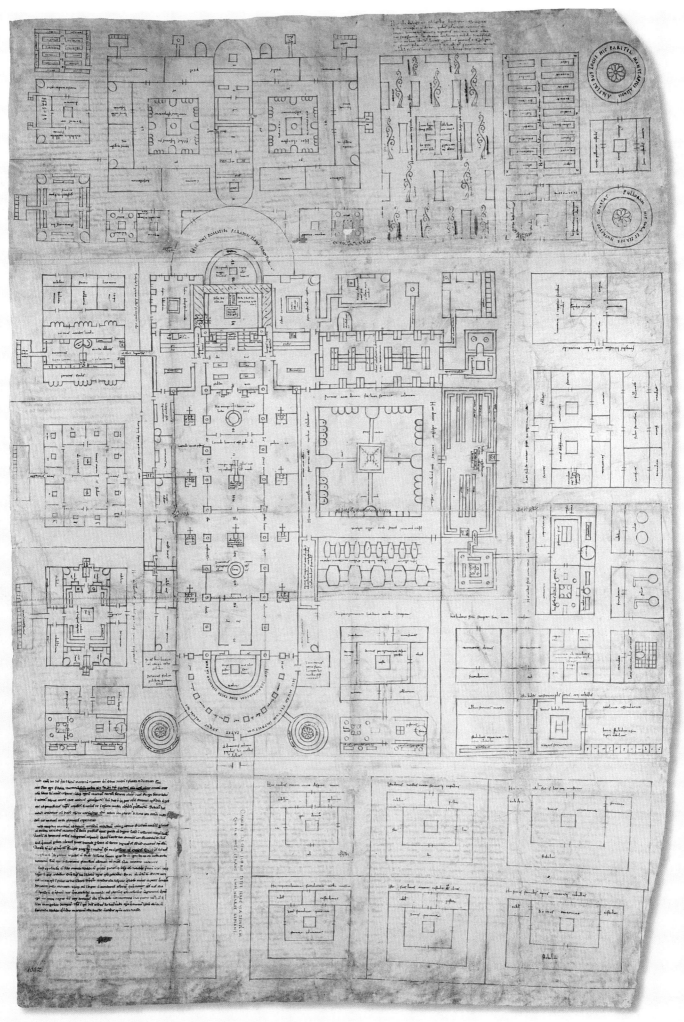

CHAPTER THREE

AD
800-1200
The kings take command

The making

The years between 800 and 1200 saw a new pattern for Church and State. It began on Christmas Day AD800 when Charlemagne was crowned in Rome by the Pope as the first Holy Roman Emperor

The kings of Europe saw themselves as hallowed by an anointing as Christian rulers. Charlemagne got the Pope to crown him. Alfred the Great set out to spread Christian learning throughout England. Edward the Confessor built Westminster Abbey, which became the royal shrine of the kingdom.

It was still touch and go whether Christian civilisation would win through. Vikings burnt monasteries, Muslims conquered Spain and occupied Jerusalem. The unrivalled Byzantium Empire saw the violence of icon-smashing, followed by a scandalous split with Western Christianity that was never healed.

In bad times individuals could still reach new heights. Anselm experimented to see how far intellect could reach towards God. Art too expressed new sensibilities, as in the carvings at Autun, or in the development of monastic chant.

In the worst failure Christianity triumphed. The life of Thomas Becket ended in bloody murder at the hands of the king's friends. Yet this event marked the beginning of his fame as one of the most widely revered saints in Europe, and it showed that kings could not just remake Christianity in their own images.

The coronation of Charlemagne by Pope Leo III in St Peter's, Rome, from the 14th-century *Grandes Chroniques de France*. Charlemagne's biographer Einhard claimed that the Frankish leader would not have entered the church if he had known what was going to happen

Inside the main entrance of St Peter's, Rome, there is set in the floor a large circular slab of porphyry. It was on this, located near the altar of an earlier St Peter's, that Charles I, King of the Franks and the Lombards, knelt on Christmas Day AD800 to be crowned by the Pope as Roman Emperor – the revival of an office which had lapsed in the West after the deposition of Romulus Augustulus in 476. The Pope, having placed a crown on the new Emperor's head, knelt before him and did him homage. The people of Rome acclaimed him *imperator et augustus*.

This dramatic event was not quite as significant as it might have appeared. The empire of Charlemagne, as he came to be called, already covered the greater part of Western Europe and his ability to protect its borders would still depend on his military might. His authority was not recognised in Eastern Europe, where the Christmas Day ceremony caused some annoyance. Yet the crowning did enhance his status as a Christian ruler, with the implication that God was on his side; and the Pope benefited, too, since the Emperor was bound to be committed to protecting him and the Catholic Church. It was a symphony of Church and State that continued to be performed, more or less harmoniously, in Europe for the next 1,000 years.

Charlemagne's lasting work, however, was in passing on learning. He was not himself well-educated, having started too late. But he filled his court with distinguished scholars from all parts of Europe who wrote and translated books and turned his ideas into practical policies. Previously, the Franks had been an ignorant people but Charlemagne inaugurated a programme of learning that lasted for 100 years and provided some of the tools for the Renaissance of the 14th-16th centuries.

But the years of his reign between 771 and 800 as King of the Franks had been spent largely in extending his kingdom, to embrace Lombardy, in Northern Italy, Bavaria, parts of northern and central Europe, and extending south to northern Spain. Always his patronage of the Church, learning and the arts was inseparable from his political aims.

He had come into the kingdom after King Pepin III died in 768. The kingdom was divided between Charles and his brother Carloman. But Carloman died in 771, leaving Charles as sole ruler. He subjugated the pagan Saxons in Germany by brutal repression accompanied by mass Baptisms of the vanquished.

Strong, centralised government became the order of the day thr oughout the kingdom. In a General Admonition issued in 789 Charles promulgated 82 articles on Church policy. Schools were to be established, the chief of them associated with cathedrals and monasteries. Study of the classics of Greece and Rome was ordered and Latin was

# of Christendom

restored as the literary language. A school at the palace was opened to ordinary people as well as to the nobility, probably the first school to give a classical education to the laity. Uniformity of worship, based closely on Mass-books brought from Rome, was promoted, with the help of the English scholar Alcuin (*see page 68*).

It was a remarkable achievement but the years that followed turned out to be unhappy. Political and economic disintegration left a difficult legacy to his son, Louis, when Charles died in 814. The first Emperor was buried in the cathedral at Aix-la-Chapelle (Aachen, now in Germany). There, 28 successive Emperors were crowned to an office of ebbing power.

EYEWITNESS

Charlemagne in bed

Charlemagne's earliest biographer Einhard describes his habits and crowning moment

During his meal he would listen to a public reading. He took great pleasure in the books of St Augustine, especially *The City of God*. He was so sparing in his use of wine that he rarely drank more than three times in the course of his dinner. After his midday meal, he would remove his shoes and undress completely, just as he did at night, and rest for two or three hours. During the night he slept so lightly that he would wake four or five times and rise from his bed. When he was dressing he would invite his friends to come in.

He learnt Latin so well that he spoke it as fluently as his own tongue: but he understood Greek better than he could speak it. He paid the greatest attention to the liberal arts, and he had great respect for those who taught them, bestowing high honours upon them. He applied himself to mathematics and traced the course of the stars. He also tried to learn to write. He used to keep writing-tablets under the pillows on his bed, so that he could try his hand at forming letters at odd moments; but, although he tried very hard, he had begun too late in life and made little progress.

Charlemagne cared more for the church of the holy apostle Peter in Rome than for any other sacred and venerable place. He poured into its treasury a vast fortune. However, throughout his whole reign of 47 years he went there only four times to fulfil his vows and to offer up his prayers.

These were not the sole reasons for Charlemagne's last visit to Rome. The truth is that the inhabitants of Rome had violently attacked Pope Leo, and had forced him to flee to the king for help. Charlemagne really came to Rome to restore the Church, which was in a very bad state indeed, but in the end he spent the whole winter there. It was on this occasion that he received the title of Emperor and Augustus. At first he was far from wanting this. He made it clear that he would not have entered the cathedral that day at all, although it was the greatest of all the festivals of the Church, if he had known in advance what the Pope was planning.

An Englishman at the court of Charlemagne

O f the international company of scholars attracted to the court of Charlemagne in the 8th century, the most brilliant was an Englishman, Alcuin of York. He had a deep and extensive knowledge of the literature of ancient Greece and Rome, as well as of the writings of St Augustine of Hippo, St Benedict and St Gregory the Great – just what was needed for encouraging the revival of learning in the Europe of that time. He was also a highly gifted teacher and there is some evidence that it was his influence that took Charlemagne to Rome for coronation as Emperor.

Alcuin was born in about 737 into a noble family in Northumberland. His English name was Ealhwine. He was educated at the cathedral school in York (the successor to which still operates), by then a famous centre of learning, where he was taught by Archbishop Egbert, a pupil of Bede's. York also had a remarkable library and served as a European clearing house for the distribution of classical volumes acquired from Rome and other places in Italy.

After ordination as a deacon and profession as a monk, Alcuin became Librarian, but while returning from a visit to Rome in 781 he called on Charlemagne and in the following year joined his court. The rest of his life, apart from two short visits to York, were spent in France, where in 796 he was given a job as Abbot of the renowned monastery of St Martin at Tours.

His pupils in Charlemagne's Palace School included the king and members of his family, as well as nobles, some ordinary people and scholars who later taught bishops, priests and monks elsewhere. Alcuin is said to have been responsible for a royal edict that the clergy should study the classics before turning to the Bible. He himself wrote several books on biblical interpretation and during his years at Tours brought together a number of editions of the Bible, containing variant readings, to form a single Latin text.

Besides this, he wrote teaching manuals on grammar, rhetoric, dialectic and mathematics, as well as poems and some biographies of saints. Another keen interest was the ordering of worship; this led him to revise the official Roman table of Bible readings and to adapt for use in France a service book authorised by Pope Gregory the Great in the 6th century.

The countering of heresy occupied some of his time, too; he wrote many letters which were preserved and are now an important source of information on the period; and his closing years were spent copying manuscripts borrowed from the library at York.

He also produced the epitaph for his own gravestone: "My name was Alchuine, and wisdom was always dear to me."

A king writes...

King Alfred explains how, though he could not read Latin, he translated important Latin works into English. This account comes from his own preface to his translation of the *Pastoral Care* by Pope Gregory, the man who sent Augustine to convert England. First, Alfred surveys the state of English learning when he came to the throne

I wondered extremely that the good and wise men who were formerly all over England, and had perfectly learnt all the books, did not wish to translate them into their own language. But again I soon answered myself and said: "They did not think that men would ever be so careless, and that learning would so decay; so they did not translate books."

Then I considered how the law was first known in Hebrew, and then, when the Greeks had learnt it, they translated the whole of it into their own language, and other books besides. And again the Romans, when they had learnt it, they translated the whole of it through learned interpreters into their own language. Therefore it seems a good idea for us also to translate the books with which people ought to be most familiar into the language which we can all understand. And you ought (as can easily be done if we have peace enough) to see that all the children of free men now in England (those who are rich enough to be able to devote themselves to it) be put to their lessons (while they are not ready for any other occupation), until that they are able to read English well. And those who are to continue their studies should be taught the Latin language.

When I realised that the knowledge of Latin was in decay throughout England, but that many could read English, I began, amid the many troubles of this kingdom, to translate into English the book which is called in Latin *Pastoralis*, and in English *Shepherd's Book*. I sometimes took it word by word and sometimes according to the sense, as I had learnt it from Plegmund my archbishop, Asser my bishop, and Grimbold and John my mass-priests. When I had mastered it to the best of my understanding, I translated it into English as far as I could interpret it.

I will send a copy to every bishopric in my kingdom; and on each there is a clasp worth 50 mancus. And I command in God's name that no man take the clasp from the book or the book from the cathedral.

The copy of Alfred's translation of Gregory the Great's *Pastoral Care* sent to Worcester

THE MAIN EVENTS AD800-1200

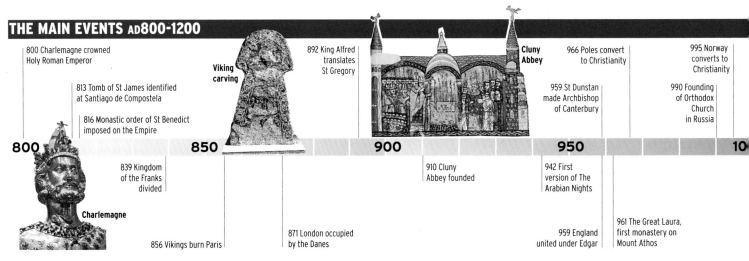

800 Charlemagne crowned Holy Roman Emperor

813 Tomb of St James identified at Santiago de Compostela

816 Monastic order of St Benedict imposed on the Empire

Charlemagne

839 Kingdom of the Franks divided

Viking carving

856 Vikings burn Paris

871 London occupied by the Danes

892 King Alfred translates St Gregory

910 Cluny Abbey founded

Cluny Abbey

942 First version of The Arabian Nights

959 St Dunstan made Archbishop of Canterbury

959 England united under Edgar

961 The Great Laura, first monastery on Mount Athos

966 Poles convert to Christianity

995 Norway converts to Christianity

990 Founding of Orthodox Church in Russia

800	850	900	950	10

Alfred after battle

Two generations after Charlemagne, England had its own king – Alfred. Everyone knows that he beat the Danes. But at the same time he launched a national scheme for education and set it going by translating Latin books himself

King Alfred – warrior, statesman, church-man, scholar – was certainly the greatest of England's Saxon kings and many believe him to have been the greatest monarch in English history. His understanding of kingship was essentially a religious one, based on a conviction that the role of the king is to be Christ's deputy on earth and that his duty is to promote the standards of the Kingdom of God, remembering always that he is himself under the judgment of God.

Yet events in Alfred's world posed a constant challenge to his theocratic view of society. The Viking invasions of England were at their most successful, and the Christian culture of its kingdoms might well have been completely destroyed. Alfred, King of the West Saxons, had suffered several defeats. But he turned the tide against the pagan Danes at the Battle of Edington in AD878 and not only required their king to be baptised, but himself stood as a godfather.

This was followed by the re-organisation of the army and, more importantly, the navy to prevent further invasions. Fortified centres were established throughout the kingdom. By 886 the Danes were confined to the North of England, which they were permitted to rule under Alfred's over-lordship, and he had received the submission of all the English who were not under the Danes. London was occupied. He became therefore the first King of the Angles and Saxons – the first King of the English.

Alfred believed that the pagans from the North had been sent by God as a punishment for neglect of the study of the Bible and other improving works from antiquity. He had found few at the beginning of his reign who were literate in both English and Latin. Education must be revived not simply for its own sake but in order to strengthen the Church and the nation and as an insurance against further divine retribution.

Alfred tackled the problem by sending to Mercia (the mid-English kingdom), Wales and the continent for competent scholars who came together to form in Winchester a circle of court intellectuals. Their task was to educate the clergy, the nobles and the judges, and by the creation of a vernacular literature make it possible for ordinary English people to understand the laws of Church and State.

The king's own educational needs were as great as those of many of his subjects. He was born in Wantage in 849 and received no formal education during his childhood. At the age of 38 he was still unable to read Latin, but he took advantage of a period of peace, 887–892, to try to remedy this.

One of the earliest contributions he made was the translation of the first 50 Psalms. Then came a translation of Gregory's *Pastoral Care*, which for many centuries provided guidance for parish clergy, though Alfred was more interested in its admonition to bishops to educate the laity. A translation of the *Consolation of Philosophy* by Boethius (*see page 48*) followed, and tradition asserts that he was also responsible the translation of part of Bede's *Ecclesiastical History*. Certainly he managed to see translated into English the 5th-century history by Orosius, which combated the idea that the Roman Empire fell because it was undermined by Christianity; thus Alfred pre-empted the contrary labours of Edward Gibbon nine centuries later. He was the only king before Henry VIII who wrote a book.

Alfred believed that the pagans from the North had been sent by God as a punishment

Alfred saw to it that more able bishops were eventually appointed and given greater authority. Some of these served on the king's council where th ey were very influential. Alfred drew no distinction between the sacred and the secular, or between the Church and politics.

The wide-ranging scheme for educating everyone that he devised included the study of man's origin and destiny. The arts, particularly metalwork, jewellery and carving, experienced a great flowering during his reign.

The coin above is inscribed "Aelfred Rex", and during the 28 years of Alfred's reign (AD871-899) he turned himself not merely into a triumphant warrior but also a patron of learning. We still have the very manuscript (*left*) of his translation of St Gregory's *Pastoral Care* which he directed to be inscribed "*Theos boc sceal toWiogora Ceastre*" – This book is to go to Worcester. He strictly instructed the Bishop of Worcester to keep it safely on the chain provided

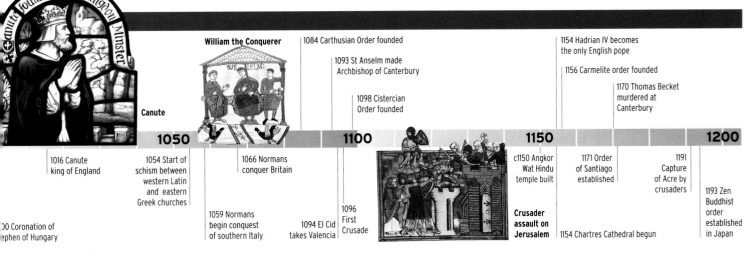

Canute	**William the Conquerer**	1084 Carthusian Order founded		1154 Hadrian IV becomes the only English pope
		1093 St Anselm made Archbishop of Canterbury		1156 Carmelite order founded
		1098 Cistercian Order founded		1170 Thomas Becket murdered at Canterbury
1050		**1100**		**1150**	**1200**
1016 Canute king of England	1054 Start of schism between western Latin and eastern Greek churches	1066 Normans conquer Britain	c1150 Angkor Wat Hindu temple built	1171 Order of Santiago established	1191 Capture of Acre by crusaders
					1193 Zen Buddhist order established in Japan
00 Coronation of phen of Hungary	1059 Normans begin conquest of southern Italy	1094 El Cid takes Valencia	1096 First Crusade	**Crusader assault on Jerusalem**	1154 Chartres Cathedral begun

Carrying the king's body with honour

England before the Conquest built up a rich literature in its own language. The popular story of the martyrdom of King Edmund by Danish invaders was full of striking events – the saint shot full of arrows till he looked "like a porcupine", his severed head being guarded by a wolf and then miraculously crying out to be reunited with its body. It was the sort of story that appealed to a master of the Old English tongue, Aelfric, Abbot of Eynsham, who lived from about 955 to 1020. The Feast each November 20 of Edmund, King of the East Angles, martyred by the Vikings in 870, was popular at the time of Aelfric. The shrine at Bury St Edmunds to which the king's body had been translated (pictured here from the Life of St Edmund, c.1130) in 903 was a place of pilgrimage. Aelfric, pronounced "Alfritch", wrote a popular cycle of sermons for saints' days from which the extract below is taken.

Then those wicked men [*Danish Viking invaders*] bound Edmund, and shamefully insulted him, and beat him with clubs, and afterward they led the faithful king to an earth-fast tree, and tied him thereto with hard bonds, and afterwards scourged him a long while with whips, and ever he called, between the blows, with true faith, on Jesus Christ; and then the heathen because of his faith were madly angry, because he called upon Christ to help him.

They shot at him with javelins as if for their amusement, until he was all beset with their shots, as with a porcupine's bristles, even as Sebastian was.

Then Hingwar, the wicked seaman, commanded men to behead him, and the heathen did. For while he was yet calling upon Christ, the heathen drew away the saint, to slay him, and with one blow struck off his head; and his soul departed joyfully to Christ. So then the seamen went again to ship, concealing the head of the holy Edmund in the thick brambles, that it might not be buried.

Then after a space, when they were gone away, came the country-folk who were still left there, to where their lord's body lay without the head, and they all went seeking at last in the wood, seeking everywhere among the thorns and brambles if they might anywhere find the head.

There was eke a great wonder, that a wolf was sent, by God's direction, to guard the head against the other animals by day and night. They went on seeking and crying out, as is often the wont of those who go through woods: "Where art thou now, comrade?" And the head answered them, "Here, here, here." And so it cried out continually, answering them all, as oft as any of them cried, until they all came to it by means of those cries.

There lay the grey wolf who guarded the head, and with his two feet had embraced the head. They were astonished at the wolf's guardianship, and carried the holy head home with them, thanking the Almighty for all His wonders. Then the country-people afterward laid the head by the holy body, and buried him as they best might in such haste, and full soon built a church over him.

Then again, after a space, after many years, when the harrying had ceased, and peace was restored to the oppressed people, then they came together, and built a church worthily to the saint, because frequently miracles were done at his burial-place, even at the bede-house where he was buried.

Then desired they to carry the holy body with popular honour, and to lay it within the church.

Then there was a great wonder, that he was all as whole as if he were alive, with clean body, and his neck was healed which before was cut through, and there was as it were a silken thread about his neck, all red, as if to show men how he was slain. And so he lieth uncorrupt until this present day.

Now

Dunstan was the domina the monk himself surviv

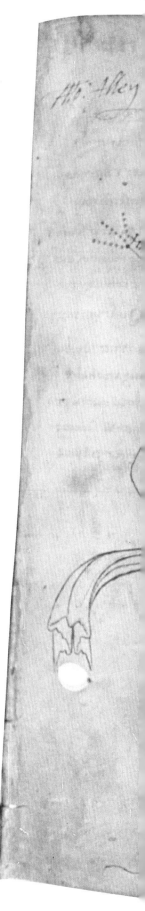

watch over me, Dunstan

rsonality in 10th-century England. The king relied on his wisdom. A touching 1,000-year-old manuscript drawing penned by
monstrating Dunstan's reliance on the wisdom of Jesus Christ

This drawing from Dunstan's own hand shows Christ as "the Wisdom of God and the true ruler of men". The monk himself is shown in a conventional attitude of worship; above the little figure is written "Watch over me, Dunstan"

Dunstan lived through the greater part of the 10th century, was Archbishop of Canterbury for 28 years, and for much of this time the most influential figure in England in both Church and State. Regarded as a saint in his own lifetime, he combined the vision of a Christian leader with the wisdom of a statesman. He was also a gifted musician, painter, illuminator and metalworker – he was later traditionally depicted holding the devil with a pair of blacksmith's tongs. The religious ceremony he devised for the coronation of King Edgar at Bath in AD973 provided the basis for all the subsequent coronation services in England.

Dunstan was born in 909 and was brought up in Somerset, where his father owned land adjoining Glastonbury Abbey. The abbey housed a community of priests who ran a school to which Dunstan went for his earliest education. Family influence secured him a position in the court of King Athelstan, but after a time he returned to Glastonbury as a monk and a priest.

In 940 he was made abbot and adopted the the rule of St Benedict. He saw this as the beginning of a movement that would enable reformed monastic foundations to spread throughout England. There was, however, a hitch in 956 when royal displeasure obliged him to go into exile in Flanders. His offence was that of dragging to the coronation the teenage King Edwy who at the appointed hour was found to be in bed with both his mistress and her daughter.

But in the following year he was recalled to England by King Edgar of Mercia and Northumbria to become Bishop of Worcester and London, and when, following the early death of Edwy, Edgar became King of all England he made Dunstan Archbishop of Canterbury.

The two men embarked on a thorough reform of Church and State. Since the king was only in his twenties, he leaned heavily on the archbishop for guidance. In return he enthusiastically backed Dunstan's proposals for Church reform. An important development came at a synod in Winchester in 970 when the bishops and abbots adopted the *Regularis Concordia* – a code of monastic observance that covered worship, the duties of abbots, processions and domestic matters (such as permitting fires to be lit in winter). This mirrored similar reforms taking place in Europe, but it was unique in prescribing prayers for the king and his family at monastic services.

Although Dunstan was not present at the synod, his influence dominated the proceedings and the leadership came from two of his colleagues, Ethelwold, Bishop of Winchester, and Oswald, Bishop of Worcester. The reforms came to have a great effect on the life of the whole Church in England. Many of the monks became bishops, and between 975 and 1066 every English diocese was at one time or another ruled by a Benedictine monk. These men were effective teachers of the parish clergy, and a new vitality was evident everywhere.

After the death of King Edgar in 975 the succession was disputed. Dunstan's influence declined, but he remained a faithful pastor of the diocese of Canterbury, and lived to crown two more kings. On Ascension Day 988 he preached in the cathedral and two days later died, surrounded by his monks.

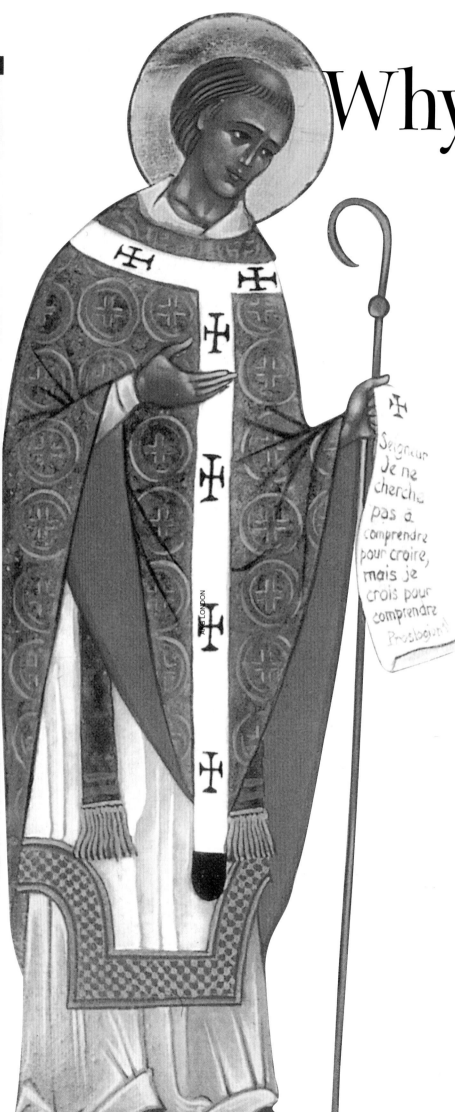

EYEWITNESS

The problem that kept Anselm awake at night

The first truly personal biography in the Middle Ages is that of Anselm by his fellow monk Eadmer. Here he explains how Anselm came to write the two books that outlined his intellectual search for God

He composed a small book, which he called the *Monologion* because in this he alone spoke and argued with himself. Here, putting aside all arguments of authority from holy scripture, he enquired into and discovered by reason alone what God is, and proved by invincible reason that God's nature is what the true faith holds it to be, and that it could not be other than it is. Afterwards it came into his mind to try to prove by one single and short argument the things which are believed and preached about God, that he is eternal, unchangeable, omnipotent, omnipresent, incomprehensible, just, righteous, merciful, true, as well as truth, goodness, justice and so on; and to show how all these qualities are united in him. And this, as he himself would say, gave him great trouble, partly because thinking about it took away his desire for food, drink and sleep, and partly – and this was more grievous to him – because it disturbed the attention which he ought to have paid to matins and to divine service at other times. When he was aware of this, and still could not entirely lay hold on what he sought, he supposed that this line of thought was a temptation of the devil and he tried to banish it from his mind. But the more vehemently he tried to do this, the more this thought pursued him.

Then suddenly one night during matins the grace of God illuminated his heart, the whole matter became clear to his mind, and a great joy and exultation filled his inmost being. Thinking therefore that others also would be glad to know what he had found, he immediately and ungrudgingly wrote it on writing tablets.

From this, therefore, he composed a volume, small in size but full of weighty discourse and most subtle speculation, which he called the *Proslogion*, because in this work he speaks either to himself or to God. This work came into the hands of someone who found fault with one of the arguments in it, judging it to be unsound. In an attempt to refute it he wrote a treatise against it and attached this to the end of Anselm's work. A friend sent this to Anselm who read it with pleasure, expressed his thanks to his critic and wrote his reply to the criticism. He had this reply attached to the treatise which had been sent to him, and returned it to the friend from whom it had come, desiring him and others who might deign to have his little book to write out at the end of it the criticism of his argument and his own reply to the criticism.

An image of St Anselm (*right*) made in Bec, the Normandy abbey where he settled in 1059. The inscription on the scroll he carries reads, "Lord, I do not seek to understand that I may believe, but I believe that I may understand" – a sentence from his philosophical enquiry into belief in God, to which he gave the name *Proslogion*

Why

did God become man?

In the 11th century scholars could move with ease from one country to another. Anselm left his home in Italy to study in Normandy and became Archbishop of Canterbury. He tussled with kings but he always found new energy to continue his intellectual questioning

Anselm, the most persistently enquiring theological mind of his era, was born in 1033 in the Alpine town of Aosta. His mother was a native of the town, probably an heiress, and the family were kinsmen of the Count of Savoy, the effective ruler in the region. Anselm's mother died when he was young. He was not close to his father Gundulf, and he left Aosta in about 1056, travelling north across the Alps. After three years' wandering, he settled, in 1059, at the Benedictine abbey of Bec, in Normandy. The Prior of Bec, Lanfranc, was Europe's leading scholar, and, according to the historian Orderic Vitalis, almost all the monks at Bec were philosophers.

Anselm's biographer Eadmer describes him as a keen student, "wearying his body with late nights, with cold and with hunger". He became well grounded in the textbooks of 11th-century logic, the works of Aristotle then known and those of Boethius (see page 48), later called the *Logica Vetus*. In about 1060 Anselm became a monk.

Within three years, he had written his first important work, an advanced introduction to dialectic (logic) to which he gave the title *De Grammatico*. A dialogue between master and pupil, the treatise raises, in an apparently casual fashion, the logical problems of the day. When, in 1063, Lanfranc left Bec to become Abbot of St Stephen's, Caen, recently founded by Duke William of Normandy (soon to be King of England), Anselm, aged 30, succeeded him as Prior of Bec. For the next seven years he dedicated his energies to the duties of the monastic life, with no time for writing.

But in 1070, when Lanfranc left Caen to become Archbishop of Canterbury, Anselm again began to write, and to preserve, letters, as well as *Prayers and Medi-tations* for those outside the community at Bec, notably William the Conqueror's daughter Adelaide. By 1078, when he became Abbot of Bec, Anselm had produced his first two great treatises, *Monologion* and *Proslogion*. Within a year or two, these were known all over Europe, and had made Anselm's name.

It was principally on the business of his monastery that in September 1092 Anselm arrived in England. By Christmas he was at Westminster Abbey, waiting for an interview with King William Rufus, and by March 1093 he was in Gloucestershire, when the king fell gravely ill. Anselm arrived to hear the king's last rites. The matter of filling the vacant see of Canterbury arose, and the king at once named Anselm.

Already 60, he was to have a stormy career as archbishop. An old sheep, he observed shrewdly, had been yoked to an untamed bull; and it was not long before tension broke out, over Anselm's refusal to accept the pallium, the symbol of his office, from the king rather than Pope Gregory.

A compromise was reached, but when William then refused to allow Anselm to go to Rome to discuss the reform of the English Church, Anselm left, in October 1097, and did not return to England until after William's death in 1100. In exile he completed his greatest theological work, *Cur Deus Homo*. Under Henry I he again went into exile, until 1107. Anselm died in 1109, reviled by Canterbury's monks for failing to establish primacy over York. Yet it was among them that he was happiest, "just as an owl is glad when she is in her hole with her chicks".

Faith in search of understanding

Anselm fearlessly applied rigorous logic to explore and explain the teachings of Christianity about the existence of God, his mysterious nature and the way in which the crucifixion of Jesus redeems mankind

Anselm's intellectual search for God not only remains the highest point of philosophical culture of the Benedictine Order, but has remained a challenge even to secular philosophers. Bertrand Russell remembered how he had suddenly been convinced by Anselm's "ontological argument" for the existence of God one day in the street in Cambridge.

Much of Anselm's work is cast in the form of a dialogue, a form, for him, to be used, as Plato used it, to draw out meaning and to give structure to a body of thoughts. The two sides in Anselm's dialogues are always master and pupil, not representatives of two rival schools of thought.

But Anselm's originality lies in the confidence with which he explores the nature of God, the Trinity, the Incarnation and Redemption through the medium of reason, or dialectic. In doing this, he was resuming a theological discipline that had hardly moved forward in Western Christendom since the time of St Augustine's death in AD 430.

The three treatises

Anselm's first great treatise, the *Monologion* (a monologue), is in essence a philosophical soliloquy or a meditation (*exemplum meditandi*) on the qualities of the Trinity, and is closely dependent on Augustine's *De Trinitate*. His second treatise, the *Proslogion*, is chiefly concerned with the qualities of God as Unity. Intended both as a meditation for the believer and a proof for the unbeliever, it is only very slightly dependent on Augustine, and is altogether more personal and vivid in expression than the *Monologion*. Anselm's original title for the *Proslogion* was *Fides quaerens intellectum* (faith in search of understanding), which better than any other phrase describes Anselm's theological programme.

The work arose out of Anselm's desire to formulate a single argument which would in itself suffice to prove that God exists, and in the first three chapters of the *Proslogion* he sets out what has become known as his ontological argument, his argument for God's existence.

The form of words Anselm needed for his proof were buried in Seneca's *Quaestiones Naturales*, a rare book, of which there were two copies at Bec in the 12th century: "God is that than which nothing greater can be thought." If, Anselm's argument goes, God is that than which nothing greater can be thought, then he must exist not merely as a concept in the mind, but also in external reality. Were he to exist only as a concept in the mind, and not in reality, he would not be that than which nothing greater can be thought.

Anselm's finest theological achievement was his sophisticated treatise on Redemption, *Cur Deus Homo*, begun during his early years as Archbishop of Canterbury and completed in exile, in the mountains near Capua, in 1098.

Its composition, prompted by a desire to clarify the meaning of the Crucifixion, sets out to provide a proof, from which there can be no appeal, that the Incarnation was a fact – and not just a fact, but a necessary fact, the only possible means of Man's Redemption.

War and peace

At this period Spain was on the edge of Christendom. The Moors had conquered the whole peninsula in AD711 except the mountains of the north. From there began the centuries-long battle for reconquest by the Christian forces

T he Moorish invasion of the Iberian peninsula in AD711 never succeeded in taking the mountains of Asturias in the north. Soon afterwards, in 722, Pelayo, a Visigothic nobleman, led an Asturian army to victory at Covadonga. But it was to be more than 700 years before the peninsula was to be entirely free of Moorish rule.

Christian practice was not extinguished under Muslim rule. The Koran acknowledged Christians as "People of the Book". Though Islam won converts, the majority stuck to their religion. Because they adopted Moorish customs, they were known as Mozarabs, from the Arabic *musta' rib* or "would be Arab".

The liturgy of the Mozarabic Christians retained ancient usages and developed independently. But in the mid-11th century a legate from Pope Alexander II (reigned 1061-73), by name Hugo Candidus, visited Spain and energetically replaced Mozarabic rites with the Roman order of Mass. It was only through the intervention of the historically minded Cardinal Francisco Ximenes de Cisneros (1436-1517; *see page 122*) that the Mozarabic rite was preserved at all, though its use became limited to one chapel in the cathedral of Toledo.

In the meantime the coming of the legate Hugo meant more than the revision of the liturgy. Pope Alexander sanctioned a crusade by the northern princes of Spain; recaptured territory was to be nominally under the feudal suzerainty of the Pope. The energetic reformist Pope Gregory VII (reigned 1073-85) wished to extend this principle; his influence was soon felt in Aragon, Navarre and Catalonia. King Alfonso VI of Castile accepted at least the introduction of the Roman liturgy in his kingdom, and Gregory was to live to see the recapture of Toledo by Alfonso in 1085. To Toledo flocked scholars in

HENRI STIERLIN

A Mozarabic miniature of the Apocalypse from the *Beatus of El Escorial*, second half of the 10th century. John the Divine is delivering one of his messages to the seven churches, represented by an angel

search of ancient texts preserved by Arabic writers. Among them was Adelard, born in Bath and widely travelled in Sicily, Palestine and Syria. He spent many years in Toledo in the first half of the 12th century translating and commenting on Aristotle and Plato, as well as writing a treatise on falconry. The Italian-born Dominic Gundisalvi, who became archdeacon of Segovia, translated the *Metaphysics of Avicenna*, an important element in the reintroduction of Aristotelian thought to the West. Gundisalvi worked with the help of a Jewish scholar who translated Arabic word for word into Spanish ready to be rendered into Latin. Another early 12th-century scholar, Hermann of Carinthia, rediscovered Ptolemy's *Planisphere*, and a contemporary, Robert of Chester, translated the *Algebra* of Al-Khwarizmi. These two even turned their hands to a translation of the Koran, commissioned by Abbot Peter the Venerable of Cluny.

It was from Cluny in Burgundy, with its reformed variety of Benedictine monasticism, that new monasteries grew up in Spain. Their foundations were supported by King Ferdinand I of León (reigned 1035-65) and grew during the reign of Pope Urban II (reigned 1088-99), a former Cluniac monk.

The Cluniacs encouraged pilgrimage to Santiago de Compostela. This shrine, boasting the relics of St James, had been attracting pilgrims since the tomb of the Apostle was thought to have been discovered in AD813. It is hard to imagine that the discovery was anything more than wishful thinking. But Santiago grew ever stronger as a magnet for pilgrims from all over Europe; along the route through northern Spain, churches and towns grew up. The image of St James – Santiago – was set up as a patron to win victory over the Moors.

As Christian territory expanded, fine Romanesque cathedrals were built, as at Salamanca, Zamora and Avila (where the apse formed part of the city walls). It was into this atmosphere of rejuvenated Christianity that Dominic, the founder of a revolutionary order of preaching friars was to be born in about 1170 in the central kingdom of Castile (*see page 98*).

Slowly the "crusades" in the 12th century, helped by knights from Provence and Genoa, retook the Balearics and Zaragoza. Lisbon and most of Portugal were reconquered from 1147. But the pace slackened in Spain until Pope Innocent III (reigned 1198-1216) declared another Spanish "crusade". With French support this resulted in a celebrated Christian victory at Navas de Tolosa in 1212. The Moors were finally vanquished in 1492.

The Moors crossed from North Africa into Spain in 711 and swiftly conquered the peninsula. Visigothic nobles fled to the Pyrenees and the mountains of Cantabria, in Asturias, from which they started the reconquest, gaining their first victory at Covadonga in about 722.
The "discovery" of the relics of St James at Santiago de Compostela in 813 brought pilgrims and new churches across the north. Toledo, the former Visigothic capital, was retaken in 1085, but the crusade continued until 1492, when the Moors were finally defeated

75

Smashing the icons

Outraged housewives killed the official sent to destroy the icon of Christ outside Hagia Sophia in Constantinople in AD726. Worse violence was to come in a century-long war to smash the icons or to save them

In the East, a bitter religious controversy that had raged for more more than a century was finally resolved in AD843. This was the rejection of iconoclasm. Iconoclasm – literally "breaking of images" – was an imperial-inspired attack on the veneration of religious images, an assault driven by both political and spiritual considerations.

Reverence for images of the holy family and the saints, especially those icons reputed to have miracle-working properties, had become a strong feature of Christian life in the East. It was part of the daily pattern of worship of a whole civilisation. The early Byzantine emperors had no objections to the pictorial representation of Christ; rather by depicting him on one side of coins and themselves on the other they emphasised the divine source of their power.

But by the early 8th century, a movement began which asserted that the use of icons was idolatrous. It was no longer accepted that the worship given to icons was merely relative – that it was God being worshipped by the reference of a picture to Jesus Christ, God made man, or by seeing the glory of God reflected in images of his saints. The iconoclast reaction was most widespread in the eastern parts of the Empire, where there was the strongest influence from the Monophysite heresy (which in practice undervalued the human qualities of Jesus) and from Judaism and Islam – religions which prohibited the making of images.

In 717, Emperor Leo III of Byzantium, a soldier who had made his reputation commanding eastern regiments, came to the throne. Supported by the army, he began in 726 to repress the use of images. He ordered that the giant gold icon of Christ that stood over the bronze gates of the Imperial Palace, facing Hagia Sophia, be pulled down. The order caused a riot, and a group of outraged housewives killed the official in charge of the demolition.

Undeterred, in 730 Leo decreed that all religious imagery, except the Cross, was forbidden. Icons were whitewashed, liturgical vestments burnt, relics smashed. Although Leo wished in part to assert his authority over the Church, his motives seem to have been primarily theological. When Pope Gregory II wrote to suggest that Leo leave religion to the experts, the emperor sent ships to arrest him. Fortunately for Gregory, they sank on the way to Rome.

The iconoclastic policy was continued by Leo's son, Constantine V, a man of unorthodox religious views who even forbade use of the title "saint". Constantine sought to give the imposition of Iconoclasm more weight than his own interpretation the Second Commandment – "Thou shalt not make unto thee any graven image, or any likeness of any thing that is in heaven above, or that is in the earth beneath". In 754, he summoned a synod and told the Church that religious iconography was wrong; by showing Christ as human, he asserted, icons either failed to express his divine nature or confounded it with the human.

The persecution now raged fiercer than ever. The object of the persecutors was much wider than merely the use of icons. Monasticism was itself attacked – monks had their beards set on fire and libraries were burnt. Every nun and monk in Thrace was forced to choose between marriage and deportation to Cyprus. Many monks fled to the West, taking icons with them, and John of Damascus (see left), the most articulate of the Iconodules, as the supporters of icons were called, was excommunicated.

Then, in 780, on the death of Constantine, his Iconodule daughter-in-law, Irene, became Regent. A council of bishops that she called was forcibly broken up by soldiers loyal to Constantine's memory. But in 787, at Nicaea, a council that included legates from Rome formally reversed the position adopted at Constantine's synod 30 years before. Their decree drew largely on the writings of John of Damascus.

The balance was tipped once more in favour of the Iconoclasts in 813 when, taking account of popular discontent aroused by military defeat, the destruction of images again became state policy. But the persecution was much less intense this time, and at the Council of Constantinople in 843 the Empress Theodora reaffirmed the ruling given at Nicaea and finally put an end to the controversy. The freedom to worship God with the help of images was restored.

The meaning of icons

The enemies of icons accused their supporters of idolatry. But the tradition of using icons in prayer carefully distinguished between the artefacts and what they represented. They became a pathway to heaven

The Greek word *eikon* means "image", or "likeness", and images of Christ and holy men and women had great importance in the Byzantine and later Orthodox churches. Whether frescoes, mosaics or paintings in oil on wood, they are among the most enduring forms of European art. Their aim, however, is not artistic, but to be an aid to devotion. Moreover, icons are held to be a direct point of contact between the worshipper and the person depicted.

Some of the early Fathers of the Church frowned on images because of the danger of their being confused with pagan idols. But it could also be argued that there was an analogy between the way that in the Roman Empire the image of the emperor had been considered a manifestation of his divine presence, and a similar but legitimate relationship between icons and the saints they portrayed.

A Muslim protector

The contentions of the iconoclasts were most successfully countered by the theologian St John of Damascus (c657–749), whose ideas still underpin teaching on the meaning of icons. It was by a quirk of history that John, who served as an official to the khalif Abdul Malek in Damascus, should have been able to write in favour of images thanks to a Muslim ruler. The khalif's religion forbade images but his patronage protected John against the wrath of an unorthodox Christian Emperor.

John argued that since Christ had become visible flesh, it was permissible to show respect to his human nature. To venerate images was not to worship the objects themselves but to pay honour through them to the figures to which they referred. "Christ," he wrote, "is venerated not in the image, but with the image." An icon is like a reflection in the mirror; not the essence of a person but an identical image demonstrative of their presence. The writings of John of Damascus were taken up enthusiastically in the Latin West as well as the Christian East.

Icons came to be seen as metaphorical channels through which prayer could pass straight to heaven, and understanding down to earth. This led to the characteristic stylisation of icons, notably the lack of perspective, with the face turned outwards to receive prayer. It was and is the aim of icon painters to produce spiritual beauty, not superficial representation

Christ the Saviour, a 13th-century icon from the Serbian monastery of Chilander on Mount Athos, Greece. Iconoclasts believed that by showing Christ as human (*Theanthropos*, or God-man), icons either failed to express his divine nature or they confounded his divinity by giving it a human form

Teaching the Slavs to write

Conversions in eastern Europe began with
Cyril and Methodius and an alphabet
especially devised for the Slavs, and
culminated in the coronation of St Stephen,
the first king of Hungary

The vast territory of Eastern
Europe, including Russia, was
essentially pagan and the scene of
constant tribal warfare before attempts
at Christianisation in the 9th and 10th
centuries. Two brothers, Cyril (826-69)
and Methodius (815-85), earned the
title Apostles of the Slavs through their
work in Eastern Europe. They came
from a Greek family and were educated
in Constantinople, where Cyril
subsequently became a brilliant
professor of philosophy. Methodius was
appointed governor of a Slav province
in the Byzantine Empire.

Both then became priests, and in 862
the Emperor sent them to engage in
missionary work in what is now
Moravia. Before they set off, however,
Cyril invented an alphabet sometimes
known as Glagolitic, designed for the
purpose of putting the Slav language
into writing. This marked the beginning
of Slavonic literature. The alphabet used
today in Russia is generally known as
Cyrillic, after Cyril.

German resentment

The mission to Moravia was successful
but it ran into difficulties when
confronted by missionaries from
Germany who regarded Moravia as
their territory. During a visit to Rome in
869 Cyril died, and Methodius was
made a bishop. But on his return to
Moravia he was put in prison for two
years at the instigation of the German
bishops. Only the Pope's intervention
secured his release. Methodius

continued his
work,
obtained
permission
from the Pope
for worship to
be conducted
in Slavonic,
rather than in
Latin. He was made
Archbishop of Pannonia
and Moravia and his followers, led by
Clement Slovensky, moved into
Bulgaria. Here Christian missionaries
had been at work since the 4th century,
as the remarkably well preserved church
dedicated to St George in Sofia now
vividly testifies. Clement Slovensky's
band were well received, he was made a
bishop, Prince Boris, the ruler, was
baptised and it was soon reported to
Pope Nicholas I that "a great majority
of the Bulgarians are converted to
Christianity".

But the matter was taken out of the
Pope's hands in 870 when a Council
held at Constantinople decreed that
Bulgaria should come under the
authority of the Eastern hierarchy.

The Russian conversion

The development of Christianity in
Russia came almost a century later.
When the Viking invaders of Rus, as it
was then called, established Rurik of
Jutland as King of Novgorod in 862
and thereby initiated the beginning of
the Russian state, the country was
pagan. During the next 100 years there
was no significant missionary incursion,
but in 977 Prince Vladimir, who was
ruling from Kiev, decided that the nation
needed a monotheistic religion and entry
into the civilised world, preferably that
of Europe.

Ambassadors were therefore
dispatched to neighbouring countries
to enquire about religious beliefs and
practices. Those who went to
Bulgaria, where there was a small
Muslim community, reported that this
religion was "not good", while others
who ventured as far as Rome "saw
no beauty" in the Latin Mass. But
those who went to Constantinople
reported: "We do not know whether
we were in heaven or earth; upon earth

there is
no such sight
or beauty. We do not know
what to say; we only know that there
God is present among men and that
their service is the best of all."

Not surprisingly, Vladimir opted for
Christianity in its Eastern form – a
momentous choice that was to
determine the course of the cultural
political, and religious life of Russia for
the next 1,000 years – and beyond.

Vladimir was himself baptised and his
subjects followed suit, sometimes at the
point of the sword. The brutality which
had been a feature of the prince's rule
was tempered. The subservience of the
Church to the State in Russia has
continued ever since.

Although it had come from the
Byzantine world, Russian Christianity
quickly took on a character of its own.
The services and parts of the Bible were
translated into Slavonic. The religious
art used in the churches, of which a
large number were built, also developed
a distinctive style. The bishops, however,
were appointed by Constantinople.
Contact with Rome was maintained for
a time, becoming much more difficult
after the Great Schism between the
Latin and Byzantine churches in 1054.

Stephen of Hungary baptised

The conversion of Hungary also owed
everything to the decision of a ruler.
King Stephen I (975-1038) was baptised
as a boy by Bishop Adalbert of Prague,
who was later martyred. In 1000 he was
crowned first King of Hungary with a
crown sent by Pope Silvester II; this
crown, used for coronation until 1916,
remains Hungary's most treasured
possession.

Stephen then worked energetically for
the conversion of his subjects, not
hesitating to use violence against the
reluctant. He created 10 bishoprics as
well as the archbishopric of Esztergom
and some monasteries. The close link
with Rome then established continued
until the present century.

Left: St Cyril and St Methodius, from a
19th-century German engraving.
Above: The crown of King Stephen of Hungary

From Vikings to saints

The Archbishop of Canterbury, Alphege, was captured by Vikings and murdered in AD1012 when his ransom was not paid. But within a few years the Viking king Canute had demonstrated his piety with a pilgrimage to Rome. And within a generation Westminster Abbey was built by Edward the Confessor

Danish raids, which had devastated England during the 9th century, were resumed in 980, and continued with increasing force for the next 30 years. An early and most notable casualty was the Archbishop of Canterbury – Alphege – who was regarded as a martyr. He was born in 954, became a monk at Deerhurst in Gloucestershire and was then appointed Abbot of Bath. Highly regarded by Archbishop Dunstan, he succeeded the great Ethelwold as Bishop of Winchester in 984 and was translated to Canterbury in 1006. Six years later a Viking raid on Kent extended as far as Canterbury where Alphege was seized and held for ransom on a Danish ship at Greenwich for seven months. On Easter Day 1012 he was barbarously murdered by the army during a drunken feast. The enormity of their action was quickly recognised by the murderers who allowed Alphege's body to be carried reverently to London for burial in St Paul's. The name of Alphege was invoked by Becket at the moment of his own martyrdom (*see page 91*).

Peace remained elusive until 1016 when the Danes overran most of England and in the following year succeeded in getting their 21-year-old king, Canute, acknowledged as King of England. The bishops, abbots and noblemen swore fealty to him in return for the promise of good government, and this is what they got. Although he had been baptised in Germany, his devotion to Christianity was initially somewhat suspect. But he accepted King Alfred's concept of the king as an agent of God and employed Lifing, the Abbot of Tavistock and Bishop of Crediton, as a personal adviser. Following an admonition from Pope Benedict VIII, conveyed to him by the Archbishop of Canterbury, Canute assured everyone that he intended to govern righteously, and in 1020 he proclaimed a new policy. The sheriffs were instructed to pay attention to the bishops in the administration of justice, and offenders against church law were to be punished. The alliance of Church and State was revived.

During a visit to Rome in 1027 for the coronation of Conrad as Holy Roman Emperor, Canute successfully protested to the Pope against the high fees charged to Archbishops of Canterbury when they received the pallium – a woollen cape symbolising their authority – and he also obtained the promise of safe conduct for pilgrims ▶

King Canute and Queen Aelfgifu present a gold altar cross to the New Minster, Winchester, from *The Book of Life*, c1030

from England to Rome. Subsequently Canute enforced the payment of tithes and other church dues, and restated that priests should remain celibate, and that Sunday be observed as a day of rest from business. All his subjects in England were to learn the Creed and the Lord's Prayer, and pagan worship among Danish immigrants was forbidden. The Code in which much of this was enshrined appears to have been drafted by Wulfstan, the Archbishop of York, but it represented Canute's views and intentions, which also found expression in two letters which he addressed to all his subjects in 1020 and 1027, and in which he reminded them of their duty to God and the Church.

Having evicted King (later Saint) Olaf from the throne of Norway in 1028, Canute became the head of a considerable empire, which he ruled from England and to which he sent a stream of missionaries (*see page 82*). Although he was apt to treat his enemies with dreadful brutality, he was, for his time, a model Christian king and left England at peace, with all its people feeling secure.

The death of Canute in 1035 at the age of 40 was followed by a period of confusion. Harold I, an illegitimate son of Canute, reigned for a short time and he was followed by Hardicanute, another of Canute's children, who proved to be an unsatisfactory king and died at a wedding feast in 1042. The male line of the Danish royal house now ended, and on the day following Hardicanute's death, Edward – a son of King Etheldred the Unready – was proclaimed King of England. He would

Canute decreed that priests should remain celibate, and that Sunday be observed as a day of rest

be known as Edward the Confessor. Born in 1005, he had been living in exile in Normandy, where he received a Norman education, the influence of which remained with him for the rest of his life. His 25-year reign proved to be remarkably peaceful. A rebellion by the Danish Earl, Godwine, was put down in 1051, and, in an act of reconciliation, Edward restored him to his position afterwards. A minor Viking raid on Kent and Essex in 1048 was defeated, and a Northumbrian revolt which brought the rebels as far as Northampton in 1065 ended when the king mollified its leaders. However, his pacific nature, combined with a shortage of money, led him to run down the navy, with serious consequences in 1066.

Edward loved and fostered the Church and lived an ascetic life. Following his death some monks claimed that, although married, he had lived as a celibate. Either way, he was widely regarded as a holy man and this was reflected in a vow, made while in exile in France, that if he ever returned to England he would go on pilgrimage to Rome. In the event, the English court advised against his leaving the country, so he asked the Pope for a dispensation. This was granted on condition that he built a church dedicated to the honour of St Peter. A small monastic building was found on Thorney Island in the marshes near the Thames, and Edward replaced this with Westminster Abbey, to be served by Benedictine monks and to become the royal church. A palace was built nearby, and the capital moved from Winchester to London.

Edward was too ill to attend the ceremony of dedication of the abbey on 28 December 1065. He died a few days later. His body was buried before the high altar, and in 1163, when he was canonised, it was transferred to a shrine there which attracted pilgrims from all over Europe, as it still does today.

King Edmund, martyred by the Vikings, holds an arrow and next to him stands King Edward the Confessor, builder of Westminster Abbey, against a rich gold background in a detail of the 14th-century Wilton Diptych

The warriors of the north were the last peoples in Europe to accept Christianity. They came to it through the example of martyrs, and through defeat in battle

The last heathens of the North

Christianity did not reach Scandinavia until the 10th century, though it had produced a saint and had a few small Christian communities during a brief flurry of missionary activity a hundred years earlier. Anskar (AD801-865) – known as the Apostle of the North – was born near Amiens, in France. He became a monk in his local monastery, then moved to Germany and in 826 to Denmark, where the king and 400 of his subjects had become Christians while living in exile in Mainz. Anskar was next invited by some merchants to visit Sweden, where he was welcomed by the king and built the first Christian church in Scandinavia, at the Viking centre of Birka, near modern Stockholm. On his return to Germany in 832 Anskar was made Bishop of Hamburg, with responsibility for all Scandinavia, and in 848 the Pope appointed him Archbishop of Bremen. Back in Denmark in 854 he converted Erik, the King of Jutland, but he got little response to his preaching and after his death Denmark and Sweden reverted to paganism.

The next known move came from England where King Canute decided in about 1020 to send missionaries to his Danish dominions and got the Archbishop of Canterbury to consecrate a number of bishops. This led to a clash with the Bishop of Hamburg, who believed these bishops were trespassing on his territory, but Canute stood his ground and secured what was to be the first of many victories of the Church over the State in Scandinavia. By 1104 Denmark had its own Archbishop and when in 1147 Pope Eugenius III issued a Bull authorising the Christians of Northern Europe to mount a Crusade against their own heathen, the Danes were in the forefront of the battle – directed mainly against Prussia and some Baltic countries.

About the year 1000 an English monk, Sigfrid, led a mission to Sweden and baptised King Olaf, but otherwise met strong resistance and made little progress. Nearly

Olaf Haraldsson used less violent means of persuasion and had bishops and priests brought from England to share in the mission, but he was overthrown by his enemies in 1030 before the evangelisation could be completed. By 1152, however, the Norwegian church was sufficiently well established for the king to remove it from Danish jurisdiction and enable it to have its own hierarchy responsible directly to Rome.

While King Olaf Tryggvason had been trying to impose Christianity on his subjects in Norway, missionaries recruited by him were preaching in Iceland. Good progress was being made until civil war was threatened between those who accepted and those who opposed Christianity. The matter was referred to a wise old man for decision and after much thought he pronounced the new religion good. So it was accepted, with some concessions to the pagans which were withdrawn in 1016 when Iceland became Christian, with two bishoprics.

Vikings led by Erik the Red, who had been outlawed in Norway and Iceland, settled in Greenland in the late 10th century. Erik's son, Leif, had been baptised in Norway during the time of King Olaf Tryggvason, and he was encouraged by his father to build a church. The first bishop was sent from Norway in 1123 and he soon became the civic as well as the religious head of the community – a practice that continued for three centuries.

The Finns – of a race very different from that of the Scandinavians – were first introduced to Christianity in 1155 when King Erik of Sweden and his army occupied their country. The king, who was accompanied by Bishop Henry of Uppsala, an Englishman, demanded that the population be baptised and, when he returned to Sweden, left the bishop behind to complete the task. Progress was much slower than anticipated, however. In the end Bishop Henry – now regarded as the founder of the Finnish Church – was martyred. The conversion of Finland was achieved at the end of the 13th century.

The conversion of Lithuania took even longer. It is not known when Christianity first reached this land of warlike rulers and ever-changing frontiers, but there is evidence of some Christians there in 1244.

Pope Eugenius III issued a Bull authorising the Christians of Northern Europe to mount a Crusade against heathens

100 years later another king, Inge, tried to have his subjects baptised and to abolish pagan sacrifices, but with limited success. It was not until the reign of King Sverker (1130-55) that Christianity got the upper hand. He sent for Cistercian monks, who established two monasteries.

Norway first encountered Christianity through one of its people – Olaf Tryggvason – who had been trained as a Viking warrior in Russia and in 990 found himself in the Scilly Isles. There he was greatly impressed by a Christian hermit and, having been baptised by him, returned to Norway where he was soon elected king. He thereupon tried, by fair means and foul, to bring his subjects to baptism, but with no great success, and the work was continued, following his death, by King (later Saint) Olaf Haraldsson.

Seven years later the king, Mindaugas, was baptised as part of the terms of an alliance with neighbouring Livonia, which had an archbishop and three bishops. But when Mindaugas died in 1268, Christianity went with him. This inspired the Order of Teutonic Knights to embark on a military crusade designed to remedy the situation. A confused war, involving neighbouring countries, ensued and it was not until 1386, when Prince Jogaila accepted baptism in order to unite Lithuania with Poland, that paganism there was finally defeated.

A stave or mast church in Norway from the second half of the 12th century. Built of timber using shipbuilding techniques, from the 11th to the 16th centuries, they were probably based on Viking ceremonial halls. More than 300 were built and 34 are preserved

East splits from

Rome and
Constantinople
drifted apart
politically and in
religious practice. But
unity was repeatedly
patched up until in
1054 a diplomatic
disaster resulted in a
split that was never
healed

The iconoclast controversy of the 8th century (*see page 76*) had torn Byzantine Christianity in two. But it had also increased strain on the ties between the Roman and Byzantine worlds. Over the next two centuries there was a progressive, though not inevitable, deterioration in relations that eventually led to an irrevocable split between the two halves of Christendom.

One underlying cause of this was that the papacy increasingly began to look to the new powers of the West rather than to Constantinople for protection from its enemies. In 732, in order to ensure that they conformed to his iconoclastic precepts, the Eastern Emperor Leo III had removed the ecclesiastical provinces of southern Italy and the Balkans (which he ruled, and where Greek was spoken) from the jurisdiction of the Bishop of Rome (the Pope) and had given them to the Patriarch of Constantinople.

This show of strength contrasted unfavourably in the papal mind with the weak Byzantine military position in northern Italy, where Ravenna was soon to fall to the barbarian Lombards. The threat of a similar fate befalling Rome encouraged the papacy to loosen its ancient ties to Byzantium and seek alliance with the growing might of the Franks. The coronation by Pope Leo III of Charlemagne as Emperor in the West in 800 was a sign that the Latin Church was willing to take its destiny into its own hands.

Yet few of those at the coronation would have doubted that the Byzantine and Roman Churches were one entity, even if the Pope and the Patriarch might have had differing views on the importance of the ecclesiastical primacy accorded to Rome.

Then in 858, following the downfall of the dowager empress Theodora, Patriarch Ignatius of Constantinople was replaced by Photius, president of the Imperial Chancellery and a layman; in a week he was advanced from tonsured cleric to bishop. In Rome, Pope Nicholas I, influenced by wild tales of Ignatius's disgrace, refused to recognise Photius's election, and in 863 declared Ignatius reinstated. The two churches were now openly in schism.

Matters were then made worse by developments in Bulgaria, a powerful military society that covered much of the Balkans and over which Rome and Constantinople had long vied for influence. Its ruler, Boris X, had been baptised by Byzantine missionaries, but when his request for a native bishop was scornfully rejected by Photius, he turned to Pope Nicholas. The Byzantine Church was furious at what it regarded as Rome's interference, and scandalised when it learnt that papal envoys in Bulgaria were insisting on the use of the word *Filioque* in the Nicene Creed.

It was not that Christians in the Eastern Empire necessarily rejected the teaching that the Holy Spirit proceeds from the Father *and* the Son (*Filioque*); it would take a pretty theologian to argue otherwise, though some rose to the challenge. The introduction of the additional clause had developed innocently in the Spanish church from the 6th century and by 800 had been adopted in Charlemagne's chapel. But the principle still embraced by both the Byzantine and Roman Churches was that no additions should be made to the Creed painfully hammered out in 381 at the Universal Council of Constantinople. The Pope himself had specifically refused in 809 to add the *Filioque* clause.

But in 867 Photius, already declared deposed by the Pope on quite different grounds, in turn declared Pope Nicholas a heretic for countenancing the use of the *Filioque* in Bulgaria. Photius persuaded an imperial coun-

West

Constantine IX Monomachus became Emperor and third husband of the Empress Zoe on their marriage in 1042, shown here in the 11th-century Scylitzes chronicle. The following year he appointed Cerularius patriarch presiding over events that led to the final split between the Catholic West and the Orthodox East

cil to depose Nicholas. Before it could act, the Emperor – Michael III, son of the dowager empress Theodora – was murdered by his lover and successor, Basil, who replaced Photius once more with Ignatius. On Ignatius's death 10 years later, a more moderate Photius again became Patriarch. A reconciliation with Rome followed, and at a Church council in 879 all additions to the Nicene-Constantinopolitan Creed were forbidden. But the root problems between East and West remained unresolved.

Differences came to a head again in 1054 and again the *Filioque* was at issue, but the central problem was the desire of Rome to assert its primacy in the Church, and the corresponding desire of Byzantium to retain its autonomy. A venomous correspondence was pursued between Pope Leo IX and Patriarch Michael Cerularius, appointed by Constantine IX Monomachus in 1043. It resulted in Leo dispatching a legation to Constantinople, led by the high-handed Cardinal Humbert.

The visit was a diplomatic disaster. Cultural differences guaranteed failure. At one point the Greeks even seemed to be accused absurdly of removing the *Filioque* from the creed.

On July 16 1054 Humbert ran out of patience. Flanked by his fellow legates, he marched up to the high altar of Hagia Sophia during the divine liturgy and laid on it a Bull of Excommunication against Cerularius. Cerularius responded in kind. Constantine's attempts to heal the rift failed. The universal Church was split by a schism that has lasted to this day.

Squalor in the city of Rome

Rome was in decay after being repeatedly sacked. As buildings crumbled in the empty streets, a succession of popes came in with their concubines or were murdered by rivals. It took a great man like Gregory VII to turn the tide

The city of Rome had dwindled and decayed since the first barbarian invasion of AD410 when its population stood at 800,000. By 500 it was only 100,000 and when it was devastated by Totila in 543 the population fell to 30,000. By 800, after a resurgence at the time of Gregory the Great, the population was probably back down to 40,000.

This meant the decay of public buildings, of public order, of reliable food supplies, of a stable cultural life. Some of the old imperial buildings were plundered by the powerful families of Rome who used the material to build the great fortified mansions that towered over the mean streets.

If the crowning of Charlemagne by Pope Leo III in AD800 set a seal on the new Western Emperor's own status, it did little to help the Pope. He had succeeded a strong leader, Hadrian I. Hadrian's family resented the interloper in the jealous politics of the city, and stirred up a riot which ended in Leo being almost blinded.

Rome was on its own. The Eastern Emperor held court at Constantinople, and struggled to keep control even of the Greek-speaking parts of Italy. Charlemagne and his successors had their seat far away at Aachen. Rome's remaining status came from its imperial past, its position as a place of pilgrimage, and the presence of the Pope, the successor of St Peter.

Now there was a new threat: Islam. In 846 Saracen pirates sailed up the Tiber, 500 horsemen disembarked, galloped inland and ransacked the city. The tombs of Saints Peter and Paul were plundered of their gold and silver adornments. Pope Leo IV responded between 848 and 852 by surrounding the Vatican with a wall 40 feet high punctuated by 44 towers.

Murder and concubinage

Churches were built under Pope Nicholas I (reigned 858-67), but after his death Rome's darkest age began. The 10th century saw a series of short-lived popes and antipopes. Some were murdered, others mutilated. Though there were good popes, most were the placemen of the Western Emperor or of the Roman families. Reigning in pomp and treating their enemies with cruelty, they might last only until they were murdered or deposed. Pope John XII (reigned 955-64) died aged 27, it was said of a stroke as he lay in bed with another man's wife. One anti-Pope was

even said to consort with evil spirits in the woods near the Vatican.

But in 1073 came a respite when Hildebrand became Pope Gregory VII. He set about re-establishing spiritual values and cleaning up the clergy, issuing decrees against clerical concubinage, against simony (buying and selling of clerical benefices) and against lay investiture (whereby the Western Emperor or royal princes installed abbots and bishops).

Divine intervention

This last reform enraged the Emperor, Henry IV, who in 1076 declared the Pope deposed and got some bishops to excommunicate him. Gregory retaliated by excommunicating Henry. But it did not escape general notice that Archbishop William of Utrecht, one of those who had excommunicated Gregory, died suddenly and that his cathedral was hit by lightning after Henry celebrated Easter there.

In 1077 a council was called at Augsburg in an attempt to heal the rift between Pope and Emperor. On his way there, Pope Gregory, having taken refuge in a friendly castle at Canossa in the Apennines, was met by a chastened Emperor Henry (who had found that disgruntled princes were refusing to obey him unless he was reconciled to the Pope). In a memorable scene, Henry stood outside the castle barefoot in the snow begging absolution, which eventually Gregory gave him.

But a few years later Henry again declared Gregory deposed, appointed an antipope in his place, and, after a three-year siege, captured Rome. Gregory and the city were saved by the martial figure of Robert Guiscard, the Norman Duke of Apulia (*pictured right*). He forced Henry to return to Germany. But both sides had destroyed large areas of the city. Gregory was exiled, and died.

In 1188 Clement III agreed to recognise the city as a *de facto* republic with the right to declare war and appoint senators; and he devoted some of the papal income to maintain buildings and pay officials. In exchange the senators swore loyalty to the Pope and agreed to recognise his temporal powers.

War for Jerusalem

In 1095 thousands of ordinary people answered the call to recapture Jerusalem; they were massacred by the Turks. An army of European knights fared better, but with strange consequences

It had come as a shock when Jerusalem, the site of the Resurrection of Jesus, was seized by the armies of Islam in AD638. Its new rulers allowed Christian pilgrims to visit the holy city for much of the succeeding centuries. But among Christians the ideas was never entirely given up of recovering the Holy Land. Western Europe was becoming more organised and among the martial Normans many younger sons, driven by land hunger, had begun to conquer territory in southern Italy, and in England. But the trigger for the First Crusade was an appeal to the West in 1095 by the Byzantine Emperor Alexius Comnenus for help in recovering his kingdom, much of which had been captured by Egyptians and fierce Seljuk Turks.

Alexius hoped for a small mercenary force. But the response to Pope Urban II's speech at the Council in Clermont, France, calling for the liberation of Jerusalem, was enormous. Thousands of ordinary people, many moved by genuine piety, set off for a destination a world away. The first contingent to arrive at Constantinople was the so-called People's Crusade, an ill-disciplined force led by Peter the Hermit, a strange figure from Amiens. The Byzantines, embarrassed by the rabble, ferried them across to Asia. They were promptly destroyed by the Turks (though Peter survived another 20 years).

The main Crusader force, about 30,000 men, began to collect soon afterwards. It had four main leaders: Godfrey of Bouillon (in Lorraine), accompanied by his brother Baldwin; the Norman adventurer Bohemond; Raymond, Count of Toulouse; and Robert of Flanders, cousin of the English king, William Rufus. They swore to restore to Byzantium any territory they took, and set out across Anatolia fully armed in summer heat. Having captured Nicaea, in July 1097 the Franks, as Easterners called

them, won a victory at Dorylaeum. Later, Baldwin accepted an offer to rule the Armenian kingdom of Edessa.

After a long siege that divided the leaders, Antioch fell in June 1098 and was given to Bohemond. The rest – perhaps half the original force – marched on Jerusalem, now in the hands of the Egyptian Fatimids, arriving in June 1099. The city seemed impregnable. On July 8 the Franks solemnly processed in penance around its walls before proceeding to the Mount of Olives. Siege towers were then brought up, and on July 13 Godfrey's men gained a foothold on the walls. The gates were soon opened and the population slaughtered. Against enormous odds, the Crusaders had taken Jerusalem.

The Franks quickly set up a feudal state, the Latin Kingdom of Jerusalem. By 1130 it covered much of modern Israel, Jordan, Lebanon, Syria and south-west Turkey. In 1144, the ruler of Mosul, Zengi, captured Edessa, and for 150 years the Franks were on the defensive. The Second Crusade, preached by Bernard of Clairvaux, was raised to retake Edessa, but despite another large response it failed, in part due to the rivalry of its leaders, Louis VII of France and Conrad III of Germany. Its failure heartened the Muslims, soon united by a new ruler of Egypt, Saladin. In 1187 he annihilated the Frankish army, including the quasi-monastic knights, the Templars and the Hospitallers. Jerusalem soon surrendered.

The Third Crusade, begun in 1188, was again marked by the rivalry of its leaders, Philip II of France and Richard the Lion Heart. The latter recaptured the port of Acre and beat Saladin at Arsuf, but problems in England called him home and the Franks had to be content with a peace treaty. Thereafter crusading became ineffectual. The nadir came in 1204 when the Fourth Crusade, diverted by the Venetians, sacked Constantinople.

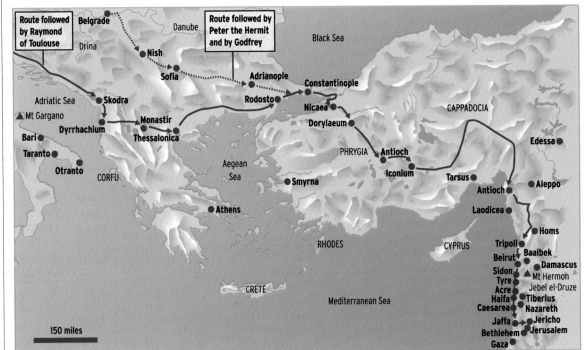

Above: the crusader routes, taken by Peter the Hermit on the disastrous "People's Crusade", and by the subsequent force led by Godfrey of Bouillon and Raymond of Toulouse, which went on to take Jerusalem in 1099. Left: The taking of Jerusalem from a French mid 14th-century edition of the *History of Deeds in Foreign Parts* by William of Tyre, who was born to French parents in Palestine around 1130 and became Archbishop of Tyre in 1175.

Normans, Greeks and Muslims

In the exotic island of 12th-century Sicily a Norman ruler governed in the Pope's name over Greek-speaking and Arabic-speaking people. For two generations architecture and learning flourished

There was another Norman Conquest besides that of England in 1066. At about the same time, this other Norman conquest overran Sicily and the lower part of the Italian peninsula. It produced a short-lived kingdom of amazing splendour that stood at the cross-roads of the three great civilisations of the medieval Mediterranean: the Latin Christendom of Western Europe, the Greek Byzantine Christendom of Eastern Europe, and Islam. It combined elements of each in a luxuriant cultural hybrid.

Normans had not many generations before been pagan Vikings. They had settled in Normandy and first came to the southern Mediterranean as military adventurers. In 1016, it is related, a band of Norman soldiers on their way home from a pilgrimage to thc Holy Land arrived in southern Italy to visit a shrine of the Archangel Michael. These pious mercenaries were immediately enlisted to fight in a local revolt against Byzantine rule. The revolt failed, but the Normans stayed on, offering their military services to whatever local warlord was in need of them. Southern Italy was unstable and fragmented and the Normans were always in demand. In each war they fought they were paid with grants of land and dukedoms until, within a generation, they became a local power themselves.

In 1061, the Norman-Italian count Roger de Hauteville led an expeditionary force into Sicily, the population of which was mostly Arab and Muslim. Capturing this green and fertile volcanic island, which was separated from the toe of Italy by 50 miles at the narrowest point of the Straits of Messina, was a natural next step for the Normans, not least because the Pope, Nicholas II, had exhorted the faithful to rid the island of its infidel inhabitants and reclaim it for Christendom.

In the realpolitik of the time, that pronouncement meant that the island should be taken in the name of the Latin Christendom of Rome, and not fall into the orbit of the rival Byzantine Empire of the East. Despite the political disunity of the island, which, like southern Italy, was held by a patchwork of rival princes, the conquest of the island was slow and arduous and bloody. Sustained by religious zeal (going into battle behind a papal banner), Roger and his small army subdued the island through violence, calculation and the imposition of effective government administration in the areas he captured.

He sent camels, looted from the defeated Arabs, as

Christ himself is shown crowning Roger II (dressed in distinctly Eastern clothing, and with his hands in the conventional attitude of prayer) as King of Sicily in this mosaic of 1148 from the church of Martorana in Palermo. Like many Christian rulers, Roger was anxious to show his authority came from God. By a quirk of history he had the Pope's backing too for his unusual island commonwealth

tribute to the Pope, and these exotic beasts were paraded through the streets of Rome. But it was not until 30 years later that the last Saracen stronghold fell and the conquest was complete. Though Roger de Hauteville acknowledged papal authority, he jealously guarded his own prerogatives over a territory that he had, after all, taken by his own efforts, fair and square.

In 1098, Pope Anacletus II found himself in a weak political position (he was in competition with an antipope) and wanted a strong Christian ally in the southern Mediterranean. This prompted him to grant Roger and his successors the powers of Apostolic Legate to the Holy See, which meant granting them papal powers within their own dominions, without reference to Rome. This curious state of affairs gave a quasi-religious aspect to Norman rule in Sicily. It gave the ruler the power to appoint bishops and establish monasteries, and this the Normans did, in their own distinctive style.

Roger de Hauteville's son, Roger II, was crowned king of Sicily, Calabria and Apulia on Christmas Day 1130 in Palermo Cathedral. This splendid ceremony took place 113 years after the first Norman adventurers landed on Italian soil. Roger II established himself almost as a kind of priest-king, wearing a royal crown and holding a papal crozier. A mosaic portrait of Roger II in the Martorana church in Palermo shows him being crowned at the hands of Jesus Christ. He borrowed the Byzantine idea

Arabic was an official language, and coins were struck pronouncing Mohammed the prophet of God

that the king stood at the boundary of heaven and earth, joining the two spheres together in his awesome authority. The king had an abstract claim to the throne of Jerusalem, which added to the lustre of the monarchy.

Though Roger promoted the Latin church in Sicily, he allowed freedom of worship to his Greek Christian, Muslim and Jewish subjects, and allowed each community to flourish. The kingdom was held together by a feudal system supported by an elaborate code of law; otherwise, as Gibbon wrote, "his administration displays a liberal and enlightened mind above the limits of his age and education". Arabic was an official language, alongside Latin, Greek and French. Even after the conquest and the establishment of the kingdom, coins continued to be struck with inscriptions on one side in Arabic script, pronouncing Mohammed the prophet of God.

Roger's reign was the high noon of the Norman kingdom of Sicily. His intellectual curiosity made his court in Palermo one of the great centres of learning of the medieval world, where Christian and Muslim scholars met and exchanged ideas. With Roger's patronage, the Arab geographer al-Idrisi wrote his description of the known world, which posterity entitled *The Book of Roger*. In the monasteries of his kingdom, monks translated into Latin works of Greek antiquity which had been lost to the Christian West for centuries. Roger commissioned churches and palaces and inscribed his grandeur on their high walls in mosaics which are the masterpieces of the form, and which happily survive.

It lasted, at its high form, for about 60 years, and then, sadly, seemingly inevitably, fizzled out. Roger was succeeded first by William "the Bad", then William "the Good". William II was not good enough to prevent rival barons waging civil war, which destroyed the peace that held the communities within the kingdom together. He died without an heir, and in due course was succeeded by the Emperor Henry VI, a German, who had married into the Norman dynasty and claimed the island as part of a dowry. His only interest in the splendour of Roger's kingdom was in its value as plunder. By 1189, it was all over.

Becket: the man behind the martyr

The unfathomable character of Thomas Becket adds a tantalising mystery to the stirring drama of his martyrdom

Towards the end of the 12th century, the perennial tussle between kings and uncompromising churchmen was played out in a memorable way between Henry II of England and Thomas Becket. It ended in the murder of the Archbishop of Canterbury (as Becket had become) explicitly upholding the cause of the Church. Behind this well known story is a character that is difficult to fathom. Unlike his contemporary St Bernard, Becket never showed his feelings in personal letters, for example.

Becket was born in 1118 in Cheapside, the prosperous heart of London where his father, a Norman, lived as a merchant. The boy was said to have has a stutter. He grew tall and handsome, and was notable for his quickness and tenacious memory. He delighted in hawking. His many enemies never accused him of being unchaste, but then it has been pointed out that the only three people he was known to have loved were his mother (who died when he was 20), and the two men he served: Archbishop Theobald of Canterbury and King Henry.

Thomas Becket was appointed Archdeacon of Canterbury in 1154. A year later he was made Chancellor of England. He shone as an administrator, fought as a soldier, and was a magnificent figure as he rode with his hounds and his falcons. Then in 1162, aged 44, he was given a position he had not sought, as Archbishop of Canterbury. He suddenly changed.

Though Becket had long been a cleric, he now, for the first time, took the Christian life absolutely seriously. He was, he said, "no longer a follower of hounds, but a shepherd of souls". He still lived in splendour, but he wore a hairshirt and gave great sums to the poor. But a deeper conversion came apparently only after he had been wrangling for some time with the king over the rights of the Church.

The feudal duties of an archbishop towards king and pope were no simple matter. Becket wanted an English Church free to remain in untramelled communion with the Pope. He edged back and forth until one day he withstood the king at Northampton, and fled for his life into exile, not to return for six years, and then to his death. What he had been told the day before that crucial day at Northampton, by the priest who heard his confession, was, according to a biographer: "If you wished, you could easily escape from all danger and not only mitigate the king's anger, but make him your friend. You refuse to do so because you choose rather to seek the will of God. The affair is no longer in your hands, but in God's."

During his six-year exile Becket did two things. He hardened in his intransigence over the principle of denying the king control of the Church; in pursuit of this he

This is the earliest representation of the murder of Thomas Becket. It comes from a volume of his collected letters made in Canterbury around 1171, the year after his death.
Top: the knights interrupt the archbishop at dinner and, below, with Grim holding his cross, Becket receives the fatal blow

fired off excommunications that sometimes lacked prudence, let alone charity, against clergy who showed any signs of compromising. He also followed a regime of monastic rigour, fasting, rising early, praying.

His death (*described right*) at the hands of four knights prompted by Henry's impatient words against him made him a martyr instantly. The Pope formally canonised him after only three years. A saga was composed about him in Iceland; churches were dedicated to him from Castile to Armenia. And Canterbury became one of the foremost places of pilgrimage in the world.

EYEWITNESS

The murder of Thomas Becket

Between 2.30 and 3.30pm on December 29 1170, four eyewitnesses saw the murder of Becket and later wrote accounts in Latin. They were William FitzStephen, Edward Grim (who carried the archbishop's processional cross that day, and received a sword cut in one arm), John of Salisbury and William of Canterbury. This compilation of their accounts is based on that made by the historian David Knowles.

The four knights arrived when the archbishop was at dinner. As the knights began to shout, Becket said: "It is useless to threaten me. If all the swords of England were over my head, your threats would not shift me from God's justice and obedience to the pope."

An uproar followed, and the knights left the room calling on those present to defy the traitor and prevent his escape. The archbishop started up and followed them to the door, where he heard them telling his servants that the king released them from fealty to the archbishop. "What do you say?" he exclaimed. "Speak! speak! I shall not run away." He then turned calmly back and sat down.

John of Salisbury, as always the candid friend, complained: "You have always been like that. You always act and speak entirely on your own, without taking advice."

The archbishop took him up good-humouredly. "What would you then, master John?"

"You should have summoned your council. You must realise those knights simply want an excuse for killing you."

"We must all die, master John," replied Thomas, "and we must not let the fear of death make us swerve from justice. I am ready to accept death for the sake of God and of justice and the Church's freedom – far more ready to accept death than they are to kill me."

"It is all very well for you to say that," was John's reply, "but the rest of us are sinners and not so ready for death."

"God's will he done," said the archbishop quietly.

As they were speaking, the knights, now fully armed, began to batter their way into the archbishop's lodging, and the monks implored him to take refuge in the church. He refused: "What are you afraid of, my fathers?" When they insisted he still sat on: "You monks never have any spirit in you." Then as the din increased they began to drag him resisting towards the church.

He refused to move till his cross-bearer was found. Then, driving the others before him, and walking slowly behind his cross he entered the cathedral. The monks began to bar the door, but Thomas forbade them: "Christ Church is not a fortress. Let anyone who wishes enter."

Then, as a cry was raised that armed men were in the cloister, "I will go to meet them," he said. But the monks carried him towards the high altar. The aisle was full of monks and townspeople, and as the knights strode in they collided in the dusk with those rushing hither and thither.

"Where is the traitor Thomas Beketh [*sic*]?" they shouted.

Then, when no reply came, "Where is the archbishop?"

Thomas came forward. "Here am I, no traitor, but a priest ready to suffer in my Redeemer's cause. God forbid that I should flee from your swords or depart from what is just. But do not dare to touch any of my people."

He then retired a few steps and stood by a pillar, with a few monks by him. "Reginald, Reginald," he said to FitzUrse, "is this your return for all that I have done for you?"

The knights rushed at him and tried to hoist him on the shoulders of William Tracy to carry him outside. The first to touch him was FitzUrse. "Unhand me, Reginald," exclaimed the archbishop, "you are my sworn vassal." Then, struggling with him: "Unhand me, pander!" He shook himself loose, seized FitzUrse by the mail coat and sent him reeling back. "I will not leave the church. If you wish to kill me, kill me here."

Then, as they delayed to strike, he covered his eyes and bowed his head. "To God and blessed Mary, St Denis, and St Alphege I commend myself and my Church." At the fourth stroke he fell full length, his hands outstretched as if in prayer.

An enamelled reliquary chasse from Limoges, from around 1195, said to contain a relic of Becket

Eve carved in stone

Church carvings reached an apogee in the 12th century. Among the finest sculptors was Gislebertus who worked on a cathedral in Burgundy

This extraordinary deep-relief of Eve was carved by one Gislebertus for the cathedral at Autun between about AD1125 and 1135. There she lies, intelligent and voluptuous, one hand to her cheek, the other grasping the forbidden fruit. The cathedral church is dedicated to St Lazarus, a relic of whom it boasted. It was a place of pilgrimage. The reconstructed cathedral, one of many being built all over Europe, was consecrated by Pope Innocent II on December 28 1130. The sculptor, whose name we know from his chiselled signature, "*Gislebertus hoc fecit*", carved other subjects for this Burgundian church of a style transitional between Romanesque and Gothic. Christ sits enthroned in glory over the doorway. On the capital of a pillar the Holy Family are seen

fleeing to Egypt, the donkey's mane, the leading rope, the cloth of the Virgin's dress all combed into shape by the chisel.

On another capital the Three Wise Men lie tucked up under a neatly draped coverlet in one bed, their crowns on their heads, the star above them. The perspective is twisted through 90 degrees between one end of the bed and the other, so that one looks down on their pillow at the bed head, but at the side of its foot.

This is carving that is thoroughly designed, convincingly naturalistic but retaining the stoniness of its medium.

Autun stood at the centre of Burgundy in the 12th century. Elsewhere in the dukedom similar carvings can be found – at Vézelay, for example, or Cluny. In the carvings of Gislebertus we find a craftsman of outstanding ability working within a cultural convention. The sculptures decorate the church and remind pilgrim worshippers of the Bible stories about which they heard from their parish priests.

Eve, from a lintel over the North Door of the cathedral of St Lazarus in Autun, France. It measures 52 inches by 28 inches

93

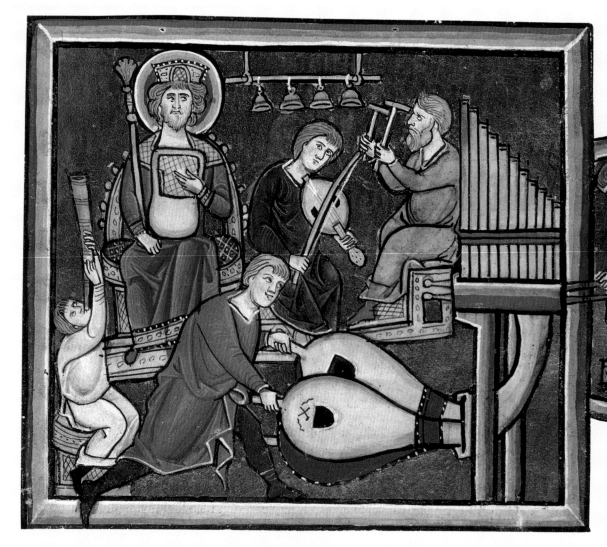

King David and his musicians are shown (*left*) gathered around an organ, with a bellows-pumper, in this 13th-century illumination from the Beatae Elisabeth Psalter. Although the organ was known to the ancient world, and treasured in the early Middle Ages (Pepin III, King of the Franks, was given one as a gift in 757), its use was largely secular until at least the 10th century. The organ shown in the 9th-century Utrecht Psalter (*below*) seems to be a scribe's misunderstanding of a Mediterranean hydraulic organ. By the 12th century the ascetic Cistercian abbot, Aelred of Rievaulx was complaining of organs being objects of curiosity, but a century later it was generally agreed that organs were the only instrument that should be allowed in church

The seduction of music

Churchmen did not want music to distract from prayerful worship. Unaccompanied chant was for centuries the only music-making allowed. But by 1200 harmony and organ music were established.

St Augustine of Hippo (354-430) expressed an ambivalence about music shared by many churchmen: "When I happen to be moved more by the singing than what is sung, I confess to have sinned grievously, and then I wish I had not heard the singing." He did concede, though, that "by means of the delight in hearing, weaker minds may be aroused to a feeling of devotion."

So, while the Church in the early Middle Ages was the principal forum for the development of music, there were restrictions to ensure that the art remained the servant of religion. Liturgical music was confined to chants and hymn singing, and instruments excluded from services. The various forms of

chant had been standardised by Pope Gregory the Great (590-604).

Gradually the custom of drawing out the melody in the Alleluias was developed until the extension (the "sequence") became a separate piece of music, with its own words. The earliest known composer of sequences was Notker Balbulus ("The Stammerer", c840-912); the form would later stretch to the *Dies Irae*, which is attributed to Thomas of Celano who died in 1255.

Especially original were the sequences of Hildegard of Bingen (1098-1179), the abbess of Rupertsberg in Germany, who was also known for her visions. She composed both verses and music. Her *Ordo Virtutum* was really a sacred music drama in plainsong.

Strict Gregorian plainsong was unharmonised. Part-singing dates from the 9th century; its principles were further elucidated by Guido d'Arezzo (c997-1050). In the 11th century the harmonising voice began to move independently of the main tune, at first in pitch and eventually in rhythm also. Part-singing flourished in the 12th

and 13th centuries at Notre Dame in Paris, and in England at Worcester Cathedral. A manuscript at Winchester from about AD1000 contains some of the earliest extant examples of two-part composition.

A system of writing down music had evolved from the 9th century. At first scribes simply placed acutes and graves above the text to show rises and falls in pitch. These accents developed into neumes, signs indicating relative pitch by their high or low position. Around 1000, a line was introduced to indicate the tone "f". From there it was a short step to the musical staff. With the development of rhythmical notation, composing and performing became separate arts, and musicians could build their own traditions, independently of the demands of the Church.

Monasteries transformed

Bernard of Clairvaux counselled popes and called a Crusade that was destined to fail. But he gave impetus to a monastic movement that transformed medieval life and its very landscape

The beautiful ruins of monasteries in rural English settings – Fountains or Rievaulx – were foundations of the Cistercian Order. The monks of this movement observed the Rule of St Benedict. They said their prayers, sang in the choir, performed manual labour; as the foundations developed, their farm hands tended thousands of sheep. The Cistercian family of abbeys derived from the mother house at Cîteaux (two hours' walk from Nuits-St-Georges in Burgundy), and Cîteaux owed its very nature to Bernard.

Bernard of Clairvaux (as he became known) was at the heart of the greatest monastic revival the West has seen. He was born at Fontaines near Dijon, in Burgundy, in 1090, one of six sons of a nobleman. His mother died when he was 17, and he was moved to begin the "long path to complete conversion".

At 22 he joined the monastery of Cîteaux. This reformist abbey, founded in 1098, had almost failed through poverty, austerity and disease. Bernard brought with him 27 relations, including four of his brothers. After two years, the abbot of Cîteaux, Stephen Harding, sent Bernard to found another monastery at Clairvaux, in Champagne. By the time of Bernard's death, aged 63, Cîteaux had 339 houses and Bernard's own monastery of Clairvaux had 68 daughter houses. One of Bernard's monks became pope; others sat in bishops' thrones from York to the Mediterranean.

For a year in his early monastic career illness made Bernard so repulsive to his fellow monks at table or in choir that he had to live in a hut. He was plagued by blinding headaches. His stomach, perhaps damaged by fasting, rejected solid food for most of his life and in later years he would vomit without respite. But his character was a forceful one.

When he thought that Henry of Blois, Bishop of Winchester and brother of King Stephen, had displayed a

A new simplicity

Bernard stood for the reformed but humane rule of the Cistercians, whose mother house was at Cîteaux.
This vied with the older rule of the monastery of Cluny.
Both traditions were based on the Rule of St Benedict.

Cluniacs
Beginnings: Cluny founded 910
Liturgy: Lengthy sung monastic office, occupying most of the day
Architecture: Large ornate churches
Situation: Often in a town
Work: Any honourable occupation that could fit in monastic timetable
Study: No time available for scholarship
Food and clothing: More choice than Benedict recommended
Possessions: Owned estates
Novices: Professed as monks within weeks

Cistercians
Beginnings: Cîteaux founded 1098
Liturgy: Psalms said slowly; long prayers trimmed
Architecture: Plain, unadorned churches
Situation: In uninhabited countryside
Work: Physical labour; no talking in the cloister
Study: Spiritual reading and private study
Food and clothing: No flesh-meat; less choice
Possessions: No monastic estates allowed at first

love of riches, he denounced him in well-chosen scriptural phrases as a "whore" and a "wizard". He combated from the pulpit what he perceived to be the dangerous theology of his contemporary Peter Abelard and he called for the condemnation of another theologian, Gilbert de la Porrée, for undermining the understanding of the nature of Christ.

Bernard was drawn into world affairs, though he wanted to stay in his monastery. In 1130 he had supported Innocent II against the antipope Anacletus. When a monk of Clairvaux was elected Pope in 1145 as Eugenius III, Bernard wrote a book on his duties, warning against corruption in the Vatican. Eugenius in return recruited Bernard to preach in southern France against the persistent heresy of Albigensianism, a variant of the old dualistic Manichaeism which had beguiled Augustine of Hippo more than 700 years before. Bernard died in 1153 only days after Eugenius.

It comes as some surprise to find in Bernard's writing a genuine appeal to the heart. He wrote in an admirable style and he clearly wanted devotion to God to include the emotions as well as steely will. His book on Christmas approaches the baby Jesus with tenderness; he was devoted to the Virgin Mary. He compiled a commentary on the sexually poetic Song of Solomon from the Old Testament.

For all his self-denial – sitting weak and emaciated writing in his cell beneath the noisy day-stairs of his monastery – Bernard was a vital part of the humanist renaissance that characterised the 12th century. It is another side of the spirit that produced the carvings at Autun (*see page 92*).

St Bernard, Abbot of Clairvaux, from the *Heures d'Etienne Chevalier* by Jean Fouquet (*c*1425-80). Bernard founded this monastery in Champagne and some 40 years later, at the end of his life, it had 68 daughter houses. His followers are sometimes called Berdardines. Bernard was given the title *Doctor mellifluus*, "the honey-sweet teacher", and his emblem is a beehive

CHAPTER FOUR

AD
1200-1500

Francis sets off

A spiritual explosion

The High Middle Ages left some of the finest artistic works mankind has known. Dante's *Divine Comedy* put vernacular poetry at the highest level. His orderly vision was echoed by the cathedral-builders in stone (with outstanding examples still standing in England). In painting the Renaissance developed the sublimity of Cimabue into the humaneness of Mantegna.

Similarly elevated ideas in theology were seen in the syncretic genius of Thomas Aquinas, who produced a harmony between the philosophies of Plato and Aristotle with the help of non-Christian thinkers such as Avicenna and Maimonides. Aquinas, holy in his own life, exemplified medieval man at his best.

Aquinas belonged to a religious order recently founded by Dominic, and a parallel foundation by Francis of Assisi put an emphasis not on theology but poverty. Sympathy with the poor also informed new organisations devoted to charity in the 15th century.

The pestilence that swept Europe in the 1340s and the schisms and heresies that appeared a little later did not destroy the integrated pattern of medieval religious devotion.

But intolerance in Spain and Florence were early signs of a coming crash.

Right: *Dream of St Gregory*, the 25th of 28 scenes of the Legend of St Francis in the church of San Francesco, Assisi. In the dream Francis appears to Pope Gregory IX and convinces him that his stigmata are real

a spiritual explosion

At the beginning of the 13th century the life of Christian Europe was transformed by the invention of a new kind of dedicated preacher – the friar. Francis of Assisi attracted vast numbers simply by taking the Gospel literally. In parallel, Dominic founded an order of friars that would make use of new insights of theology gained by Thomas Aquinas. It was the simplicity of Francis that made the first impact

Francis of Assisi, the most obviously Christ-like and popular of all the saints, transformed the Church's mission in the towns of 13th-century Europe, and thereafter provided a model of Christian discipleship in its purest form. The secret of his influence was simple: he was obedient to the commands of Christ, taking the Gospels at their face value. This led him to embrace total poverty and to concentrate his preaching on the poorest of the poor. His devotion to the crucified Christ led to his receiving the marks (known as stigmata) of crucifixion in his own body. In the picture here he is depicted showing the wound in his side to Pope Gregory IX in a dream.

Francis, the son of a wealthy cloth merchant, was born in the Italian town of Assisi in 1181. As a young man he helped in his father's business and enjoyed a riotous personal life, but both came to an end when he was caught up in a local war and held prisoner for 12 months.

When peace came he went on pilgrimage to Rome, where he was deeply affected by the sight of the beggars outside St Peter's. He exchanged his fine clothes with one of them and spent the rest of the day begging. Returning to Assisi, he lived as a hermit in caves and ruined churches, some of which he restored, and one day while attending Mass he heard in the Gospel reading: "Preach as you go, saying, The kingdom of heaven is at hand. . . Take no gold, nor silver, nor copper in your belts, no bag for your journey, nor two tunics, nor sandals, nor staff; for the labourer deserves his food." He took this as a personal call and embarked on a mission to save the souls of the poor.

A century later there were upwards of 25,000 Franciscan friars (brothers) preaching from 1,400 friaries in most of the burgeoning towns of Western Europe. They offered what amounted to a new expression of the Christian religion. Never before had a mission entered so fully into the lives of the urban poor in order to demonstrate the love of Christ by means of lives as well as by sermons. They were to encounter some problems.

In 1209 when Francis had 12 followers he asked Pope Innocent III to approve a simple Rule governing their community life. It consisted of no more than a few Gospel texts, and the Pope was dubious, but he ▶

decided to take a chance on it and gave his verbal consent. Thus encouraged, Francis sent his friars out two by two to Italian towns, and later further afield. By 1217 it was necessary to divide the movement into provinces, each with a supervising minister.

Francis himself went to Egypt in 1219 in a vain attempt to convert the Muslim leader, the Sultan, and he arrived back in Italy to find the friars sharply divided. Some wished to keep to the letter of Christ's commands, while others – the majority – believed that the developing mission needed Bibles, service books and, in some circumstances, church buildings. Francis was in no doubt as to which choice to make, and a formal rule approved by Pope Honorius in 1223 prescribed poverty both for individual friars and for the entire Order – no money, no property.

In 1230, however, the provincial ministers asked the Pope for an interpretation of the rule that would allow a "spiritual friend" of a friary to hold property in trust and administer money on its behalf. This was granted and marked the beginning of what was to become a formal division in the Order.

Shortly before his death in 1226 Francis had compiled a Testament in which he reiterated the need for poverty

A formal rule prescribed poverty for the entire order – no money, no property

and simplicity of life, but this was later declared null and void by the Pope. Following the canonisation of Francis as a saint in 1228, his body was transferred to a large new church built in his honour in Assisi.

In spite of the problems and divisions, the movement continued to grow throughout the 13th century. A women's branch was formed and a Third Order enabled lay people to embrace Franciscan ideals in their ordinary lives. Some of the greatest medieval theologians were Franciscans.

It was a movement that, in spite of its austerity, expressed Christian joy. Francis designed the first Christmas crib, and his hymn *Canticle of the Sun* expresses his affinity with nature. He loved animals and birds, and he is thought to have been an influence on artists of the period, bringing a whole new naturalism to Western art, starting with Giotto, who was born 20 years after his death. Francis himself was the first major poet to write in Italian.

Decline set in during the 14th century due partly to the disputes, partly to growth in material prosperity, partly to the Black Death (*see page 110*). But the Order has at times experienced revival, not least in the 20th century.

In the meantime a more intellectual movement began – the Dominicans.

Dominicans: the dogs of the Lord

In the years when the poor Franciscans were spreading throughout Europe, a parallel movement began. The Dominican friars combined with their poverty a devotion to intellectual study that made them a powerhouse of orthodox theology. Their guardianship of Church teaching gave rise to a play on words – they were the *'Domini canes'*, the dogs of the Lord

A kind of preaching friar dedicated to learning as well as to poverty was founded by Dominic. His Order of Preachers, known as Dominicans, undertook the combating of heresy and became the intellectual powerhouse of the medieval Church. It was a different emphasis from that of the contemporary Franciscans.

Born in 1170 into a pious family at Caleruega, in Castile, Dominic was educated first by an uncle who was a priest and then at Palencia University, where he proved an unflinchingly dedicated yet cheerful student. He once sold his books to provide food for the poor during a famine; but unlike St Francis, whom he probably never met, Dominic went through no stage of rebellious youth and his commitment to a life of poverty began less as a personal statement than as a matter of policy.

He became a canon of Osma Cathedral, near his home town before being asked to accompany his bishop on a diplomatic mission to Denmark for King Alphonso VIII. It was while talking all night to an innkeeper at Toulouse that Dominic encountered Albigensianism, a collection of heresies rooted in the perception of the flesh as evil. The heretics, who had been well established in the region for several generations and enjoyed strong political support, lived by a strict code of conduct which made a sharp contrast to the style of the monastic abbots who periodically arrived to convert them.

The only way to succeed, concluded Bishop Diego and Dominic, was to mount a continuous mission by preachers who, in the tradition of the apostles, travelled everywhere on foot and begged for food from door to door. Dismissing their retinue, they set about the task with a relish in which Dominic displayed a notable talent for eliciting tears of repentance.

The preachers' efforts were eventually rewarded by a fortnight-long debate with the heretics. This involved written submissions, one of which, written by Dominic, was thrown into a fire three times without burning. The heretics refused to be convinced that this was a miracle; and the lay adjudicators (sympathetic to the Albigensians) refused to reach a judgment. But as a result of their gradual success, Diego and Dominic found themselves supervising a group of female converts in what became

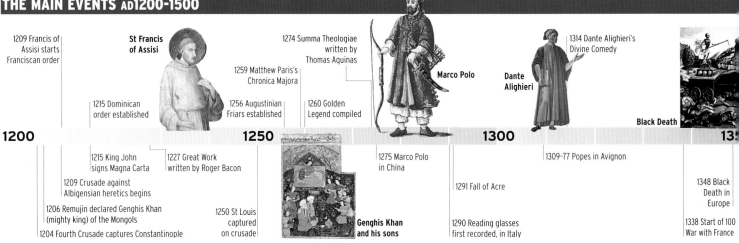

THE MAIN EVENTS AD1200-1500

1209 Francis of Assisi starts Franciscan order

St Francis of Assisi

1274 Summa Theologiae written by Thomas Aquinas

1314 Dante Alighieri's Divine Comedy

1259 Matthew Paris's Chronica Majora

Marco Polo

Dante Alighieri

1215 Dominican order established

1256 Augustinian Friars established

1260 Golden Legend compiled

Black Death

1200 **1250** **1300** **13**

1215 King John signs Magna Carta

1227 Great Work written by Roger Bacon

1275 Marco Polo in China

1309-77 Popes in Avignon

1209 Crusade against Albigensian heretics begins

1291 Fall of Acre

1348 Black Death in Europe

1206 Remujin declared Genghis Khan (mighty king) of the Mongols

1250 St Louis captured on crusade

1290 Reading glasses first recorded, in Italy

1338 Start of 100 War with France

1204 Fourth Crusade captures Constantinople

Genghis Khan and his sons

The Dominicans proved an alternative to the churchmen who were dumb dogs that would not bark

the first Dominican convent at Prouille. A more dramatic development was the murder of a papal legate in the region, which resulted in a crusade against the Albigensians led by Simon de Montfort. Dominic befriended de Montfort, but restricted himself to spiritual duties during the fighting. At the siege of Toulouse he was credited with saving some 40 English pilgrims whose boat had capsized on a river by the fervour of his prayers when he was called to the shore.

After Diego's death and Dominic's assumption of the leadership, the preaching institute was sufficiently firmly established by 1215 for him to set off with high hopes to the fourth Lateran Council. This was a universal gathering of bishops called by Pope Innocent III partly to find an answer to the state of the Church's pastors, who, he found, were "dumb dogs that cannot bark". The answer surely seemed to be the followers of Dominic, the *Domini canes* ("dogs of the Lord"). Yet although Innocent was sympathetic, preaching was regarded as properly the task of the hierarchy, not a new body of poor friars. The council declared that any new religious order must live by an existing rule of life.

Dominic returned to his band, now consisting of some 16 members, which decided to adopt the flexible Augustinian Rule. They introduced a system of dispensations to ensure that preaching and study were given priority over the recitation of the office (the psalms sung at intervals throughout the day). Back in Rome the following year, Dominic made a strong impression with his austere sanctity and Lenten sermons and obtained the first of a series of bulls confirming the order and its goals of checking heresy and carrying the Gospel to the ends of the earth.

The Black Friars, as the Dominicans were also called, on account of the black mantle worn over their white habit, were strategically placed both to open schools and to lecture on scripture and theology in the new universities which were springing up across Europe.

In the next five years, Dominic's inspiring administration sent members of the order to a number of countries. He was about to set off on a mission to Hungary in 1221 when he fell fatally ill, worn out by continuous travels on foot as well as by his habit of praying all night in church. His diet often consisted of only a small piece of fish or a couple of egg yolks. Although little given to confidences, he admitted on his deathbed that he was a virgin, yet had preferred talking to girls rather than old ladies.

St Dominic, a detail of a fresco, *The Mocking of Christ* (1442), by Fra Angelico in San Marco, Florence

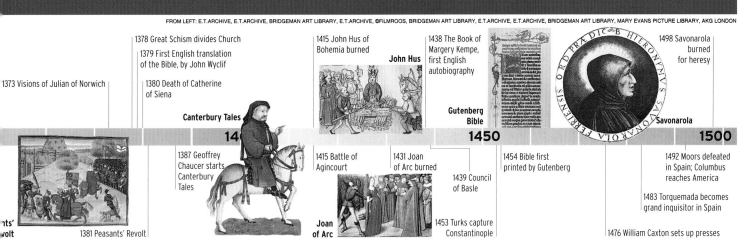

FROM LEFT: E.T.ARCHIVE, E.T.ARCHIVE, BRIDGEMAN ART LIBRARY, E.T.ARCHIVE, ©FILMROOS, BRIDGEMAN ART LIBRARY, E.T.ARCHIVE, E.T.ARCHIVE, BRIDGEMAN ART LIBRARY, MARY EVANS PICTURE LIBRARY, AKG LONDON

1373 Visions of Julian of Norwich

1378 Great Schism divides Church

1379 First English translation of the Bible, by John Wyclif

1380 Death of Catherine of Siena

Canterbury Tales

1387 Geoffrey Chaucer starts Canterbury Tales

1381 Peasants' Revolt

1415 John Hus of Bohemia burned

John Hus

1415 Battle of Agincourt

1431 Joan of Arc burned

Joan of Arc

1453 Turks capture Constantinople

1438 The Book of Margery Kempe, first English autobiography

Gutenberg Bible

1439 Council of Basle

1454 Bible first printed by Gutenberg

1498 Savonarola burned for heresy

Savonarola

1492 Moors defeated in Spain; Columbus reaches America

1483 Torquemada becomes grand inquisitor in Spain

1476 William Caxton sets up presses

1450

1500

Beliefs under strict scrutiny

The second generation of the order of friars founded by St Dominic produced one of its greatest figures, Thomas Aquinas. He was one of the most penetrating thinkers of all time.
He also had a devout faith. He integrated the two in an unprecedented way, with the aid of the pagan Aristotle, two Muslim commentators and a Jewish philosopher

It is fortunate for us that in 1265 at the age of 40 Thomas Aquinas turned down the offer of the Archbishopric of Naples, and decided instead to compile what was to become his masterpiece. The *Summa Theologiae* is not quite as long a work as might be suggested by the 60 volumes of the current edition published by the English Dominicans. But it does present all sides of theology, from the existence of God to the psychology of men, in a marvellously rounded and connected way.

The idea of such a *Summa* (summing up) was not new. University students found a compilation covering their whole course valuable. But only Thomas could have made it what it is: theology finely adjusted between the rather poetic Platonic approach of St Augustine and the newly recovered, more realistic metaphysics of Aristotle. It might seem a small claim to say that Thomas demonstrated that faith and reason were not mutual enemies. But in his day there was a popular theory that it was possible to think that one proposition was true in secular philosophy and simultaneously to believe by the light of faith another proposition that contradicted it.

More subtly there was a school of philosophy, encouraged by the clever logician Peter Abelard (1079-1142) and later to be disastrously developed by William of

Thomas got into trouble for reconciling Aristotelian philosophy with Christian thought

Ockham (1285-1349), that asserted that no true metaphysical thought could even be attempted. For these philosophers, words were empty of content, and ideas had no universal application. This approach has an echo in the sterility of modern-day logical positivism, popularised by A. J. Ayer. Thomas's approach fruitfully outflanks such a dead end.

Thomas had only nine years before his death to complete his *Summa*. He just about made it; the last books, which are now known as "The Supplement", were posthumously compiled from his earlier theological work, a commentary on the book by Peter Lombard called *Sentences*. But before he died Thomas had covered the great themes in a new way. His first consideration is: "Does God exist? It would seem not..." He then analyses the implications of creation, and traces man's return journey to God, the dispenser of goodness, through the only possible route, Jesus Christ, the incarnate God.

Aquinas had a deep appreciation of Holy Scripture and an encyclopaedic knowledge of the writings of the early writers of the Church. (One of his earlier works was the

Catena Aurea, "Golden Chain", a compilation of commentaries on each chapter of the Gospels by the Church Fathers.) But essential to his system of thought is his understanding of being – of existence as we tend to call it. He outlined this fundamental concept in a separate work called *De Ente et Essentia*. This idea made possible his application of the principle of analogy: similarities between created beings up the scale between the simplest forms and God who created them.

Aquinas was also lucky to be living at a time when much of Aristotle had once more been discovered. Nor did he spurn the interpretations of non-Christian commentators on Aristotle. These were principally two Muslims, Avicenna (Ibn Sina, 980-1037) from Kazakhstan and Averroes (Ibn Rushd, 1126-98) from Spain, and a Jew, Moses Maimonides (ben Maimon, 1138-1204), also from Spain.

Thomas got into trouble with some Church authorities for reconciling Aristotelian philosophy with Christian thought. At one point Aristotle was forbidden as a text for lecturers to use as a set book in the University of Paris, for the instruction of arts students (though not for theology students). Posthumously, Thomas was briefly condemned for his philosophical adoption of Aristotle. But his success was in integrating faith and reason, grace and nature, charity and friendship.

The *Summa* is intended as a beginner's book, a series of lecture notes for theological students. Following the disputatious convention of the day it sets out a wide selection of arguments against orthodox Christian teachings and brings to bear the best responses to them. All the time that Thomas was writing the *Summa* he had to travel about, following the papal court from Anagni to Orvieto, from Orvieto to Viterbo, moving from Paris to Naples, away from books, dictating when time permitted to companions from his Dominican brotherhood. Other distractions included his family's tragic political struggles, and urgent requests for advice from popes, the King of France and the Master General of his religious order.

Thomas was declared a saint in 1323, and a doctor of the Church in 1567. His theology was adopted by Church authorities as perennially applicable. If this at times led to a plodding textbook attitude to his thought, in the 20th century logicians, metaphysicians and theologians of various schools, not all traditionally Catholic, have drawn new developments from him.

Thomas Aquinas sits enthroned in this 14th-century fresco from Santa Maria Novella, Florence. On his right is St John the Evangelist and on his left another Gospel-writer, St Matthew. At his feet are pagan philosophers, with the Arabic writer from Spain, Averroes, in the middle

Thomas Aquinas: a fat man with big ideas

Thomas Aquinas was only 49 when he died in 1274, leaving his masterpiece, the *Summa*, almost complete. It is not a work full of jokes, but from other evidence Thomas sounds a very likeable man.

He was fat, but had a lightness of touch. He recommended to his fellow Dominican friars that they should be pleasant in their community life. His poetry is not sentimental but full of powerful considerations (such as the forgiveness of the Good Thief by Jesus, crucified next to him, which is used as an image in one telling line of his Latin hymn *Adoro Te Devote*, "Devoutly I adore you", still sung today).

He was born in 1225 at Roccasecca near Pontecorvo in central Italy. His was an aristocratic family, but he wanted none of that, deciding firmly, after finishing his schooling at the great Benedictine abbey of Monte Cassino, that he would be a Dominican friar. (*See page 98 for the founder, Dominic, who had died when Thomas was nine*.) His noble family was shocked by his decision and he was kidnapped by his brothers and locked up for a year, but he persisted.

His life with the Dominicans was given to a routine of prayer and study. He was also gifted at preaching in the Neapolitan dialect. But it was his intellect that was astounding. The early Dominicans were renowned for their learning and Thomas throve as he studied under Albert the Great (who outlived him) at Cologne. He then went to Paris, the foremost European university of the day, and spent years teaching at Dominican houses of studies at Rome, Orvieto, Viterbo and Perugia.

He wrote a great deal that was not only of point in its day but proved to be of lasting value. After experiencing an unexpected trance on December 6 1273 he said that all of his his writings seemed like chaff. He wrote little more and on March 7 1274 on his way to the Universal Council of Lyons, he died in the Cistercian Abbey of Fossanuova not far from his birthplace. On his deathbed he had been commenting for his companions on the biblical Song of Songs.

To the Seventh Heaven

With the Italian Renaissance came one of the great poems of Western culture, Dante's *Divine Comedy*. It embodies the ordered medieval view of the cosmos and the highest theological insights of the time

Dante's masterpiece, *The Divine Comedy*, is not just about dead people being tortured in Hell. The visionary journey through Hell and via the Mountain of Purgatory to the circles of Heaven takes a week: from the Thursday before Easter, AD1300, to the following Thursday.

Dante explained the meaning himself in a letter to his patron Can Grande della Scala: "The subject of the whole work, taken merely in the *literal* sense is 'the state of the soul after death straightforwardly affirmed', for the development of the whole work hinges on that. But if, though, the work is taken *allegorically*, its subject is: 'Man, by the exercise of his free will

deserving good or ill, becoming liable to the rewards or punishments of Justice.'"

Dante was talking about a way of reading a book that was familiar to his contemporaries from their reading of the Bible. In the Bible or in *The Divine Comedy*, all interpretation begins with the literal reading. In Dante's case, the additional allegorical reading does not become clear simply by saying "Virgil stands for Human Wisdom", as Bunyan's Slough of Despond stands for what its name suggests. Dante's figures are more like natural symbols, or mythical figures in a symbolic drama.

In the poem the narrator, Dante (allegorically the Christian Sinner), finds himself, in the middle of the biblical span of three-score years

and ten, aged 35, in AD1300, in a dark wood, on the edge of the pit of Hell. In his journey through Hell he is led by Virgil (Human Wisdom, incapable by itself of reaching heaven), who then takes him almost to the summit of the mountain of Purgatory. From there his guide is Beatrice, his unattained love (she is a Bearer of God, like Divine Grace or the Church). She takes him through Heaven, ever nearer God, until her role is subsumed by Mary the Mother of Jesus, the original God-Bearer. At the centre of Heaven God himself combines image and reality.

On the way, no doubt, Dante has much to say of the diseased body politic of his own city-state, Florence, which readers today often find uninteresting, because they cannot know the

characters to whom the poet refers. Dante, who lived from 1265 to about 1321, was in his latter years a political exile. We may decide that he was a good man; there is evidence that he was capable of intense feeling. But it is unnecessary to know much about his life to appreciate his poem.

In Dante's hands, powerful images are knitted into a poem widely acknowledged as a summit of Christian art. What other is greater? *The Divine Comedy* exemplifies high medieval thought of two kinds: one, the cosmology accepted by contemporary Christian civilisation; the other, a poetic understanding through the theology of the time, notably that of Thomas Aquinas, who explained why the free will of men and women moves them nearer to God or ▶

'One point I saw, so radiantly
  bright,
So searing to the eyes it
  strikes upon,
They needs must close before
  such piercing light'

Beatrice shows Dante the light of heaven,
one of Giovanni di Paolo's
15th-century illustrations for *Paradiso*

isolates them from him. Aquinas had a concept of created things existing through participation in the very being of God; Dante took this and built a poem round it.

In the third part of *The Divine Comedy*, "Heaven", Dante meets Aquinas. He is in the company of Albert the Great, Dionysius the Areopagite, Orosius, Boethius, Isidore of Seville and Bede – names that crop up in earlier chapters of *AD*. Aquinas takes Dante further, closer to God, with Francis of Assisi and Dominic.

None of the mechanism of the poem means that Dante really thought that he could find a cavern leading down to Hell in the middle of the Earth. He did, though, accept the Ptolemaic astronomical system, with the planets circling the Earth (just as 700 years later we take for granted the post-Copernican model, with the Earth orbiting the Sun). He was aware of the vast distances to the stars; he knew more of the apparent movement of the heavenly bodies than most people do today. He knew about the effects of gravity; when in his fiction he reaches the centre of the Earth, he begins to climb *up* towards the Antipodes.

In the cosmology of the time, Hell was thought of as at the centre of the Earth, for that was the farthest point physically from the influence of God. There was a deliberate play, in the thought of the day, on the idea of love being the same as appetite, which is the same as a power of attraction: fire leaps upwards towards the Sun; earth drops downwards towards the Earth. The planets circled the Earth, moved by the power of the heavenly spheres above them. Beyond the outer sphere of the fixed stars was the empyrean which, like some invisible shell, moved everything below it. And God encompassed all. It was love that made the world go round; it was by their appetite towards beings higher than themselves that the planets moved.

It was a cosmology familiar to Augustine in the 4th century, to King Alfred in the 9th, to Milton in the 17th. Only after the decay of the medieval world-vision was space to take on in imagination an empty god-forsaken formlessness.

Who's who in Dante's Hell

Brunetto Latini (1220-94). Florentine statesman, friend and instructor of Dante. Sodomite; in the 7th Circle with the Violent against Nature.
Pope Celestine V (1214-96). Abdicated in 1294. Dante puts him in the vestibule of Hell with the Futile. He was declared a saint in 1313.
Ganelon. Betrayed Roland and the rearguard of Charlemagne's army in Spain (AD778). In Cocytus, a frozen lake at the bottom of Hell, with the traitors.
Mohammed (570-632). In the 8th Circle as a sower of discord, according to a common medieval idea that he was a Christian schismatic.

... and who's who in Heaven

Godfrey of Bouillon (c1061-1100). Crusader and ruler of Jerusalem. In the 5th Heaven with those distinguished for fortitude.
Petrus Comestor (died 1179). Wrote *Historia scholastica*, a study of the Bible. In the 4th Heaven, with those distinguished for prudence.
Trajan (53-117). In legend restored to life by the prayers of Gregory the Great and so enabled to gain the grace of Christ. In the 6th Heaven, with those distinguished for justice.
Bernard of Clairvaux (1090-1153). Holy monk and spiritual writer. Prays to the Virgin Mary to intercede for Dante so that he might see God.

7 The windows
Windows in the side aisles, with another row above the archways into the nave, filled the whole of the 80ft height of the nave with light. The windows of Canterbury were famed for the stained glass with scenes from the life of Jesus and Old Testament episodes prefiguring them

6 The nave
The nave was rebuilt from 1391 to 1405. It was then unobstructed by benches, and gave plenty of space for pilgrims

5 The choir
This is where the monks of the monastery attached to the cathedral sang psalms of the liturgical office every day. Built under Archbishop Anselm from 1096, only the shell survived a fire in 1174, when it was rebuilt

Adam delving in a 12th-century window now at the west end of the cathedral but once part of a series showing ancestors of Jesus in the choir and Trinity Chapel

Canterbury Cathedral

1 Bell Harry
The central tower, Bell Harry, 249ft high, was the last main feature of the cathedral to be built (1494-1503). The lower course of windows gives light to the centre of the cathedral beneath; the bells can be heard far away, from their housing behind the high upper windows

Canterbury Cathedral is typical in having been added to during the medieval centuries. It occupies the site of a church built during Roman times and reconsecrated by St Augustine of Canterbury in AD602. Nothing of this remains. As the seat of the leader of the nation's Christians, Canterbury always had a prime status. Different architectural styles developed from the Norman (choir and crypt beneath, completed in 1130) to the Perpendicular (the central tower, called Bell Harry) finished just after 1500. The cathedral was supported by a community of monks who lived in a large monastery to the north of the church. Some of the monastic buildings still survive. The shrine of St Thomas Becket (died 1170) made it one of the leading places of pilgrimage in Europe. The people entered at the west end (*left*), and worshipped in the nave, facing the focus of the high altar (*to the east, right of the choir*), where Mass was celebrated. The choir was used daily by the monks. Even further east was the highly decorated shrine of St Thomas, now destroyed, which could be reached via the side aisles. The stained-glass windows of the Trinity Chapel portrayed the crucifixion, death, resurrection and ascension into heaven of Jesus, and the coming of the Holy Spirit at Pentecost.

2 The Pavement
The Pavement was laid down in front of Thomas Becket's shrine in 1220. It shows the labours of the months and virtues triumphing over vices

3 Trinity Chapel
The Trinity Chapel, built within 14 years of Thomas Becket's martyrdom in 1170, is where the great shrine to the saint was set up. The floor level (above a crypt beneath) is 16 steps higher than the choir, making it strikingly visible from the far west end of the nave

4 The Corona
The Corona was built at the same time as the Trinity Chapel. It is 515ft from the entrance in the west. St Augustine's Chair, for the enthronement of archbishops, stood here from the 13th century

Footfalls in the cloister

Monasteries provided employment and exports from their thousands of sheep. But the greater part of the monks' lives continued to be spent chanting psalms in the choir

In 1320 the monastery of Christ Church, which ran Canterbury Cathedral, owned 13,730 sheep. Each sheep brought in about 8d (eightpence was a thirtieth of a pound) a year; so Christ Church would earn £457 1s 4d a year from its flocks. Christ Church was an old-fashioned monastery of Benedictines, or Black Monks. The newer Cistercian monasteries that made farms out of wasteland in the 13th century had sheep runs supporting even larger flocks, at Fountains or Rievaulx in the north of England. Marketing the wool could be a sophisticated deal. It might be sold as a futures commodity to merchants, and in 1276 Fountains Abbey was actually mortgaged to Italian money-lenders on the receipt of four years' advance payment for the wool crop.

It was not, of course, the real business of a monk to be a sheep farmer. Most of the shepherding and administration would be done by lay brothers, or increasingly by tenants of the monastic estates. But churches, or cathedrals, had to be built and the roof mended, so economics always crept in.

The centuries between 1200 and 1500 were in some ways the high point of monasticism in England and continental Europe. Monasteries not only administered eight English cathedrals and kept thousands of acres under well-managed cultivation, they also gave employment and alms to the poor. To the mind of their contemporaries, though, the most important task of the monks was to praise God and pray for the nation.

An underlying theme of the authority on monastic history, David Knowles, in *Religious Orders in England* (1216 to the Reformation, published 1955), is that the level of spiritual commitment was not as high in this period as under such exemplary monks as Ailred of Rievaulx (1109-1166). The rule of thumb applied was that when the numbers of the lukewarm monks equalled that of the saintly, the monastery was in decline.

But the old monasteries of the Black Monks throve, and there were new foundations by the Cistercians apart from houses of Austin Canons, Carmelites, Premonstratensians, Gilbertines (founded by the 12th-century counsellor of kings, Gilbert of Sempringham, from Lincolnshire, who lived to over 100) and the strict, hermit-like Carthusians. If there was a falling off in fervour, it was indicated by such things as individual monks using books as if they were their own property or having pocket money to spend and taking holidays away from the monastery in country granges. There was glass in the windows, and more monks went to the universities. More officials from the monastery would be absent, administering farms. Meanwhile the abbots had separate

The prior, the haystack and the jumbo town band

est crotu̅ ui̅ q̅ tot faginan̅t reddicib; ad farracend̅ | relict
Elephaf gr:mone
proceden̅t obuia̅m
muti Ricardo uff
Imperatoꝛe̅ fre

The municipal band of Cremona, one of the many engaging drawings by Matthew Paris in his 13th-century *Chronicles*

LEFT: PITKIN UNICHROME. ABOVE: BY PERMISSION OF THE MASTERS AND FELLOWS CORPUS CHRISTI COLLEGE, CAMBRIDGE

Matthew Paris, monk and historian, had a lively curiosity. He noted how an earthquake on December 21 1248 brought down a roof at Wells Cathedral; how on another day most of Newcastle burnt down; how the French being besieged by the Saracens were obliged to eat their own horses during Lent; how the prior of Bentley near Harrow, Middlesex, died when a hay stack fell on him.

Matthew Paris was born about 1200, and spent the years between 1217 and his death in 1259 at St Alban's Abbey. It was not the biggest or richest Benedictine monastery, but being a day's journey from London on the Great North Road, it had a stream of interesting visitors and stabling for 300 horses.

Matthew asked everyone who came what they could tell him for his chronicle. He soon gained a reputation; Henry III visited the

monastery at least nine times and Matthew provides a drawing of the king carrying a relic of the Holy Blood in procession at court.

Matthew does not digest his material first as Bede had done but throws it all in the pot. He was once asked to visit Norway to establish the best practice for a Benedictine monastery there. This he found most interesting, and records a close escape from death by lightning at Bergen.

By great good fortune Matthew's two big volumes, written and illustrated by his own hand, escaped the destructions of the 16th century. There is much in them of historical importance. There are also charming pictures – of countrymen threshing, St Francis preaching to the birds (the earliest depiction known), camels, and the ox and ass at the nativity, of beastly Tartars roasting people to eat, Becket's head being cloven by a sword, and crusading knights

battling it out. There are maps of the Holy Land and Hadrian's Wall, and a lively picture of the municipal band of Cremona riding an elephant during Frederick II's siege of Parma.

When not in church or his scriptorium, Matthew sculpted, and, while none of this has survived in Britain, an oak panel made for Faaberg church in Norway might be his work. Though he went on until his death, he meant to end his chronicle in 1250, and wrote on his parchment page that year some lines that have been translated:

Matthew's chronicle here ends
And the jubilee year sends
Repose down from the skies.
May repose to him be given
Here on earth and up in heaven
When he there shall rise.

lodgings in the monastery. All this might not match the standards of Anselm or Ailred, but it is no scandal. The monks' lives were harder in some ways than might appear. One of the liturgical hours at which they sang psalms was in the middle of the night. This meant breaking their sleep every night. It was cold most of the time in winter; only in the calefactory, a common room, was there an opportunity to warm up in the hour of recreation. There was fasting every Friday and in seasons such as Lent. The reformed orders ate no flesh meat; the monks would be hungry after manual labour, and the medieval appetite enjoyed flesh meat when it could be had.

There were isolated incidents of monks being absent without leave in taverns, of some being out at night, even

keeping a mistress. We know about these offences from the periodic visitations of monasteries by the authorities, as imposed after the Fourth Lateran Council in 1215.

In the 14th century Chaucer's monk in *The Canterbury Tales* is jolly enough, but worldly wise and fond of eating and drinking; at the same time Langland sees some of the usefulness of monks, at work in their cloisters copying manuscripts of good books. Both writers had harsher words for gadabout friars.

Monasticism was constantly renewing itself. In 1500, the generation before all the monasteries and houses of friars were dissolved by order of the king, the most revered orders were the Carthusians, as strict as ever, the Observant Franciscans, upon whom the royal family depended for spiritual advisers, and the Brigittines at Syon, Middlesex, the first stone of whose monastery Henry V laid in 1415.

The cloisters of Gloucester Cathedral, where the monks of the medieval foundation would wash before choir duties

Reverence for bones

If the saints were in heaven, the remains of their holy bodies were fit to be honoured on earth. This idea led to a vast expansion in devotion to relics in the Middle Ages. Sometimes relic-hunters did not stop at theft

In 1247, King Henry III of England was delighted to receive a relic of the Holy Blood of Jesus, sent in a handsome rock-crystal reliquary by the masters of the Knights Templars and Hospitallers of Jerusalem. He kept vigil the night before its reception in London, fasting on bread and water with many candles and solemn prayers.

The next day he ordered all the most powerful men in the country to gather at St Paul's Cathedral. They assembled in fine array, with lighted candles and clergy in procession before them bearing crosses. The king, humbly dressed in a simple cloak with no hood, carried the holy relic on foot all the way to Westminster Abbey. Two assistants steadied his arms lest he stumble on the road with his precious burden. He deposited the relic in the Abbey, which was filled to the doors with bishops, abbots and monks tearfully singing. In a sermon, the Bishop of Norwich did not omit to point out that the relic had been sent from Jerusalem because of the "holiness of the lord King of the English, who was recognised as the most Christian of all Christian princes".

He was not the only ruler to realise that relics could reflect glory on their guardians. Henry's brother-in-law and enemy in war, Louis IX of France (later declared a saint), built the Sainte-Chapelle in Paris to house the Crown of Thorns. This, with a portion of the Cross and a nail of the Passion, he had acquired through his expeditions as a crusader. Henry's successor as King of England, Edward I, himself helped to carry the bier of St Hugh of Lincoln when it was translated in 1280 to a shrine in the Angel Choir of Lincoln Cathedral, which had been expressly constructed to house it. There was a special solemnity of ceremony for the translation of relics – that is, the transferring them from a burial place to an honourable shrine in a church or cathedral.

Some translations were less honourable. Relics of the True Cross had followed an ever more complicated path of translation, exchange or recovery from infidel capture ever since Helena, the mother of the Emperor Constantine, discovered it in the 4th century buried in Jerusalem (its authenticity proved by miraculous cures). In the succeeding centuries many small relics of the True Cross were reverenced throughout Christendom, though it is by no means true that a ship could be constructed from all the timber.

But it was an uphill struggle by church authorities to prevent the naive multiplication of relics. In the early 13th century the Council of Lyons forbade the veneration of recently found relics without the approval of the pope. The other general prohibition was the sale of relics on account of their holy properties; this, it was held, amounted to simony.

Relics attracted pilgrimages. The tomb of Thomas Becket at Canterbury was one of the most popular in Europe. Apart from the Holy Places in Jerusalem and the tomb of St Peter in Rome, the most frequented place of pilgrimage was Santiago de Compostela in north-west Spain. Cologne boasted the Three Kings.

By the late 15th century devotion to images of saints was more popular than to their relics alone. If relics of great saints were only to be seen after an arduous pilgrimage, every parish could have a picture of its patron saint. Yet at the beginning of the 16th century, the patron of Martin Luther, the Elector Frederick the Wise of Saxony, had a vast collection of relics in the church of his castle at Wittenberg. There were 17,443 relics to be precise, ranging from a saint's little finger to the complete mortal remains of one of the Holy Innocents martyred by King Herod.

Within a generation a view was to prevail that was expressed in vigorous language by Nicholas Shaxton, Bishop of Salisbury (1485-1556), who denounced the false relics he had confiscated, "namely stinking boots, mucky combs, ragged rochets, rotten girdles, pyld purses, great bullocks' horns, locks of hair and filthy rags, gobbets of wood under the name of parcels of the holy cross and such pelfry beyond estimation".

Looking forward to the resurrection of the body

There is something grisly to some people's way of thinking in displaying bits of dead bodies in churches. But the medieval reverence for relics derived from belief (expressed in the Creed) in the resurrection of the body. At the end of the world, the saints' bodies will rise again to be reunited with their souls in heaven. This idea had encouraged devotion to the remains of martyrs from the earliest days (*see page 19*). "We honour the relics of the martyrs," St Jerome had said, "in order the better to adore God, whose martyrs they are." From the time of the first martyrs, the Eucharist had been celebrated at the site of their tombs. As time went by, every altar incorporated a niche for the remains of a saint; it reflected the participation in the Eucharist of the Church in heaven as well as the Church on earth.

Gregory the Great had sent relics to St Augustine of Canterbury along with sacred vessels, altar linen and priestly vestments. The Second Council of Nicaea (AD787) insisted that relics were to be used in the consecration of every church. But there were not enough saints' bodies to go round, so churches had to be content with even a small relic.

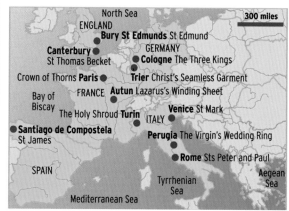

Popular shrines of the Middle Ages included the relics of the saints' bodies and objects connected with the life of Christ and the saints. At St Ursula's, Cologne (*right*), hundreds of relics decorate the whole wall. The ornate statue-reliquary of St Foy in Conques, France (*left*), was designed to reflect heavenly glory

The decay of Christe

The Black Death killed nearly half the population of England in just 18 months. To some it seemed like the end of the world, but the unity of Christendom was under attack from quite other causes

The plague now known as the Black Death reached England in 1348. Within 18 months, according to the best modern estimates, 47 per cent of the population of England had died. This pandemic was caused by the bacterium *Yersinia pestis*, later responsible for the Great Plague of London in 1665. It is called bubonic plague because of the swellings or buboes it causes in armpit or groin. Sometimes it took the form of the more rapidly fatal pneumonic plague, infecting the lungs. This plague is spread by the fleas of rats.

For three years, from 1347 when it reached Constantinople from central Asia, it swept Europe, killing perhaps 25 million. To some it seemed like the end of the world. One friar in Ireland (*Eyewitness, right*) thought it possible no man would survive it. The spread of the disease was unnervingly unpredictable. By the autumn of 1348 it was raging in London, but St Alban's Abbey, only a day's journey from the capital, was not infected till the

following April. By that time, seafarers had carried the plague as far as Bergen in Norway.

The Archbishop of York ordered solemn processions to ask for God's mercy in July 1348. The Bishop of London took the practical step of buying a plot called No Man's Land and walling it about as a burial ground. By the end of 1349 the worst was past. On December 28 the Archbishop of Canterbury directed prayers to be said in thanksgiving. Surprisingly the plague seemed to have little effect on the attitudes of the nation. Preachers used it to exemplify the suddenness of death. Some asked in puzzlement what they had done to suffer this sudden apocalypse. But, perhaps being accustomed to death, people did not seem either to gain or lose faith in God. From Chaucer a generation later (apart from the *Pardoner's Tale*), one would hardly guess that almost half the population had perished within living memory.

The first effect of the plague was social disruption. Where the village priest had died it interrupted regular

Death embraces monk, farm labourer, friar, king and cardinal in a late 15th-century fresco in the church of La Ferté-Loupière, France

ndom

churchgoing. Where a monastery had been badly afflicted it could mean that manuscripts were left uncopied, farms untended, the poor unrelieved of hunger. Some villages ceased to exist. Some parishes were amalgamated. The population did not recover for a century. The plague attracted eccentric movements. In continental Europe confraternities would perform public penance by flagellating themselves, which the Church did not favour.

There are the pictures of the Dance of Death, such as the one here from La Ferté-Loupière some 80 miles south of Paris, to remind us of how the plague struck princes and beggars, bishops and ploughmen. But these images were commonplaces of religious art. The hearty wish of lay people before the Reformation was to avoid an unprovided death. The plague might go, but death was always with them.

DIATHEO

Waiting for death to come

John Clynn, a Franciscan Friar in Ireland, writes of the plague that reached the country in 1348.

Since the beginning of the world it has been unheard of for so many people to die of pestilence, famine or other infirmity in such a short time. This pestilence was so contagious that those who touched the dead or the sick were immediately infected and died, so that the penitent and confessor were carried together to the grave.

Because of their fear and horror men could hardly bring themselves to perform the pious and charitable acts of visiting and burying the dead. Many died of boils, abscesses and pustules which erupted on the legs and in the armpits. Others died in a frenzy, brought on by an affliction of the head, or vomiting blood. This amazing year was exceptional in quite contradictory ways – abundantly fertile and yet at the same time sickly and deadly.

Among the Franciscans at Drogheda 25 brothers died before Christmas, and 23 died at Dublin. At Kilkenny the pestilence was strong during Lent, and eight Dominicans died between Christmas and March 6. It was very rare for just one person to die in a house, usually husband, wife, children and servants went the way of death.

I, seeing these many ills, and that the whole world is encompassed by evil, wait among the dead for death to come. I leave parchment for continuing the work, in case anyone should still be alive in the future and any son of Adam can escape this pestilence and continue the work thus begun.

Wyclif's rebellion

In the late 14th century, an Oxford theologian, John Wyclif, was denounced as a subversive, but many of his ideas were picked up later during the Reformation

A dyer's youngest daughter

John Wyclif (1330-84) fostered ideas that deeply influenced the Protestant Reformation in Europe in the early 16th century. But some of his beliefs were too extreme ever to be adopted by the Church of England. Wyclif was educated at Balliol College, Oxford, was made a doctor of divinity in 1362, preached fiercely, ran the risk of imprisonment for his views, but ended his life as a country clergyman. One of his ideas that subverted the medieval establishment was that men could exercise "dominion", meaning possession of goods or of authority, only if they were in a state of grace, free from mortal sin.

This seemed to resurrect Donatism from 1,000 years before, against which Augustine of Hippo had fought (*see page 38*). It meant that no one would know if they had been validly baptised – who could say if the baptiser was in a state of grace? Moreover Wyclif urged that since Church authorities were sinful they should give up all their possessions.

Wyclif wrote voluminously. On the Eucharist he asserted that the bread and wine remain unchanged even after Christ becomes present in the sacrament. This was seen as contradicting what the Church had been teaching explicitly since the condemnation of Berengarius under Gregory VII 300 years before.

Network of poor priests

Wyclif proposed that the Bible should be interpreted not by the Church but by everyone (*see right*). From the late 1370s he set up a network of "Poor Priests" (later not priests at all but lay preachers) to spread his ideas to the rural poor; he valued the preaching of holy but ignorant men above that of the learned. After the Peasants' Revolt of 1381, Wyclif's teachings were condemned by a synod of bishops at Blackfriars. But before any action was taken against him, Wyclif suffered a stroke at his parish of Lutterworth in Leicestershire. He died on the last day of 1384.

In 1415, the Council of Constance, declaring itself a Universal Council of the Church, condemned 45 errors ostensibly drawn from Wyclif's writings, such as "*Ecclesia Romana est synagoga satanae*" –The Roman Church is a synagogue of Satan. In 1428 Wyclif's body was dug up and burnt, but his influence continued, through the Lollard movement, and through the Bohemian John Hus, who incorporated his writings wholesale into his own books, where they attracted the attention of Martin Luther and Ulrich Zwingli, the instigators of the Protestant Reformation.

An English Bible

Wyclif's name even in his own time was associated with translating the Bible into English, although most of the work was done after his death in 1384. He certainly wanted the Bible in English, as part of his plan of radical evangelisation. Such translation was not prohibited, for not only had the Anglo-Saxons long ago put the Gospels into English, but recent translations for devotional use were also in circulation.

The two men most active in the production of Wyclifite translations were John Purvey (died after 1421) and Nicholas of Hereford (died 1417). Nicholas did not spoil his career by his enterprise, becoming chancellor of his diocese. He ended his life as an austere Carthusian monk. He had worked on translation with Wyclif at Oxford, probably breaking off in about 1382 when the University was in a tumult over Wyclif's sermons. Purvey, a more shadowy figure, continued the work after Wyclif's death, completing a version. He is last heard of in 1421 in prison yet again, on heresy charges.

The translations were from the Latin Vulgate; Wyclif knew no Greek or Hebrew. They contain no bias against orthodox doctrine, and their later condemnation was for the heretical Lollard introductions prefaced to the manuscripts in which they were circulated. Before long, the whole practice of translation came to regarded as dangerous (*see page 134*).

A page from the first English Bible, attributed to Wyclif, though most work was done after his death

In the 14th century the Western Church was badly hit by the exile of popes in Avignon and then by the Great Schism between rival popes. In the middle entered the compelling figure of Catherine of Siena

When the Archbishop of Bordeaux, Bertrand de Got, was elected Pope Clement V in 1305 he tried to please the King of France by being crowned in Lyons. Italy was in such chaos that he then decided to stay in Avignon for a while. For the next 70 years the papacy remained in exile from Rome. The refusal of successive popes to return home was a scandal to many. Into this scene stepped the remarkable character of Catherine of Siena.

Catherine was born in about 1347, the 21st child of a prosperous dyer in Siena. She came under heavy pressure from her parents to marry, but resisted. Contemporary biographers record that she ate practically nothing; meat dishes made her sick. Perhaps she would be classified as anorexic nowadays. But she knew what she wanted, which was to live a life of prayer. She became a lay member (a tertiary) of the Order of St Dominic and, though living at home, acquired the habit of contemplative prayer.

She attracted a collection of followers, including the English Austin Friar, William of Flete (*see page 121*), who were known as Caterinati. After a forthright campaign she succeeded in 1377 in persuading Pope Gregory XI to return to Rome. But in 1378, Gregory died, and his successor Urban VI found himself opposed by another antipope. Catherine dictated endless letters to churchmen and secular rulers, even to the English mercenary Sir John Hawkwood (of whom Mantegna painted a memorable portrait) but to little political avail. Though Catherine was to attract a wide cult as a saint, she could achieve no solution to the papal schism, even after going to Rome to take up Urban's cause. There she died in 1380.

By then the substantial number of French cardinals, who had been used to getting their own way at Avignon, had returned there in a huff and had installed their own candidate, Clement VII. So began the era of popes and anti-popes, a schism which divided European allegiances: France, Austria, Aragon and Scotland were for Avignon; England, the Low Countries and Castile for Rome.

The next 70 years were witness to an interminable series of rival popes. One attempt to mend matters came in 1414 when the Emperor Sigismund convened a council at Constance, an international assembly of clerics and theologians. It eventually deposed three simultaneously rival popes, and substituted for them a fourth, Martin V.

Shortly before his death in 1431 Martin convoked another council. It sat at Basle, tended to oppose papal prerogatives and was dominated by theologians. At its first session not a single bishop was present. The new pope, Eugenius IV, tried and failed to dissolve the council. The Council in turn attempted to rule the pope, at last electing an anti-pope of its own (Felix V). Eugenius called

a council independently, in 1439, first at Ferrara, then at Florence. The Council of Florence achieved a short-lived reconciliation of sorts with the Church in the East. Byzantium was in a desperate position, under threat from Turkey. Whatever paper agreement was achieved became a dead letter when Constantinople fell in 1453.

Throughout these decades of schism and scandal in the Western Church, there was surprisingly little disturbance of Christian practice. There is hardly a sign of the terrible divisions in the Church in the writings of Chaucer, for example. The ploughman, the Wife of Bath, the parson or the knight know that there should be a pope in Rome, but they get on regardless of who it might be.

St Catherine of Siena before Pope Gregory XI, c1448, by Giovanni di Paolo. Catherine persuaded him to return to Rome from Avignon, but he died before making the journey

The new humanity

In the high Middle Ages, pious Christians started many new initiatives to care for the poor and sick. Their fortunes varied

As cities grew more organised the care of the poor was split between parish clergy, monasteries, hospitals (generally refuges run by religious orders), corporations, craft guilds and lay confraternities. Helping the poor had always been a distinguishing feature of Christian life, but the organisation of civil society was something that depended on the secular rulers.

An example of how care for the poor developed in the high Middle Ages is the story of John Colombini. He was born in Siena in about 1300 and gave himself to commerce with some success. His wife, though, had to put up with his bad temper. Going off in a huff after one row, he picked up by chance a book about Mary of Egypt, a saint noted for her penance in expiation of a sinful early life. This somehow set off a reaction in John Colombini.

He forsook his acquisitive ways, and when he fell sick, he insisted on sharing the hardships of the poor people in the local hospital. When he regained his health he set about turning the house into a refuge for poor people, whom he fed and washed with his own hands.

The unfortunate Signora Colombini now had to reconcile herself to her husband's new ways. With their children off their hands (the son dead; the daughter a nun), he settled an annuity on her and divided the ample remainder of his fortune between a monastery and founding a hospital. He begged for his daily bread and looked after poor people who were sick. His idealism attracted several young men from the ruling families. But the city council was prevailed upon to banish Colombini for inciting the young to "folly". He then toured Tuscany acquiring more followers.

When Pope Urban V returned to Rome from exile in Avignon he gave the organisation approval under the name Apostolic Clerics of St Jerome. But, from their frequent exclamation "Praise be to Jesus Christ", they gained the popular name "Jesuati" (not to be confused with the Jesuits, founded in the 16th century). After its founder's death in 1367 the congregation spread rapidly all over Italy, as did a parallel congregation for women founded by Colombini's cousin Catherine. But after 300 years the men had lost their early ideals, and in 1668 were suppressed by the Pope as "of little advantage to the interests of the Church". The sisterhood survived until 1872.

A more enduring foundation was made by another John, later known as St John of God. He was born in 1495 at Montemor o Novo in Portugal and grew up a shepherd. One day he set off for Africa determined to offer himself as a ransom for Christian hostages of the Moors. A priest to whom he resorted for Confession advised him to return to Spain.

In Granada he heard the preaching of the renowned John of Avila. This provoked him to give away his possessions and to go about the streets bewailing his sins like a madman. John of Avila persuaded him to take a more reasonable course of life, and he spent his days working with the poor. He found ways to help the sick, in particular the mad or mentally deficient, the unemployed, orphans and prostitutes.

He became a hero of Granada, died in 1550, and his work was continued by a congregation built up by his followers. He was declared a saint in 1690. By then the congregation had been given a new impetus in France.

By the 1920s the Brothers of John of God were giving more than two million beds a year there to the homeless, and caring for hundreds of disabled orphans. The congregation's work continues.

Brothers of St John of God, an order started by a Portuguese-born Christian who became a hero of Granada looking after the sick, the mad or mentally deficient, the unemployed, orphans and prostitutes. The brothers nursed the sick with their own hands

The rise and fall of a charitable order

The religious order known as the Humiliati had a strange history from beginning to end. It was an example of how ad hoc efforts to help the poor could prosper and then fall into decay. The Humiliati originated in a group of nobles from Lombardy who at the beginning of the 12th century had fallen foul of the Emperor Charles V. After putting down a rebellion in Lombardy he transported suspected ringleaders to Germany. There some embraced a pious life of penance and charity and adopted a drab costume. Having convinced the Emperor of the reform of their ways they returned to Lombardy, taking with them a knowledge of German knitwear production, which did much to bring prosperity to Lombard workers.

On the recommendation of St Bernard of Clairvaux some of them set up a monastery in Milan. It did well, and they received the approval of Pope Innocent II in about 1200. They proved a counter-attraction to the Cathar heretics long established among the country people, and in towns they helped form trade associations. They were known for their practical help for the poor and their holy lives. Several were declared saints after their deaths.

But as the generations passed fewer new members were recruited while wealth accumulated to the order. At one stage there were, in 94 monasteries, only 170 members. By the 16th century, with other reforms of the counter-reformation, Charles Borromeo was given the task by Pope Pius V of reforming them. For his trouble, a piqued and unbalanced member of the Humiliati attempted to murder Borromeo. After that, the Humiliati were suppressed, on February 8 1571, and their properties given to other religious orders or sold for charitable ends.

Meanwhile a parallel order of women deriving from the wives of some of the first Humiliati were having a hard time of it. They had established hospitals and refuges for lepers. When the male Humiliati were suppressed, the women's hospitals were still doing good work, but they had relied on the men's monasteries to administer their temporal affairs. Despite the odds, five independent houses of women Humiliati survived in Italy into the 20th century.

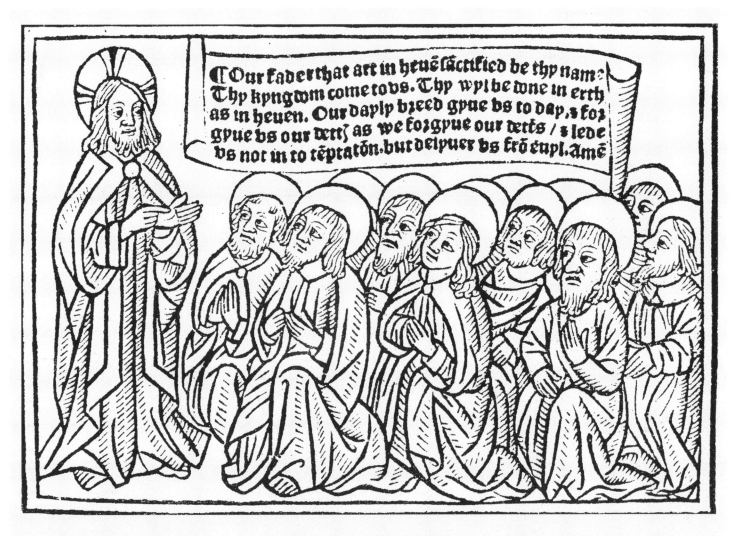

Jesus teaches his 12 Apostles the Lord's Prayer in English, from the *Arte or Crafte to Lyve Well and to Dye Well*, a bestselling prayer book printed in 1505

Learning to pray in your mother tongue

England did not lag behind the rest of Europe in exploiting printing to produce popular books of devotion for lay people

Printers and booksellers in the late 15th century catered for a growing market for prayer books in English. The invention of printing had given the trade a huge commercial impetus. Such books, known as primers, contained prayers for lay people to say while attending Mass, daily prayers and a collection of devotions relating to Jesus and his mother Mary. The spirit of these devotions is still familiar from the *Imitation of Christ*, a work which continued to appeal to Protestants as well as Catholics through the centuries after the Reformation.

Unlike the *Imitation*, however, the vernacular primers rarely survived the 16th century. As well-used manuals they fell apart; as collections of prayers to Christ present in the Sacrament, to the saints and to Jesus as represented in an image, they became objects fit for destruction in a Protestant ethos that abominated such practices.

One of the most popular books of devotion was a translation into English made by a Carthusian monk, Nicholas Love, of a work by St Bonaventure, *Meditationes Vitae Christi*, Meditations on the Life of Christ. The reader was invited to contemplate the Passion of Christ in a prayerful state of mind. The affective contemplation of the humanity of Jesus, as a brother of mankind, extended to another popular devotion in the late Middle Ages that might seem either artificial or gruesome to many today – devotion to the Five Wounds of Christ. This was often related to a legend of Gregory the Great in which the Pope while saying Mass sees a vision of Jesus displaying the instruments of the Passion (the cross, the nails, the lance and so on). In primers this image would be reproduced as a woodcut, accompanied by a rubric offering indulgences to readers who contemplated the image and recited the Lord's Prayer, the Hail Mary and the Creed. In other words devotional recitation of the prayers would win the worshipper deliverance from some of their time in Purgatory.

Anglo-Saxon roots
The most common formulation of such a prayer was the one beginning: "I adore you, Lord Jesus Christ, hanging on the Cross, and bearing on your head a crown of thorns." Following on, there are six more such prayers, divided up by an Our Father and a Hail Mary. Modern historians trace these prayers back to Anglo-Saxon times. They are found in the *Book of Cerne*, a prayer book compiled in the early 9th century.

Another bestselling collection was printed in 1505 by Wynken de Worde, the associate of William Caxton. It was called *The Arte or Crafte to Lyve Well and to Dye Well*. This was adapted from a French source, but well calculated to appeal to a lay English audience. It explained the Lord's Prayer, the Hail Mary, the Creed, the Ten Commandments, the gifts of the Holy Spirit, the works of mercy and the seven sacraments. Among its woodcuts was a series giving the Old Testament antetypes for the sacraments. The Eucharist, for example, was illustrated by a picture of the sacrifice of Melchizedek, just as a mosaic had in the church of San Vitale, Ravenna, in the 6th century (*see picture on page 23*). Another of the woodcuts in *The Arte or Crafte* was the scene above of Jesus teaching the Twelve Apostles to pray, with the Lord's Prayer clearly legible in English (rather than the Latin in which it was said at Mass).

The power of the laity at this period to provide a demand for such books is demonstrated by *The Kalendar of Shepherdes* published by the printer Richard Pynson in 1506. It gives astronomical and medical information as well as a popularly couched exposition of prayers and commandments. It also includes the satirically memorable Ten Commandments of the Devil, such as: "Be dronkyn upon the holy daye/ And cause other to synne if thou may".

Giovanni Cimabue's *Virgin and Child in Majesty* (*left*) was painted in the late 13th century, 200 years before the *Madonna and Child* by Andrea Mantegna (*right*). Cimabue's is a work on a gilt wood panel designed for devotion in a church; Mantegna's might hang in a private room. Cimabue follows the conventions of Byzantine art before him. The Virgin and child Jesus sit enthroned and face the viewer. Their sanctity is indicated by golden haloes, as is that of the six angels who stand formally in attendance. As an aid to devotion it has a close resemblance to the icons of the East (*see page 76*). Mantegna's painting of about 1465 is unconventional in technique, being painted with pigments bound in glue directly on to a canvas. But it is even less conventional in composition, showing a mother and child with no haloes or angels to indicate their holy nature. The mother holds the child Jesus close to her cheek without displaying him to the viewer. She seems lost in her own thoughts; the child is asleep. The baby is young and lifelike. The devotion evoked is intimate and humane.

A tender realism

Towards the end of the medieval period devotional art grew more personal. It recruited human emotions as a response to divine realities

'My helpers in need'

For ordinary parishioners in the Middle Ages, the saints were all around them. Toothache, childbirth and the health of horses each had its own patron

Protector of travellers

St Christopher was commonly painted on the walls of churches near the door, as here in this 15th-century mural from Breage church in Cornwall, so that parishioners leaving could invoke his protection on their travels. He was shown as a giant fording a river, with a great sprouting staff and bearing the child Jesus on his shoulder.

In the *Golden Legend* (*see right*) he is said to have been a Canaanite called Reprobus before baptism. He seeks the most powerful king to serve. At one court he sees the king cross himself with fear at the mention of the devil, so Christopher goes to find the devil. But as he walks with the devil he sees him fearfully avoiding a wayside cross, and so realises that Christ is the most powerful king.

A hermit tells him to serve Christ by helping people across a ford. One day a little child weighs so heavily on him that he asks who he is. "He who created the whole world." As a token of his heavenly guest Christopher's staff sprouts overnight.

Christopher's feast is still celebrated in the Catholic Church, though the feast of St James takes precedence in the universal calendar.

One of the most popular books ever written was *The Golden Legend*, a compilation of stories of the saints. It was originally compiled in about 1260 by Jacobus de Voragine (*vorago* is the Latin for a whirlpool). It was one of the first books printed in English, by William Caxton in 1483. Caxton was what we would now call a publisher as well as a printer, and his edition of the book included Bible stories and English versions of the readings week by week at Sunday Mass.

Jacobus (1230-98) was a Dominican friar and saw his series of saints' lives as a way of conveying Church teaching in a memorable form. In this he succeeded beyond the most optimistic hopes. More than 1,000 manuscripts of the book survive from before the age of printing, when it found a new mass market.

Few people today have read *The Golden Legend*, but the versions of the legends of the saints with which we are familiar often derive from it. We find St George delivering the king's daughter from the dragon (she leads it back into town "like a little dog" with her girdle tied round its neck). There is St Catherine, sentenced to be crushed and sliced between two great wheels that revolve in opposite directions, until under the influence of her holiness they burst apart with a crack.

In the centuries before the Reformation, the saints played a daily and lively part in the lives of parishioners throughout Europe. It did not matter so much what St Catherine had once done to the wheels, but that she was available here and now for the person asking for her to pray to God for some favour. Saints were thought to bring material as well as spiritual benefits. St Erasmus, portrayed as having his intestines pulled out on a windlass, would pray to God to cure your belly-ache. A candle lit with a prayer before a picture of St Loy (Eligius) would make your horses thrive.

It made no difference whether a saint had lived in the deepest past or, like the reputedly saintly Henry VI, had died recently; they were expected to take a personal interest in clients who cultivated a devotion to them. At Windsor, Henry VI's hat could be tried on by those who sought his intercession for headache.

In the 15th century it was customary in a last will and testament to express religious faith. One Somerset will records the friendly terms on which the testator had been with a collection of "the good saints that I have had mynde and prayers moost unto, that is, St Nicholas, St George, St John the Baptist, St Christofer, St Mary Magdalene, St Gabriell, St Erasmus, St Fabian, St Sebastian, St John the Evangelist, whom I have always honoured and loved, Sts Cuthbert and Katheryn myn advocates and my syngular helpers and socourers in this my grete nede".

Each trade had its patron saint. Each year saw a round of saints' days: February 3 St Blaise, patron of throats; March 25 Lady's Day, the feast of the Annunciation; April 23 St George; June 24 St John the Baptist; September 29 Michaelmas, the feast of St Michael the Archangel; December 29 St Thomas of Canterbury.

But saints could be invoked any day. Their images were in the parish church as constant reminders and objects of devotion. Everyone had his own saint who came with his Christian name. It was a part of life. If there were abuses and superstition, it did not worry many people until the growth of Christian humanism in the late 15th century.

St Apollonia

Apollonia was invoked against toothache, not so common in the Middle Ages before the widespread use of sugar, but terribly painful, of course, and sometimes a killer. She was often painted on the screen at the front of the nave in parish churches (such as Horsham St Faith, Norfolk, of 1528). She was a virgin martyr who died in 249 and, according to a contemporary account, had her teeth beaten out before being burnt on a pyre.

St Martin

Some 4,000 churches were dedicated to St Martin in France alone. He is usually shown on horseback dividing his cloak with a beggar (who, he learns in a dream, was Christ himself). His cloak, *capella* in Latin, gave its name to a shrine where it was preserved, giving us the word chapel. His feast, November 11, was the day livestock were slaughtered, hence the proverb: "Every pig has his St Martin."

St Roche

Roche or Rock can be identified in pictures and statues by the sore on his thigh that he generally points to, and by the dog usually accompanying him. He lived in the 14th century and gained great popularity all over Europe in the 15th century because his prayers were renowned for alleviating physical ailments. His legend has him catching the plague after tending its victims and being looked after in deserted woods by his dog.

St Nicholas

Nicholas was a 4th-century bishop of Myra in Asia Minor whose relics were stolen and enshrined at Bari in Italy in 1087. Hundreds of churches were dedicated to him. His legend has him throwing three bags of gold in at a window as dowry to help three girls marry (hence the three balls of pawnbrokers), and raising from the dead three boys cut up in a tub of brine. His feast is December 6 and by a roundabout route he was to become to some Santa Claus.

Margery Kempe

Margery Kempe (c1373-1440), a pious if neurotic merchant's wife from Lynn in Norfolk, made several pilgrimages on her own. On the way back from Jerusalem she went to Rome via Assisi. In her memoir she habitually refers to herself as "this creature"

The aforesaid creature had a ring, which Our Lord had commanded her to have made while she was at home in England, and she had it engraved: "*Jesus Cryst est amor meus.*" She was very worried about keeping this ring safe from being stolen, as she travelled through different countries. She would not, she thought to herself, lose that ring for a thousand pounds – or much more.

So it happened that she was staying in a respectable man's house. Lots of neighbours came in to talk with her, which was all meant for her improvement and growth in holiness. She gave them a description of Christ's grave [*she had just spent three weeks in Jerusalem*]. They were glad to hear all about it and thanked her warmly.

Afterwards this creature went to her room and put her ring onto her purse-string, which she carried hanging at her breast. In the morning, when she went to put on her ring, it was gone. She could not find it anywhere. She was greatly upset, and complained to the woman of the house, to this effect: "Madam, my wedding ring, Jesus Christ's wedding ring, as one might say, it has gone."

The good woman, understanding what she meant, asked her to pray for her. But she had a strange look on her face, as though she had been guilty. Then this creature took a candle in her hand and looked all around the bed in which she had slept all night. And the woman of the house took another candle in her hand and busied herself too looking all around the bed. And at last this creature found the ring under the bed on the floorboards! And with great delight she told the woman of the house that she had found the ring. Then the woman asked this creature for forgiveness, as well as she could.

Tears in Assisi

Then this creature reached Assisi, where she met a Friar, an Englishman, who said he had never heard of anyone living in the world who was so much at home with God. One day she was in church in Assisi where they were showing Our Lady's handkerchief which she wore when she was here on earth. There were many candles around it and much reverence from the people. Then this creature was filled with devotion. She wept, she sobbed, she cried with floods of tears and she was filled with holy thoughts.

She was also at church there on Lammas Day, when there is great pardon with plenary remission. She was there with the intention of obtaining grace, mercy and forgiveness for herself, for all her friends, for all her enemies, and for all the souls in Purgatory.

When this creature reached Rome, some of the people who had been travelling with her before, but who had got rid of her and would not have her travelling with them, were in Rome too. When they heard that a woman like this creature had got there, they were very surprised and wondered how she had got there safely.

Women had always greatly influenced the development of Christianity. At the end of the 14th century in East Anglia two Englishwomen, who had met one another, both wrote books about their spiritual lives

Women's constant influence

The woman reading in this painting by Rogier van der Weyden is identifiable as Mary Magdalen from the jar of ointment standing on the floor next to her. Otherwise she could be any middle-class woman of the 15th century, sitting in a clean room and saying her prayers with the help of a book of psalms or a devotional work.

Although the status of women in society depended on the prevailing culture, they had always greatly influenced the history of Christianity. Augustine of Hippo became a Christian only through the prayers of his mother Monica; Jerome, who compiled the Bible, would hardly have survived without the patronage of powerful women. England and France became Christian through the influence of two queens: behind Ethelbert, the pagan King of Kent who received Augustine of Canterbury, was Queen Bertha, a Christian already; the same is true of Queen Clotild, the wife of Clovis.

In the 15th century, Margery Kempe, like Etheria 1,000 years before (*see page 43*), travelled alone to Jerusalem and to Rome on pilgrimage. Margery Kempe (c1373-1440) was married to a merchant in the prosperous town of Lynn (King's Lynn) in Norfolk. She worshipped in St Margaret's, a fine church which is still standing.

There is no doubt that she was a little mad. She was always weeping, so much so that she was sometimes barred from churches for her distracting behaviour. Her memoirs, discovered in manuscript only this century, reveal a character not at ease. Some modern critics explain her apparently neurotic streak as the only way she could express herself in the constricting society of her time. If there is something in that, she was nevertheless often able to get other people to do what she wanted, and she travelled about Europe and the Middle East with surprising freedom.

It was nearer home that she found calming advice. She went to Norwich, some 50 miles away, to consult Julian, who was not in the least neurotic. Dame Julian (1342-1413), as Margery Kempe calls her, was an anchoress. That meant she lived in a fixed place, probably a little room attached to a church, and spent her time in prayer. Margery Kempe records visiting her for a few days. Julian counselled her, she says, "to be obedient to the will of Our Lord God and to fulfil with all her might whatever he put into her soul, if it were not against the wor-

Detail from *The Magdalen Reading* by Rogier van der Weyden (1399-1464), a typical 15th-century scene

Mother Jesus

In *The Revelations of Divine Love* Julian of Norwich wrote of her "Showings", mystical experiences, which included the way in which Jesus, though a man and God, seems like a mother

ship of God and profit of her fellow Christians". The Holy Spirit would move her in charity and chastity too, for he "makes a soul stable and steadfast in the right faith".

Julian herself wrote a much admired book known as *The Revelations of Divine Love*. It was in the tradition of English mysticism in the 14th and 15th century, of books such as the anonymous *Cloud of Unknowing* or *The Ladder of Perfection*, by Walter Hylton. Hylton (*c*1330-1396) was an Austin Canon, a kind of monk following a rule derived from St Augustine of Hippo. A contemporary Austin Friar (a member of another order following Augustine's rule), called William Flete, had spent 20 years in Italy gaining experience in the spiritual life from the saintly Catherine of Siena (*see page 112*), who had not hesitated to tell popes to mend their ways. Another Austin Canon in Walter's time was John of Bridlington, declared a saint in 1401. A few years later Margery Kempe sought advice from John of Bridlington's confessor, William Sleightholm. Another pious and powerful woman, Lady Margaret Beaufort (Henry VII's mother), requested Wynken de Worde, Caxton's collaborator, to print Hylton's book in 1494.

Julian of Norwich reflects in her own writings the best English tradition of the period. Often she refers to "St Dionyse of France" as people of her time called the Pseudo-Dionysius (*see page 53*). She might have known him from a translation of one of his mystical works enti-

'All shall be well, and all shall be well, and all manner of things shall be well'

tled in English *Hid Divinite* which was written by the same anonymous writer as the classic treatise *The Cloud of Unknowing*

She wrote her own book in order to record 16 "Showings" – visions of a kind – which she experienced over two days in 1373. Some of the Showings that she records as best she can, since words fail to do them justice, are very vivid. She sees the body of Christ on the cross change colour and wither as a cold dry wind blows over it while he dies, which seems to take a week. And yet the tone of her book is confident and joyful. Her best known insight is: "All shall be well, and all shall be well, and all manner of things shall be well."

At the end of her book she explains that she had spent 15 years wondering what the revelation was really about. All at once she understood it: "Love was his meaning. Who showed it you? Love. What did he show you? Love. Why did he show it? For love. Hold on to this and you will know and understand love more and more. But you will not know or learn anything else – ever."

EYEWITNESS

So we see that Jesus is the true Mother of our nature, for he made us. He is our Mother, too, by grace, because he took our created nature upon himself. Our Mother by nature and grace – for he would become our Mother in everything – laid the foundation of his work in the Virgin's womb with great and gentle condescension. (This was shown in the first revelation, when I received a mental picture of the Virgin's genuine simplicity at the time she conceived.) In other words, it was in this lowly place that God most high, the supreme wisdom of all, adorned himself with our poor flesh, ready to function and serve as Mother in all things.

A mother's is the most intimate, willing and dependable of all services, because it is the truest of all. None has been able to fulfil it properly but Christ, and he alone can. We know that our own mother's bearing of us was a bearing to pain and death, but what does Jesus, our true Mother, do? Why, he, All-love, bear us to joy and eternal life! Blessings on him! Thus he carries us within himself in love. And he is in labour until the time has fully come for him to suffer the sharpest pangs and most appalling pain – and in the end he dies. And not even, when this is over and we ourselves have been born to eternal bliss, is his marvellous love completely satisfied. This he shows in that overwhelming word of love, "If I could possibly have suffered more, I would have done so."

He might die no more, but that does not stop him working, for he needs to feed us. It is an obligation of his dear, motherly, love. The human mother will suckle her child with her own milk, but our beloved Mother, Jesus, feeds us with himself, and, with the most tender courtesy, does it by means of the Blessed Sacrament, the precious food of all true life. And it keeps us going through his mercy and grace by all the sacraments.

The human mother may put her child tenderly to her breast, but our tender Mother Jesus simply leads us into his blessed breast through his open side, and there gives us a glimpse of the Godhead and heavenly joy – the inner certainty of eternal bliss.

Cleansing the kingdom

At the end of the 15h century the 'Catholic Kings' of Spain, Ferdinand and Isabella, tried to make their kingdom a model Christian state, but along with their achievements came inquisition, torture and mass expulsions

In 1481, two years into his reign, King Ferdinand declared as his aim "to expel from all Spain the enemies of the Catholic faith and dedicate Spain to the service of God". Ferdinand and Isabella were to rule Spain as the *Reyes Catolicos* ("Catholic Kings" is the traditional English translation). It was a title given to them by the Pope in 1494, much like Henry VIII's *Fidei Defensor* (Defender of the Faith). The Spanish monarchs did not always do what the Pope wanted; they gradually took into their own hands the appointment of bishops, a power which he had previously exercised

Spain saw itself as Christian through and through, the very heart of Christendom. But it was utterly different from anywhere else in Europe. After establishing its own Christian civilisation, it had in AD711 been overrun by Muslims from North Africa. It then spent centuries reconquering its territory (*see chapters Two and Three*).

Any tradition of Christians, Moors and Jews practising *convivencia*, living together in the same society, was split apart by the decision in 1492 to expel any Jews who would not be baptised. Some historians have said that Ferdinand and Isabella were not motivated by racialism in this policy. It is true that they employed Jews and *conversos*, convert Jews, as trusted high officials. In 1488 they made a Jew, Abraham Seneor, treasurer-general of the Hermandad, the chief agency of tax-gathering and law and order. At least four bishops in Isabella's Castile were *conversos*, and three of her secretaries. It was fear that her religion would be contaminated that moved Isabella to embark on the monstrous and counter-productive measures of exile and inquisition.

Isabella (1451-1504) had become Queen of Castile in 1474; Ferdinand (1452-1516) became King of Aragon in 1479. They had been married in 1469 and were joint rulers of Christian Spain, but the kingdoms and cities remained jealous of their own privileges. Although kings,

'After so much travail, expense, death and bloodshed, this kingdom has been won to the glory of God'

clergy and nobles were completely identified with the Church, there was room for conflict. Archbishop Alfonso Carrillo of Toledo, for example, sent an army against Isabella at the battle of Toro in 1476 when she was fighting to establish her claim to the throne.

It seemed only natural for Ferdinand and Isabella to follow their predecessors and continue the reconquest. This culminated in their capture of Granada in 1492. A decade earlier it had been the capital of an independent

Mastermind of the Inquisition

As Inquisitor General of Spain, Tomás de Torquemada is a byword for monstrous cruelty. He was to blame for burning about 2,000 people and torturing many more. Yet he would not have recognised himself as a wicked murderer

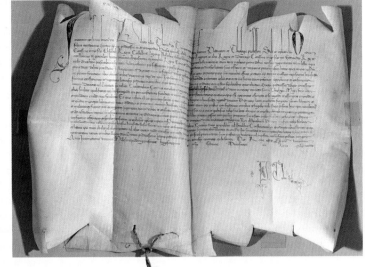

Papal Bull of Innocent VIII (1432-92) appointing Tomás de Torquemada Inquisitor General of Spain

The Spanish Inquisition came into operation in 1480. Technically it was established by a papal bull, but the Catholic Kings zealously kept its appointments in their own hands. Its task was to root out heresy – but there was no heresy to speak of in Spain. In reality it acted against converts from Judaism to Christianity who were suspected of retaining Jewish practice or of "judaising" – persuading others to follow Jewish ways.

Tomás de Torquemada (1420-1498), who was grand inquisitor from 1483 until his death, urged the disastrous step of expelling all Jews who would not convert. Perhaps 180,000 left and 50,000 converted. This just made the suspicions of the Inquisition worse – were they secretly still practising Jews? It was hard to stop the Inquisition. Pope Sixtus IV himself wrote to Ferdinand in alarm that "the Inquisition has been moved not by zeal for faith but by lust for wealth, and that many true and faithful Christians have without any legitimate proof been imprisoned, tortured and condemned as heretics". But the king was unwilling to rein in the inquisitors.

The Inquisition had no financing beyond the property forfeited by those found guilty. This was an obvious temptation for convictions to be sought with insufficient grounds. The use of torture on suspects was normal under law in most parts of Europe, but the use of anonymous denunciations was an innovation. Both elements attracted protest. Jews were not subject to the authority of the Inquisition, which could prosecute only baptised Christians. But any family of a *converso*, a convert from judaism, came under suspicion. After Torquemada's time there was an even fiercer and really corrupt Inquisitor of Córdoba, Diego Lucero. In 1500 he burnt 130 on charges of covert judaism at a swoop. In 1506 he took action against the saintly old Archbishop of Granada, Hernando Talavera, who had been Isabella's own confessor. Lucero had gone too far and Cardinal Ximenes convoked an assembly that had him sacked.

Moorish emirate of half a million people, but in 1482 the Pope had granted a bull designating the war against Granada a "crusade". When the city finally fell on January 2 1492, Ferdinand, to whom Isabella had left the fighting, sent a message to Rome: "After so much travail, expense, death and bloodshed this kingdom of Granada, which for 780 years was occupied by infidels, has been won to the glory of God, the exaltation of our Holy Catholic Faith and the honour of the Apostolic See".

The policy to the vanquished was at first lenient. Archbishop Hernando Talavera of Granada was in favour of leading the conquered Moors to Christianity by example and charity. But the Archbishop of Toledo pressed a more aggressive line. Under him, forced conversions precipitated in January 1500 a revolt by the Muslims of the mountainous Alpujarras region of Andalusia. This in turn brought an even harsher round of forced conversions which ended with an ultimatum in 1502 to all Muslims in Castile to submit to baptism or be exiled. The man who had pressed this unyielding policy, Francisco Ximenes de Cisneros (1436-1517) is full of contradictions to modern eyes. At the age of 73, while Archbishop of Toledo, he led in person an army of 15,000 into Africa and captured Oran. He had become Isabella's confessor, giving her spiritual advice, in 1492.

He steeled her resolve to expel the Jews. But he was to champion the rights of the Indians of America against the mistreatment of the *conquistadores*. (It was almost absent-mindedly that on April 17 1492, after years of delay, Isabella had approved the voyage of discovery by Columbus which had such stupendous consequences.)

And in Church matters Ximenes welcomed the reforming ideas of Erasmus (*see page 127*) and sponsored the printing of devotional works of Savonarola (who was hanged on charges of heresy, *see page 124*). He was also responsible for the renowned Complutensian Polyglot edition of the Bible in four ancient languages.

Ximenes had been trained in a hard school himself. Having been guaranteed by the Pope a benefice in the Archdiocese of Toledo, he was thrown into prison in 1473 by the same Alfonso Carillo who was to send his army against Isabella. After six years in jail, Ximenes was freed and in 1482 appointed vicar general of the diocese of Sigüenza. But two years later, now middle-aged and prospering, he threw it all up to become a humble Franciscan friar.

Having been plucked from his friary after eight years and rising to new eminence, he enforced a thoroughgoing reform of the Franciscan order. By 1507 he was grand inquisitor and a cardinal. Just before his death in 1517 he ensured the succession of Charles V to the throne. In his life he summed up the incongruous piety and cruelty of Spain at the Renaissance.

Ferdinand II of Aragon and Isabella of Castille, from about 1482, 10 years before these "Catholic Kings" drove the Muslims from Spain

morti sopra
detto Padre il di
23 maggi

Savonarola betrayed

At the end of the 15th century Florence was transformed by the fiery campaign of the friar Girolamo Savonarola. His enemies, led by the Pope, saw him hanged in public

Girolamo Savonarola was executed for his crimes against the Church in 1498; but today, 500 years later, there is a real chance that he may be declared a saint. His story is as strange as Joan of Arc's. Savonarola (1452-98) had joined the Dominicans, the Order of Preachers, in 1475. During a series of Lent sermons in 1485 and 1486 he outlined his vision of a Church purified of its corruption.

From 1490 he settled in Florence, at first with the support of its ruler, Lorenzo de Medici, who was to become an enemy whose sins Savonarola denounced from the pulpit. (The story that he denied Lorenzo absolution on his deathbed, though, has been disproved by documentary evidence.) Savonarola turned the city upside down. Florence was famed for its luxury, and he made it a

pretations of the biblical doom-sayings of Amos and Ezekiel.

He won enemies by denouncing the sins of the Pope and by advocating the convocation of a Universal Council of bishops to set the Church to rights. The Pope whom he denounced was Alexander VI, a Borgia Pope who led a colourfully scandalous life, keeping mistresses openly. Of Savonarola he was reputed to have announced: "He might be as saintly as John the Baptist, but he must die."

For Savonarola the Pope's first task was to set his own house in order. It was not just a matter of putting away his mistress and eschewing simony. "The temporal power of the Pope is at the bottom of all the evils and abuses which have slipped into the Church," he insisted. For Rome, as for Florence, he prophesied destruction as the alternative to repentance.

In the meantime, Savonarola was the darling of the people of Florence. He must have been an entrancing preacher; 15,000 a time crowded to him. They wept and changed their lives. Under a new, stricter rule the friary of which in 1491 he was made prior, San Marco (its walls painted with the beautiful frescoes of Fra Angelico), saw its numbers rise from 50 to 280, with the new recruits being the brightest and best of society.

Savonarola was no obscurantist. He borrowed money to buy a library belonging to the Medicis for San Marco, and he encouraged the study of oriental languages. He

'The temporal power of the Pope is at the bottom of all the evils and abuses which have slipped into the Church'

was a hero of such men as the intellectual firebrand, Pico della Mirandola (1463-94).

In 1495 Pope Alexander, hoping to have Savonarola arrested, ordered him to go to Bologna under pain of excommunication. He refused, and pointed out that the Pope's letter was legally flawed. On October 16 the Pope barred him from public preaching. Again Savonarola refused to comply, on legal grounds.

At the carnival celebrations before Lent in 1497 the propertied classes brought along indecent pictures, frivolous books, fripperies and even wigs to be burned in the city square in a "bonfire of the vanities". Botticelli destroyed some of his earlier mythological paintings; and to this period is attributed a new style exemplified by his *Mystic Nativity*, now in the National Gallery in London.

But a hostile element had become dominant in the city government and it turned against Savonarola, securing a bull of excommunication against him (again legally flawed, he insisted). For one last Lent, in 1498, he preached on the book of Exodus. Later that spring the city arrested him and examined him under torture. This was normal in criminal proceedings, but it was none the better for that. He was racked and hung up by his arms till they became almost useless. Once, in his agony, he shouted that he was abandoned by Christ. He immediately repented, and now saw himself as a repentant Peter.

A commission came from Rome with their minds made up and turned him over for punishment by the secular authorities. So he and two fellow friars were condemned to be hanged. Beneath the gallows in the main city square straw and wood were piled up ready to consume the corpses. Strangely, the Pope sent a document absolving Savonarola, which he accepted at the foot of the scaffold. Though the hangmen let his enemies mock, buffet and scratch him, Savonarola went to his death with dignity.

Shortly afterwards there was a popular reaction against his persecution. Men of unimpeachable orthodoxy and holiness, such as the saint Philip Neri, venerated him. On the anniversary of his martyrdom, great piles of flowers were left in the Piazza, until it was forbidden by Napoleon.

Left: Savonarola by Fra Bartolomeo (1472-1517). He was executed in 1498 after being tortured in Florence. This contemporary Italian painting (*above*) shows Savonarola and two fellow friars at the various stages of their formal sentencing, hanging and burning

theocracy patrolled by religious police who confiscated playing cards on Sundays and put prostitutes out of business. After the overthrow of the Medici and the invasion of Charles VIII of France in 1494, Savonarola ruled through a quasi-democratic Signoria or city council. He saw the King of France, also an enemy of the Pope, as the instrument of divine chastisement.

Savonarola thought that by making the Law of Christ the law of the land he was ushering in the reign of Christ on earth and the kingdom of the Holy Spirit. Savonarola's extravagant language was fired by his inter-

CHAPTER FIVE

AD 1500-1800

New worship, new worlds

The Protestant Reformation took place when Europe was being turned upside down by other forces. The year 1500 can be taken as the beginning of the Modern world. The abandonment of medieval learning, the spread of cheap printed books, the development of experimental sciences and the planting of colonial empires – all these coincided with a religious Reformation of such determination that Christendom was split into armed camps.

In each country the religious system was decided largely by the convictions or policy of the monarch. Thus in Spain the stony Catholicism of the king tolerated no dissent. In England, religious practice seesawed under Henry VIII, Mary and Elizabeth; only at the end of the 17th century was the turmoil resolved.

Giant figures strode through this period: Luther, who never intended to be a party leader; Calvin, who moulded a theocracy; Knox, who defied queens in pursuit of reform in Scotland. Others were so fired that they refused to be deterred by persecution: George Fox, who founded the Quakers; Teresa of Avila, who put the life of prayer before all else; John Wesley, who sowed conviction among thousands of working folk.

With the discovery of the New World, riches and power were grasped through ruthless conquest. Europe confronted a bewildering variety of cultures; Christendom was no longer limited to Europe.

Erasmus of Rotterdam by Quentin Metsys (1466-1530). He spent some time in England preparing his edition of the New Testament in Greek

Reform or revolt

There was nothing inevitable about the form the Reformation took in the early 16th century. In Europe Luther set it off. In England it began with Henry VIII's money and marriage problems. Before either, Erasmus made scholarly and peaceful proposals to which few listened

Erasmus is one of those figures about whom it is tempting to play the historical game: What if...? What if his ideas had eagerly been embraced, the Church cleansed and re-educated? Would Luther have been deprived of his grounds for protest? Would the Church have been saved from the almost fatal division into Protestant and Catholic that remains a scandal to the present day?

Erasmus wanted reform of worldly popes and ignorant monks. He wanted a revival of biblical studies according to the principles of the early Fathers of the Church. But he was cut out to be a party leader even less than Luther.

Erasmus, who had no real surname, was born in Rotterdam, probably in 1466, an illegitimate child, as he was painfully reminded during his upbringing by guardians. He became, largely by solitary effort, the greatest scholar of his time. He had been schooled by an association of clergymen called the Brethren of the Common Life. Though he looked back with loathing on those of his schoolmasters who were violent, he developed a style of Christianity espoused by the Brethren and made familiar to generations of British readers from translations of *The Imitation of Christ*. This was an example of the *devotio moderna*, the new devotion that regarded Jesus Christ as friend and brother as well as God.

Like Luther, Erasmus joined an Augustinian monastery but came to hate his way of life there. It perhaps accentuated a neurotic side to him. He was professed as a monk in 1488 but escaped the cloister in 1493 by becoming secretary to the Bishop of Cambrai. Thereafter he led a wandering life. It was not until 1517, aged 50, that he finally secured a dispensation from his monastic vows. He remained a priest and was not at liberty to marry even if he had wanted.

We see Erasmus's best side in his friendship with fellow scholars, though of his 12 volumes of letters, in Latin, too many are flattering, and most are written in a style intentionally artificial. His *Moriae Encomium* (In Praise of Folly), with a play on his friend Thomas More's surname, was received as an entertaining work, though hardly anybody reads it now. Books such as his *Colloquies* sold ▶

Christian humanism

Erasmus was a humanist in the best sense: learned, unsuperstitious, urbane, unheated. In his rejection of scholasticism, the conventional university theology of the Middle Ages, he was not unusual. Everybody was rejecting it, both Thomas More, the foe of heretics, and Luther, the enemy of papal authority. The kind of scholasticism against which both Luther and Erasmus turned was not the penetrating methodology of theologians such as Thomas Aquinas. It was the textbook pettifogging of the late medieval followers of William of Ockham.

One of the enthusiasms of the Christian humanists was Greek, as a medium of classical literature, and as a way of better understanding the Bible. It was because he found a group of scholars eager to master ancient learning that Erasmus spent periods in England (1499-1500, 1505-6 and 1509-14). Both John Colet, the founder of St Paul's School, and John Fisher, Bishop of Rochester and an eminent theologian, learnt Greek in middle age, partly through the encouragement of Erasmus. Erasmus also befriended and corresponded with Thomas More, the Chancellor of England, who, possibly at the instigation of Henry VIII, wrote to the University of Oxford urging it to abandon resistance to the study of Greek.

Greek does not make saints. More and Fisher ended as martyrs; Erasmus avoided having to pay such a price for his beliefs.

well, and eased his chronic lack of money. Luther, in an aside, once remarked that "to this barefaced scoundrel, God is merely funny". That is unfair, but Erasmus did value wit. When Luther threatened to denounce him in print, he replied that he welcomed the prospect, for it would at least clear him from the suspicions of one portion of his critics.

Erasmus had long resisted writing against Luther. He pointed out that he had devoted his life to the text of the Greek Bible (*see below*) and had no time also to master debates about grace and predestination. Moreover his instincts were pacific. He saw the importance of a shared belief in the Apostles' Creed and was horrified by violent disputes about theological opinion.

But at last, in 1524, he took on Luther in a book, *De Libero Arbitrio*, on free will. It was praised by both the Pope and Henry VIII, and brought a reply from Luther, *De Servo Arbitrio*, on the bondage of the will, in which he thanks Erasmus for not having "wearied me with such peripheral topics as the papacy, purgatory, indulgences and so on". Erasmus had put his finger on it: "The elect, who fear God, Luther says, will be reformed by the Holy Spirit; the rest will perish unreformed." But Erasmus could not abide such a vision of a terrible God.

"We have had enough of quarrels," Erasmus wrote in 1533, three years before his death. "Perhaps sheer weariness may bring us together in concord, to dwell in the house of the Lord as friends."

Back to a basic text

The most important work of Erasmus was to establish a good text of the New Testament in Greek. He did this by looking for the "best manuscripts" during a stay in Cambridge, using them to print a text he thought nearest the original and putting a Latin translation next to it. This Latin version differed in many points from the commonly used Vulgate, the translation into Latin made by St Jerome (*see page 40*).

Erasmus's printed version came out in 1517. It contained many misprints, for, out of lack of patience or resources, he had hurried it through the press. The Greek text of the *Complutensian Polyglot*, sponsored by the Spaniard, Cardinal Ximenes (*see page 122*) was better. But the *Polyglot* was limited to 600 copies and was very expensive. Erasmus's edition was cheaper and was often reprinted. Scholars with more refined techniques built on his work.

In justifying his search for a better text (since there was resistance from many who regarded the Vulgate as a version inspired in itself) Erasmus appealed to the Fathers of the Church, particularly Jerome, with whom he had much in common.

DETAIL OF PORTRAIT OF MARTIN LUTHER, 1529, BY LUCAS CRANACH / BRIDGEMAN ART LIBRARY

Luther's very German protest

From 1517 onwards Luther's great idea about salvation took on a life of its own thanks to the ambitions of German princes

When in 1517 Martin Luther nailed his 95 Theses against indulgences to the door of the church in Wittenberg, he did not intend to declare war on the Catholic Church. The theses were propositions for university debate, and, Luther believed, consistent with the Bible and Augustine. He was surprised and frightened by the explosion that followed.

Luther was born in 1483 in Eisleben in Saxony, the son of a miner prosperous enough to pay for his son's education. But the boy grew up tortured by his own unworthiness, too terrified to look at carvings of Christ in Judgment in his local church. One day, returning to Erfurt University,

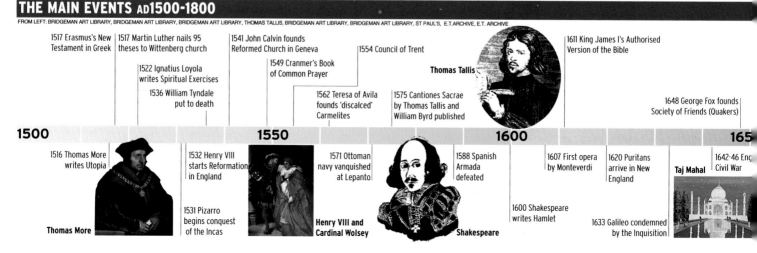

1517 Erasmus's New Testament in Greek
1517 Martin Luther nails 95 theses to Wittenberg church
1522 Ignatius Loyola writes Spiritual Exercises
1536 William Tyndale put to death
1541 John Calvin founds Reformed Church in Geneva
1549 Cranmer's Book of Common Prayer
1554 Council of Trent
1562 Teresa of Avila founds 'discalced' Carmelites
Thomas Tallis
1575 Cantiones Sacrae by Thomas Tallis and William Byrd published
1611 King James I's Authorised Version of the Bible
1648 George Fox founds Society of Friends (Quakers)

1500 **1550** **1600** **165**

1516 Thomas More writes Utopia
1532 Henry VIII starts Reformation in England
1531 Pizarro begins conquest of the Incas
1571 Ottoman navy vanquished at Lepanto
Henry VIII and Cardinal Wolsey
1588 Spanish Armada defeated
Shakespeare
1600 Shakespeare writes Hamlet
1607 First opera by Monteverdi
1620 Puritans arrive in New England
1633 Galileo condemned by the Inquisition
Taj Mahal
1642-46 Eng Civil War

Thomas More

he was knocked to the ground by a bolt of lightning and he shouted, "Help, St Anne, and I'll become a monk." In 1505 he entered the Augustinian monastery at Erfurt where his scrupulous afflictions of the soul continued.

Luther embarked on a career as professor of biblical studies at the University of Wittenberg founded in 1503 by the Elector of Saxony, Frederick the Wise. Here Luther became obsessed with a passage in Paul's Epistle to the Romans (1:17): "The just shall live by faith." He came to believe that righteousness before God is not to be had by achievement, but is a gift accepted by faith.

This delivered Luther from his "monster of uncertainty". It also undermined the theological basis for the indulgences

He became obsessed with the passage: 'The just shall live by faith'

being sold in the area by a Dominican friar, John Tetzel, whose approach was summed up by the jingle: "As soon as the coin into the box rings, a soul from purgatory to heaven springs."

When Luther's theses attacking Tetzel's activities arrived in Rome, Pope Leo X was inclined to dismiss Luther. But the Pope's Dominican advisers accused Luther of heresy. It was simply a matter of time before he was excommunicated. But Luther had time on his side. The Habsburg Emperor Maximilian was dying, and the Pope was seeking a candidate to challenge Maximilian's heir Charles V at the imperial elections. Because Luther's patron Frederick the Wise was a prime candidate, the Pope hesitated to proceed against Frederick's prize professor.

Thus Luther was not called to account until 1521, shortly after his excommunication, when he appeared (under a safe conduct) before the new Emperor Charles V at the Diet at Worms. There he famously refused to recant with the words "*Hier stehe ich…*". ("Here I stand. I can do no other.") By then religious protest had turned into political revolt, led or harnessed by secular princes of the Empire.

Meanwhile Frederick spirited Luther away to Wartburg Castle for a year. Within five years of the Diet of Worms, he had produced not only a reformed Bible, but a liturgy and hymn book for his followers. Returning to Wittenberg he found them engaged in setting rules for what was becoming a new Church. These included the ending of clerical celibacy. In 1523, Luther met a former nun, Katherine von Bora. She had refused a number of suitors, but agreed Luther would do.

· After his marriage in 1525, Luther took the Augustinian monastery in Wittenberg as married quarters. There, Katherine bore him six children, bossed him mercilessly and, he said, brewed the best beer in town.

Luther died in 1546 and was buried in the church of All Saints in Wittenberg.

Strangers among sinners

John Calvin constructed a whole system of belief and social obligations for a new society of hardline Protestantism adopted by the city of Geneva. By the time of his death in 1564 Calvinism was spread throughout Europe

John Calvin (1509-64) was the most influential of the second-generation reformers. By his interpretation of the doctrine of predestination he inspired his followers to think of themselves as an embattled minority – "strangers among sinners" – a status they manifested by obtrusive abstention from all frivolities.

John Calvin was born in Noyon, France, the son of a Church administrator. He trained as a Church lawyer and was converted to the new thinking after hearing a homily on the sovereignty of the scriptures by the Rector of the Sorbonne, Nicholas Cop. Fearing repression if he made his beliefs public, Calvin fled to Basle, where in 1535 he published his influential *Institution de la Religion Chrétienne*.

In 1536, he was persuaded to take control of the Church in Geneva, which had just broken free of the Catholic House of Savoy. However his insistence on discipline and doctrinal uniformity antagonised Genevan politicians and Calvin was expelled. He spent the next three years in Strasbourg, where he married.

Recall to Geneva
The threat of a resurgence of Catholicism in Geneva led the town's Protestant magistrates to implore Calvin to return. At first he protested he would rather "die a hundred times", but eventually he yielded and in 1541 became pastor of the Cathedral of St Peter, with a decent salary, a fine

Born in France, Calvin made his reputation in Geneva: this 17th-century portrait is from the Swiss school

house and 250 gallons of wine a year. He began his first sermon with the chapter and verse of the Bible where he had left off three years earlier.

Calvin's creation of Geneva as a model of thoroughgoing Protestantism was remarkable because he worked mainly by moral persuasion. He was also able to use his legal training to write the ecclesiastical and political constitution for the new city state.

Calvinism held a particular appeal to the rising urban bourgeoisie. By the time of his death in 1564, Calvinist Protestantism had spread widely from Scotland in the West (where it became the established religion in 1560) and into Hungary and Bohemia in the East.

AUROS-GIRAUDON / THE BRIDGEMAN LIBRARY

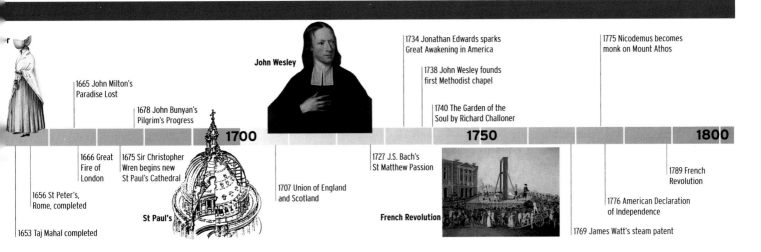

1665 John Milton's Paradise Lost

1678 John Bunyan's Pilgrim's Progress

John Wesley

1734 Jonathan Edwards sparks Great Awakening in America

1738 John Wesley founds first Methodist chapel

1740 The Garden of the Soul by Richard Challoner

1775 Nicodemus becomes monk on Mount Athos

1700

1750

1800

1666 Great Fire of London

1675 Sir Christopher Wren begins new St Paul's Cathedral

1656 St Peter's, Rome, completed

1653 Taj Mahal completed

St Paul's

1707 Union of England and Scotland

1727 J.S. Bach's St Matthew Passion

French Revolution

1789 French Revolution

1776 American Declaration of Independence

1769 James Watt's steam patent

A new kind of worship

In England the introduction of services in the vernacular in 1549 set off a rebellion. But the changes did not go far enough for others

During the first half of the 16th century the desire for change in the Church's forms of worship came to be widely felt in several parts of Western Europe. In Rome itself Cardinal Quiñones produced in 1543, at the request of Pope Clement VII, a revised version of the Breviary (the concise version of the liturgy of the hours recited by priests). His concern was to facilitate the better use in worship of the Bible.

In England the work of revision was masterminded by the Archbishop of Canterbury, Thomas Cranmer (*see page 132*), a liturgical genius and a master of the English language. Initially influenced by Quiñones, Cranmer based the First Book of Common Prayer of 1549 largely on the medieval services, particularly as used in the diocese of Salisbury.

Destruction of the altars

Cranmer, who was assisted by a committee of bishops, had however some other objectives – the services were to be in English and provide for greater participation by the laity; the five books in use were to be reduced to a single volume, and the law was to be employed to enforce uniformity of worship. Some 12 months before its publication an edict ordered the abolition of "all the images remaining in any church or chapel". None of this encouraged the happy acceptance of the new liturgy, and on Whitsunday 1549 people in Cornwall and Devon rose in rebellion. The rising spread to the Midlands and two months passed before order was fully restored, the ringleaders having been condemned to death. In London the Dean of St Paul's brought the new book into use, but the Bishop, Nicholas Ridley, who had actually been involved in its compilation, refused to use it.

In the following year the Bishop ordered the destruction of all stone and ornamented altars in London diocese and this quickly became policy throughout the country. Plain tables were substituted. Meanwhile, the Duke of Northumberland, Lord Protector during the reign of the youthful King Edward VI, noted that few statues had been removed from the parishes. Since the government also needed "a mass of money", officials were sent to plunder Communion plate, ornaments, statues, organs and bells and to ransack treasuries. The plate was sent to the Tower of London to be melted down.

The wind of theological change was blowing more fiercely from the Continent. Martin Bucer, a leading Reformer in Strasbourg, had become Professor of Divinity at Cambridge, and Peter Martyr, an Italian Reformer, was installed at Oxford. They and their followers were highly critical of the new Prayer Book because it expressed a great deal of traditional Catholic belief – in particular, that in the Eucharist Christ is present sacramentally in the consecrated bread and wine; they believed that he was present only in the heart of the believer.

The Second Prayer Book, 1552, moved firmly in the Reformed direction. Holy Communion was to be celebrated only on Sundays and Holy Days, and clergy were to wear only simple robes. But within a year the young king was dead and his successor, Queen Mary, repealed the Acts of Uniformity.

The Communion table, replacing the old stone altars on which Mass was offered, is labelled in this woodcut from Foxe's *Book of Martyrs*

Bare ruined choirs

The romantic ruins of monasteries, the 'bare ruined choirs' of Shakespeare's sonnet, are a relic of Henry VIII's ruthless grab for easy money

The dissolution of England's 852 monasteries, nunneries and friaries between 1536 and 1540 had more to do with money than with religion. Henry VIII was not opposed to religious communities as such, but his revenues had fallen well below national needs. The seizure of the monastic property was for him an easier option than the imposition of higher general taxation. The monasteries were vulnerable because some had become very wealthy and moved away from their founders' intentions.

In response there was a chain of uprisings, known as the Pilgrimage of Grace, in Lincolnshire and the North, but these were put down and 200 of the rebels were hanged.

The Suppression of Religious Houses Act of 1536 had involved 250 smaller monasteries and was presented as rationalisation, but this was quickly followed by the dissolution of all friaries and the dismantling of monastic shrines. An Act to dissolve the rest came in 1539 and was implemented with sometimes brutal efficiency by the king's Vicar General – Thomas Cromwell.

The abbots of Glastonbury, Colchester and Reading were hanged, but for the most part monks submitted meekly. Apart from the friars, they were given modest pensions and many later became parish priests. Eight monastery churches were cathedrals and these continued. Churches serving parishes stayed in operation.

The proceeds of the dissolution were used to found six new bishoprics, grammar schools in cathedral cities, Christ Church at Oxford, Trinity College at Cambridge and 12 professorships between the two universities. By far the greater part of the money was spent on coastal defences and other government projects. Much of the monastic land was sold to nobles and gentry at knock-down prices. The great abbey at Bury St Edmunds (*see page 70*) was sold for £413; it had been giving £400 a year away to the poor. Thus in four years, institutions that for 1,000 years had contributed to England's spiritual life and culture were completely destroyed.

St Swithun swept away

Richard Pollard, Thomas Wriothesley and John Williams write to Thomas Cromwell, September 21 1538:
"Pleaseth your lordship to be advertised that this Saturday, in the morning, about three of the clock, we made an end of the shrine [*of St Swithun*] here in Winchester. There was in it no piece of gold, nor any ring, or true stone, but all great counterfeits. Nevertheless we think the silver alone thereof will amount to two thousand marks… We intend to sweep away all the rotten bones that be called relics."

Left: the ruins of Castle Acre priory, Swaffham, Norfolk, one of the 852 religious houses in England dissolved by Henry VIII

SKYSCAN

The rise and fall of Thomas Cranmer

Cranmer was made Archbishop of Canterbury by Henry VIII, from whom he had to keep his marriage and his thoroughgoing Protestant aims secret. After drawing up the Book of Common Prayer he died a martyr under the Catholic Queen Mary

Henry VIII was fortunate to have an Archbishop of Canterbury who believed that his subservience to the king was in accordance with the will of God. Although there is much in the life of Thomas Cranmer which the 20th-century mind is bound to deplore, he provided the Church of England with the foundations of a reformed religion and endowed it with a Book of Common Prayer, a rich treasury of Christian worship and devotion. His death at the stake during the reign of Queen Mary secured him a place among those who have died for their beliefs and confirmed his key role in the English Reformation.

Born in the Nottinghamshire village of Aslacton in 1489, Cranmer was given a traditional Catholic upbringing and went to Jesus College, Cambridge, where he seemed destined for the life of a scholar. Early marriage ended tragically when after a year his wife, Joan, died in childbirth. But he continued his academic work and in 1520 was ordained priest.

At this time he was loyal to the Pope and critical of the Continental Reformers. Cardinal Wolsey recruited him to the diplomatic service. There was plenty of work for diplomats, since the king was looking for support in Europe for a petition to the Pope seeking the annulment of his marriage to Catherine of Aragon, the widow of his elder brother Prince Arthur. Catherine had failed to provide Henry with a male heir and he, having fallen in love with Anne Boleyn, hoped that the Pope might declare invalid an earlier dispensation that had allowed him to marry Catherine, thus annulling their marriage and leaving him free to remarry.

Cranmer supported this on biblical grounds, but the arguments of theologians and the bargaining of diplomats failed to move the Pope, and the young English scholar had to be content with a different success. While serving as ambassador at the Court of the Holy Roman Emperor, Cranmer won the heart of Margarete Osiander, the niece of a German Protestant theologian, and secretly married her.

The king, quite unaware of this, recalled him to England in 1533 to become Archbishop of Canterbury. Although he was reluctant to accept he eventually gave in, and the king secured from the Pope the authorisation necessary for his consecration as Primate of All England. From this point onwards Cranmer led Henry's campaign for throwing off the Pope's supremacy over the Church in England. He genuinely believed that the interests of the Church would be best served by acknowledging the authority of a "godly Prince", to whom the Pope had given the title Defender of the Faith, in preference to that of an alien pontiff whose dubious theological opinions were accompanied by heavy financial demands on the English parishes.

Cranmer promptly annulled the king's first marriage and pronounced his union with Anne Boleyn to be lawful. Later, when Anne also failed to produce a male heir, he annulled this marriage too, and for no valid reason. Then, having connived in and officiated at Henry's marriage to Anne of Cleves, he approved a divorce.

But although the king's marital problems consumed much of his time, Cranmer was also busy about theological questions and church reform. In 1536 he got the Convocation of Canterbury to adopt Ten Articles of Faith which were the first statements of doctrine to be issued by the Church of England during the Reformation period. These were of a fairly conservative character and were followed in 1539 by another Six Articles, issued by command of the king and designed to prevent the spread of Protestant beliefs and practices. Since one of the Articles reaffirmed clerical celibacy, Cranmer felt obliged to send his wife and daughter (who had been kept in seclusion) to Germany.

He was however coming increasingly under the influence of European Protestant theology and he encouraged the translation of the Bible into English. In 1544 he produced the first Litany in English and, following the death of King Henry in 1547, he secured permission for the clergy to marry, celebrating this by bringing his own family back from Germany and adding a son to its number.

He also embarked on a revision of the Church's worship, which led to the Book of Common Prayer in 1549, with a revised version completed in 1552. But the accession of Catholic Mary Tudor in the following year brought this, and much else, to a sudden halt. Cranmer, who had supported Lady Jane Grey's claim to the throne, was arrested, accused of high treason and sentenced to death.

The queen granted a reprieve, but only in order that he might be charged with heresy. Six formal recantations made under the threat of death were not however sufficient to save him, and in a final sermon, shortly before going to the stake, he withdrew these recantations. As he approached the fire he put his hand into the flames and declared: "Forasmuch as my hand offended, writing contrary to my heart, my hand shall first be punished."

Had Cranmer's first wife not died in childbirth, leaving him free to become a priest, the course of the English Reformation would have been different.

> 'Forasmuch as my hand offended, writing contrary to my heart,' he said, thrusting it into the flames, 'my hand shall first be punished'

Portrait of Thomas Cranmer, 1546, by Gerlach Flicke. A learned liturgist who left England sublime services, Cranmer found the question of clerical celibacy more difficult

© NATIONAL GALLERY, LONDON

The Bible in English

The Gospell off Sancte Jhon.

The fyrst Chapter.

IN the begynnynge was that worde/ãd that worde was with god: and god was thatt worde. The same was in the begynnynge wyth god. All thyngf were made by it/ and with out it/ was made noo thige/that made was. In it was lyfe/ And lyfe was the light of mē/ And the light shyïnethi darcknes/ãd darcknes cópzehēded it not.

The Authorised Version of the Bible made under James I relied heavily on previous translations made periodically in the 16th century, principally on the version published by William Tyndale in 1526 (*above*)

One day in 1607, 47 leading scholars of the Church of England gathered in the Jerusalem Chamber at Westminster Abbey to plan the production of an accurate translation of the Bible. Urged on by King James I, who had authorised the project at a conference held at Hampton Court in 1604, they completed their task in two years and nine months. Two of their number saw it through the printing press and in 1611 it was published as the Authorised Version of the Bible – a landmark in the history of English-speaking Christianity and also of the English language.

The secret of the speed with which this translation was accomplished is quite simple: the scholars made extensive use of some other English translations which had appeared during the previous century. Chief among these was the translation of the New Testament published by William Tyndale in 1526. This had been banned at the time, but no less than 90 per cent of the Authorised Version of the New Testament is the work of Tyndale, including such memorable phrases as "Ye are the salt of the earth" and "The spirit is willing but the flesh is weak". And, although imprisonment and finally martyrdom gave him time to translate only 14 of the 39 books of the Old Testament, these too were taken into the Authorised Version with only minor corrections.

Unlike John Wyclif, the 14th-century translator (*see page 114*), Tyndale went behind the Latin text of the Bible to the original Hebrew and Greek. He was himself a good scholar, educated at Oxford and Cambridge, but initially he could find employment only as tutor to the children of a wealthy Gloucestershire family. Over dinner he was apt to raise controversial theological issues and in the course of a dispute with a scholar guest he declared, in exasperation: "I defy the Pope and all his laws; if God spare my life, ere many years I will cause a boy that driveth a plough shall know more of the Scripture than thou dost."

There was no possibility of his translating the Scriptures safely in England, so he went to Germany in 1524 and quickly completed the New Testament. By now the production of printed books was flourishing, and by March 1526 copies of Tyndale's work started to reach London. In October of that year the Bishop of London ordered all copies to be seized and burned at St Paul's Cross, but these were soon replaced and copies continued to circulate.

The rest of Tyndale's life was spent as an outlaw and fugitive in Germany and the Low Countries. In 1535, having been betrayed to the authorities, he was imprisoned for 16 months near Brussels. On October 6 1536 he was, on the orders of the Holy Roman Emperor, first strangled and then burned at the stake.

Bible translation had by this time come to be regarded as subversive, for although the Gospels had been translated in Anglo-Saxon times, new versions in English enabled individuals who might have no training in interpretation to pursue their private opinions about the meaning of the Christian faith, which might well be heretical. Wyclif's own heretical teachings on other matters had merely seemed to confirm such suspicions. And heresy was always a threat to the stability of a society in which religion and the authority of the king were inextricably intertwined.

Another refugee and an assistant to Tyndale was Myles Coverdale (1488-1568), who produced in 1535 the first complete Bible in English. This was translated from German and Latin, and made extensive use of Tyndale's version. Two years later, John Rogers, who had also been an associate of Tyndale and used the pen-name Thomas Matthews, published his version, based substantially on that of Tyndale. Coverdale then revised this, and it appeared in 1539 as The Great Bible – a copy of which was, by King Henry VIII's command, set up in every parish church for public and private reading.

This arrangement was short-lived, for in 1543 Parliament decreed it to be illegal to read or expound the Bible publicly, and there were more bonfires at St Paul's Cross. But in 1549 the new Book of Common Prayer included Coverdale's version of the Psalms as given in The Great Bible, and it prescribed Bible readings that would enable the whole of Holy Scripture to be covered in one year. Yet another English version appeared in 1560. This had been excellently translated in Geneva and exposed the deficiencies of The Great Bible. It became very popular in England, though it was never officially authorised. The Bishops' Bible, produced by a committee of bishops in 1568, was deemed not to be as good as the Geneva Bible but it was used in parish churches and cathedrals until replaced by King James I's Authorised Version in 1611.

James himself was convinced that if a new translation was to be commissioned, it should contain no marginal notes, for he had noticed that "in the Genevan translation some notes are partial, untrue, seditious and savouring of traitorous conceits". He got his way, and the Authorised Version was published unadorned save by a dedication to "the Most High and Mighty" king and a translators' preface.

> **Tyndale's version included such well known phrases as: 'The spirit is willing but the flesh is weak'**

Knox blasts a stern trumpet

John Knox was utterly convinced by a radical kind of Calvinism that would change the face of Scottish worship and government. First he had to undergo imprisonment and exile

In Scotland the Reformation embraced a radical Protestantism of the Calvinist sort, and became linked with nationalism. This was to be strongly challenged under the Stuart kings, who ruled both England and Scotland, but eventually a church order without bishops and based on an austere biblical theology was firmly established. Thereafter the General Assembly became the nation's mouthpiece.

John Knox (1513-72) was a disciple of Calvin and an outstanding leader of the Reform movement in Scotland. After spending some time as a prisoner of the French, following their capture of the castle at St Andrews, he was in England as chaplain to King Edward VI. But after the accession of Queen Mary he fled to the Continent and in 1556 became pastor of the English congregation in Geneva – Calvin's city (see page 129).

In 1558 Knox wrote, among many pamphlets, his *First Blast of the Trumpet against the Monstrous Regiment of Women*, in which he explained why rule by women (such as Mary in England and Mary Queen of Scots) was "repugnant to nature and contrary to God". Within a year Elizabeth came to the throne of England. She was not surprisingly annoyed by Knox's views.

"My First Blast," he wrote ruefully, "has blown from me all my friends in England."

His influence in Scotland increased, though. While he was in Geneva he compiled a service book which he took back with him to Scotland and which was authorised for use in 1562 as the Book of Common Order. This contained various suggestions and prayers for worship, but the minister was encouraged to pray "as the spirit of God shall move his harte".

The Westminster Directory,

which replaced it in 1645 and was used also in England during the Commonwealth, was equally flexible and contained mainly general instructions, rather than set forms of worship. It strongly emphasised the use of the Bible and abolished saints' days and any ceremony for the burial of the dead.

But the Scots tired of its stark austerity and by the end of the 18th century it had more or less fallen out of use.

John Knox blasting his trumpet at Mary Queen of Scots, from a contemporary print

The making of the Church of England

Queen Elizabeth had lived through the reigns of a brother who favoured hardline Protestants and a sister who returned the kingdom to obedience to Rome. Elizabeth tried to find a middle way

On the accession of Queen Elizabeth I in 1558 England was in desperate need of religious and political stability. Since the days of Elizabeth's father, King Henry VIII, the nation had been on a religious see-saw. Shortly after her coronation, Elizabeth stopped at Westminster Abbey on her way to open Parliament. During her sister Mary's reign (1553-58) the Abbey had been re-established, after its dissolution under Henry. On this occasion, the Mantuan ambassador left an account of a telling incident. "On arriving at Westminster Abbey, the Abbot, robed pontifically, with all his monks in procession, each of them having a lighted torch in his hand, received her as usual, giving her first of all incense and holy water; and when her Majesty saw the monks who accompanied her with torches, she said, `Away with these torches, for we see very well.'"

It was clear to the monks which way the wind was blowing; ceremonial lights were anathema to Protestants. Within weeks the monks were out of the Abbey for good. Meanwhile Elizabeth sought to restore equilibrium by returning the Church to the position it held immediately before King Henry's death.

In January 1559 Elizabeth's first Parliament approved the Act of Supremacy, which revived her father's legislation against Rome and imposed an oath on all clergy and secular officials to acknowledge the queen as Supreme Governor of both Church and State. At the same time the Act of Uniformity reintroduced the 1552 Book of Common Prayer with a few alterations. These Acts of Parliament constituted what came to be known as the Elizabethan Settlement, and provided the bedrock for a distinctive Anglicanism.

A serious problem arose, however, over the bishops. Cardinal Pole, the Archbishop of Canterbury, died within a few hours of Catholic Queen Mary, and all but one of the remaining bishops refused to take the Supremacy oath. They were deposed and retired to the country or went into exile. Matthew Parker, a distinguished scholar, was chosen to be the new Archbishop and the queen was careful to ensure that he was consecrated by four bishops who were in office during the reigns of either Henry VIII or Edward VI. Continuity was important.

The parish clergy gave little trouble and most of the laity accepted the new order, though there were pockets of resistance in the North, and some, while attending the parish church on Sunday, continued to receive the sacraments from Roman Catholic priests who were in varying degrees in hiding.

The Church of England was seeking to create a middle way between what was described as "the meretricious gaudiness of the church of Rome, and the squalid sluttery of a fanatical conventicle". Thirty-Nine Articles of Religion, to which the clergy were required to subscribe, defined the Church's doctrine and a rather more hardline *Book of Homilies* (sermons) was issued to assist preachers and keep them orthodox. But any hopes of compromise and tolerance were dashed in 1570 when Pope Pius V excommunicated Queen Elizabeth and said that her subjects were no longer bound by any oaths of allegiance to her. Though few of them regarded the papal bull as legally promulgated or in fact compromised their patriotism, from now on Roman Catholics could be regarded by the state as traitors.

At the other extreme, the more radical Protestants tried to persuade Parliament to rescind the 1559 Settlement Acts and impose on the Church a more austere form of worship and a form of government that excluded bishops. The Queen quickly informed Parliament that religious matters were none of their business, but the Protestants continued to protest and the settlement of religious controversy was still a long way off.

This portrait of Elizabeth I at prayer is from Queen Elizabeth's Prayerbook, attributed to John Day, 1569. In this copy, prayers for good government have been put in the first person for her benefit

'It hath in it seeds of eternity'

In Queen Elizabeth's reign Richard Hooker produced the classic defence of Church of England belief

During the great religious controversies of the 16th-century the developing Church of England was assailed by traditionalist Roman Catholics on the one hand, and by radical Protestants, who came to be known as Puritans, on the other.

A common criticism was that the Church by law established was no more than a creation of the State and lacked theological conviction. This last charge was answered, massively, by Richard Hooker, whose book *Of the Laws of Ecclesiastical Polity* became the classic statement of the basis of Anglicanism.

Hooker was born near Exeter in 1554, educated at Corpus Christi College, Oxford, where he became a Fellow, and ordained priest in 1582. From 1585 to 1591 he was Master of the Temple – a lawyers' church – but became weary of the vicious controversy prevailing in London and secured appointment as Rector of Boscombe in Wiltshire. Four years later he moved to Bishopsbourne, near Canterbury, where he died in 1600.

It was in these two country parishes that he wrote, in magnificent English, his great defence of Anglicanism, of which Pope Clement VIII said, "It has in it such seeds of eternity that it will abide till the last fire shall consume all learning." Although the work was concerned primarily with the ordering of the life of the Church, it based its arguments on a broader philosophical theology derived from belief in God as Eternal Reason, who reveals himself to human beings in many ways.

Thus it cannot be claimed, he says, that as the Puritans were wont to claim, only those things found in the Bible are Christian truth. Neither can it be the case, as Roman Catholics claimed, that the pattern of Church life is determined by what was revealed in the past. The Church is an organic, not a static, institution and its form of government will change according to historical circumstances. Rejection of the Pope's claim to universal jurisdiction does not therefore invalidate the authenticity of the Church of England.

Hooker's work was a fairly conservative reaction to the extreme views of the Puritans. It prepared the way for the further development of Anglican theology in the 17th century and also succeeded in rescuing theological debate from the gutter.

English spirituality

After Queen Elizabeth's death a succession of writers, each with a deep spiritual life of his own, constructed a living tradition for the Church of England

After the consolidation of the Elizabethan Settlement, the Church of England in the early 17th century produced a remarkable crop of able theologians who became known collectively as the Caroline Divines because they worked during the reign of Charles I. Although they were in no sense an organised group, they had one thing in common: they were conscious of the Catholic character of the Church of England. While recognising the need for many of the 16th-century reforms, they stressed the continuity of the Church's life and they believed that the renewed emphasis on the Bible exercised by Protestantism needed to be balanced by the tradition of the Church, especially its sacramental life, and by an appeal to reason. Much of their study was devoted to the life and thought of the undivided Church during the earliest centuries of its history.

The most immediately influential among these scholars was William Laud, who was Archbishop of Canterbury from 1633 until his execution for alleged popery in 1645. But in the longer term three others of their number had a greater impact.

Lancelot Andrewes (1555-1626) had a distinguished academic career at Cambridge, where he mastered 15 languages, became Dean of Westminster in 1601, and held the bishoprics, first of Chichester, then of Ely and finally of Winchester. He was famed for his preaching, and his lengthy sermons expressed a commitment to biblical revelation and to traditional Church order. He was a holy man to whom many turned for counsel and his high doctrine of the Eucharist found expression in the adornment of his chapel with altar candles and the use of incense and dignified ceremonial in worship. His book of private prayers, *Preces Privatae*, remains a rich treasury of devotion. A contemporary described him as "Doctor Andrewes in the school, Bishop Andrewes in the pulpit, Saint Andrewes in the closet."

George Herbert (1593-1633) expressed his convictions through his work as a poet and a parish priest. He, too, had a brilliant academic career at Cambridge, where he became the university's Public Orator. Although as a young man he intended to become a priest he was diverted from this for a time when he was elected Member of Parliament for Montgomeryshire.

He supposed this might be a better way of exercising a Christian influence on society, but he was quickly disillusioned with parliamentary life, and, having taken Holy Orders, was Rector of Bemerton, near Salisbury, from

1630 until his death in 1633. The quality of his ministry during that short time became widely known and his insights into the nature of the Christian priesthood, outlined in a short book *The Country Parson*, published after his death, made him the supreme exemplar for many generations of Anglican clergymen who followed him. For Herbert, the Church was the primary sphere for living and exploring the Christian life. Whereas the Puritans encouraged individualism, his Anglicanism was a corporate faith, to be seen most clearly when priest and people came together in their parish church for worship.

He was devoted to the Book of Common Prayer, conducting Morning and Evening Prayer daily, and the Holy Communion weekly, in Bemerton church. He described the pulpit as the preacher's throne and said the priest is "the deputy of Christ for the reducing of Man to the obedience of God". *The Country Parson* consists of brief chapters on the practical aspects of pastoral ministry – The Parson Praying, The Parson's Library, The Parson Comforting, and so on – and the collection of his poetry *The Temple*, which made him a leading English minor poet, express the same kind of practical spirituality. Among his poems now sung as hymns are "King of glory, King of peace, I will love thee", "Teach me, my God and King, in all things thee to see" and "The God of love my Shepherd is." Another, titled "The Call", is reproduced, right.

A little later, Jeremy Taylor (1613-67), another Cam-bridge scholar and high churchman, had a somewhat chequered career. He was a devoted Rector of Uppingham, Chaplain to King Charles I, in prison for a time during the Civil War, in Wales writing books during the Commonwealth, and after the Restoration in 1660 Bishop of Down and Connor. His two devotional books *Holy Living* and *Holy Dying* are classics.

As for Church music, its survival at the Reformation was by no means inevitable. Hardline Protestants were for reducing it to unaccompanied Psalm-singing. But, particularly in cathedrals, the English choral tradition was by great good fortune preserved. There was, though, a new emphasis on the words. Thomas Tallis (1505-85), a bridge between pre- and post-Reformation Church music, took this into account when composing a setting of the first English Litany, which is still widely used. His contemporary John Merbecke (1510-85) wrote settings for some of the services in the new Book of Common Prayer. These were not much used at the time but they were revived in the 19th century and are still sung in services today.

Pre-eminent among post-Reformation composers, however, was William Byrd (1543-1623), a musician of great versatility who had a very large output in Latin and English and was one of the earliest to produce music to accompany the Prayer Book. He was in fact a Catholic sympathiser, wrote Masses sung in the safety of Catholic country houses and narrowly escaped imprisonment for refusing to conform to the Elizabethan Settlement, but his music captured the spirit of developing Anglicanism and his settings for Mattins and Evensong have never been surpassed.

The Children and Gentlemen (wearing surplices and copes) of the Chapel Royal in the funeral procession of Queen Elizabeth, 1603

The Call

Come, my Way, my Truth,
  my Life:
Such a Way as gives us
  breath:
Such a Truth as ends all
  strife:
Such a Life as killeth
  death.

Come, my Light, my
  Feast, my Strength:
Such a Light as shows a
  feast:
Such a Feast as mends in
  length:
Such a Strength as makes
  his guest.

Come, my Joy, my Love,
  my Heart:
Such a Joy as none can
  move:
Such a Love as none can
  part:
Such a Heart as joys in
  love.

— George Herbert

EYEWITNESS

Escape from the Tower of London

Laws in Elizabeth's reign penalised with death the saying of Mass or the return of Roman Catholic priests from abroad. John Gerard (1564-1637) trained for the priesthood abroad and returned to England in 1588. He was arrested in 1594 but in 1597 escaped from the Tower of London. This is his account

I asked John Lillie and Richard Fulwood (he was attending Father Garnet in the Tower at the time) whether they were prepared to take the risk, and, if they were, to come on a certain night to the far side of the moat, opposite the squat tower I described.

The night came. I begged and bribed my warder to let me visit my fellow-prisoner. I walked across. The warder locked the pair of us in the cell, barred the door and went off. But he had also bolted the inside door which gave on to the stairs leading up to the roof, and we had to cut away with a knife the stone holding the socket of the bolt.

At last we climbed up the stairs without a light, for a guard was posted every night in a garden at the foot of the wall, and when we spoke, it was in a faint whisper. We went up on to the tower. The boat came along and it pulled in safely to the bank. The two men got out with the rope. Following my instructions they fastened it to a stake, and listened for the sound of the iron ball we threw down to them. It was found without difficulty and the cord fastened to the end of the rope.

Perilous descent

Now a fresh difficulty arose which we had not foreseen. The distance between the tower at one end and the stake at the other was very great and the rope, instead of sloping down, stretched almost horizontally. It was impossible to slide down with our own weight.

I commended myself to God and Our Lord Jesus, to the Blessed Virgin, my guardian angel, and to Father Southwell who was imprisoned near here until he was taken out to martyrdom. I had gone three or four yards face downwards when my body suddenly swung round with its own weight and I nearly fell. I was still very weak [*from repeated torture*], and with the slack rope and my body hanging underneath I could make practically no progress. At last I worked myself to the middle of the rope, and there I stuck, seeming altogether spent.

With the help of the saints and, I think, by the power of my friends' prayers below, I moved along a little way and then I stuck again. Now I thought I would never be able to get down. But I was determined not to fall into the moat, and, thank God, I got as far as the wall on the far side of the moat. But my feet touched the top of the wall and the rest of my body hung horizontally behind, with my head no higher than my legs. I don't know how I would have got over the wall, if it had not been for John Lillie. Somehow or other, he got up on to the wall, pulled me over and put me safely down on the ground. We stepped into the boat and thanked God who had snatched us from the hands of our persecutors. We also thanked the men who had done so much and undergone such risks for us.

Rome wakes up

A Pope with four illegitimate children was the unlikely sponsor for a council which at last dealt with the abuses of the Roman Catholic Church from within

The man who convoked the Council of Trent to reform the Roman Catholic Church was a good example of the corruptions it faced. Alessandro Farnese (1468-1549) was elected Pope Paul III in 1534. His sister had been Pope Alexander VI's last mistress; he himself had kept a mistress, by whom he had four children. But suddenly in 1513 he had ended his liaison and by 1520, though still given to jolly parties and extravagant architecture, was allied with the party of reform.

Pope Paul wanted a universal council to include Lutherans, whose reconciliation he sought. For this reason the council was to be in Trent, a city on the German side of the border with Italy, beyond which no Lutheran would care to venture. But negotiations at Regensburg between Rome and representatives of Protestantism foundered in 1541; in any case, since the Pope insisted on presiding, the Lutherans chose to keep away from the council.

In the meantime, a reform commission was at work in Rome charged with producing a report on what was wrong with the Church. It presented its findings to the Pope in 1537, putting blame not so much on heretics as on such corruptions as papal sales of privileges, the pluralistic practices of the higher clergy and the poor level of education of parish priests.

A council finally opened at Trent in 1545, with four cardinals, four archbishops and 21 bishops present. The numbers were to rise to 228 bishops during the latter sessions, spread out over the next 18 years. The evils it had to undo were summarised by Cardinal Reginald Pole, a cousin of King Henry VIII: "It is our ambition, our avarice and our cupidity which have wrought all these evils on the people of God."

The council soon took practical steps such as outlawing clerical pluralism and forbidding clandestine marriages. It also spelled out some of the Church's doctrines. Naturally, justification – the process by which people are fitted for heaven through salvation by Jesus Christ – figured large in these decrees, as a subject central to the protests of Luther and Calvin. Similarly, Trent declared that in the Eucharist bread and wine were really changed into the body and blood of Christ in a manner that could "suitably" be expressed by the word transubstantiation. Trent also had things to say about purgatory and the seven sacraments, not just contradicting Protestant ▶

The Council of Trent inaugural session, December 3 1545, painted in 1711 by Nicolo Dorigat. The meeting confirmed the movement that came to be called the Counter-Reformation

teaching but also dismissing medieval speculation. Calls for a vernacular liturgy, though, were rejected as "inappropriate".

The council failed to reconcile Protestants. But it strengthened Roman Catholics' certainty of their own identity. It ordered the compilation of a fat catechism of doctrine and established seminaries to train priests. The papacy emerged cleaner and stronger.

Trent confirmed the movement that came to be called the Counter-Reformation. Many of the tendencies now favoured had been in place even before the Protestant Reformation had occurred. An emphasis on the role of the laity, on study of Scripture and on the need to do away with abuses of clerical position – all this had got under way in the 15th century.

New congregations of religious men, not confined to monasteries, came into being. The Oratorians, for example, started meeting in Rome in 1517, the year Luther pinned up his theses. The most notable newcomers were the Jesuits. Formally instituted in 1540, the Society of Jesus made great use of a system of vigorous meditative prayer known as the Spiritual Exercises, drawn up by its founder Ignatius of Loyola (1491-1556), a Basque former soldier. Taking a special vow of allegiance to the Pope, the Jesuits played a central role in re-establishing Roman Catholicism in central Europe. Within a generation they were reaching the Indies (*see page 146*).

The Jesuits were prominent in providing the sacraments for those in Britain who continued in the Roman Catholic faith when their rulers – Elizabeth I and King James VI of Scotland and I of England – embraced Protestantism. The Tudor and Stuart world was a violent one, and many Roman Catholic priests and people were executed, just as Protestants had been under Mary.

A reforming insider

Charles Borromeo showed how a Counter-Reformation new broom could sweep a diocese clean

Charles Borromeo (1538-84) was made a cardinal before he was a priest by his uncle Pope Pius IV. He took part in the last sessions of the Council of Trent, helped compile the catechism it authorised and was energetic in seeking reform.

In 1564, still only 26, he was made Archbishop of Milan, a diocese of 1,000 parishes. He set about applying the measures of Trent, establishing seminaries, starting Sunday schools to teach doctrine and ensuring the liturgy was performed in a dignified way. (He commissioned Palestrina's baroque masterpiece the *Mass of Pope Marcellus*.)

He gave away his money in alms and cared personally for the sick, acting heroically during the plague of 1576. His reforms provoked opposition. A disgruntled member of the decayed order of Humiliati (*see page 114*) tried to kill him.

Borromeo showed how a counter-Reformation diocese could be run. He died, aged 46, in the arms of his confessor, Dr Gruffydd Roberts. A devotional tract by Borromeo was found in the 18th century tucked away in the house of Shakespeare's father. Charles Borromeo was made a saint in 1610; Pope John Paul II was christened Karol (Charles) Wojtyla after him.

Teresa of Avila was alone, sick and poor. Moreover she was a woman in a man's world. But she had a sense of humour and a conviction that God was calling her to reform the practice of religion

Night in a bad inn

Teresa of Avila (1515-82) was in no good position to change the face of the religion in which she was brought up. Spanish society in her day did not countenance women making a stir in public. It was fearful of change and mindful that the Inquisition could arrest anyone suspected of spreading heresy. Moreover Teresa suffered years of ill health.

But she had a forceful character, and an engaging one too. She was born Teresa de Cepeda y Ahumada in Avila, a strongly walled city high up in central Spain. Her father was well off, but not rich. Teresa had 11 brothers and sisters; her mother died when she was 13 and this had a profound effect on her.

Teresa's achievement was to be twofold. First she was to teach a habit of prayer that brought God close – in her case it also brought visions. But she made it clear that this way of prayer was open to anybody who wanted strongly enough to follow it, and that visions were no indication of holiness.

Her second task, which brought danger and suffering, was to transform the religious order to which she belonged – the Carmelites. When she was about 20, Teresa had entered the Carmelite convent in her home town. It was a comfortable enough place, not corrupt, but not fanatical. But Teresa's health broke down. She was an invalid for 18 months and had hardly recovered when she was struck by "catalepsy" and taken for dead; she narrowly escaped burial. She regained use of her limbs slowly and was not really well until she was aged about 40.

In middle age Teresa realised she had been wasting her time. Her life was virtuous but easygoing and her prayers unconcentrated; worst of all she "took hardly any notice of venial sin". Her "conversion" in about 1555 entailed her devoting herself wholeheartedly to mental prayer. She began to experience the so-called Prayer of Quiet and the Prayer of Union – mental states she found hard to describe.

When she began to hear the occasional "locution" (an interior message) from God, it instructed her to return the Carmelite Order to the full rigour of its constitutions as set down in the 13th century. Before she could begin, she had to gain the permission of her superiors. This seemed impossible. They told her that her visions came from the Devil; they forbade her to found even a little convent.

Without being explicitly disobedient, Teresa gained the help of a number of remarkable people. One was Francis Borgia, who had bucked the trend of his notorious family and was later made a saint. Other holy men supported her reform: St Peter of Alcántara, who performed hair-raising penances, Peter Alvarez, a 25-year-old priest in the vigorous new Society of Jesus, and most notably John

St Teresa of Avila at the age of 61, by Juan de la Miseria (c1526-1616), from the Convent of St Teresa, Avila, Spain. The scroll above her head is from Psalm 89: "I will sing of the mercies of the Lord for ever"

MISERICORDIAS DOMINI ▲ IN ETERNVM CANTABO

of the Cross, a Spanish monk renowned for his poems (such as *The Dark Night of the Soul*) and for his cheerfulness in suffering.

John of the Cross (1542-91) was also determined to reform the Carmelites. He was actually imprisoned by his own order, as a trouble-maker, kept in solitary confinement, given poor food and beaten. After nine months he escaped. His reforming ideas prevailed, but again he was deposed from authority and badly treated till three months before his death.

Teresa meanwhile obtained in 1562 permission from the Pope himself to start a new convent. Her nuns were

'I have neither the health nor the intelligence to write'

called Discalced Carmelites, for they went about barefoot. So began 20 years of constant travel, founding reformed convents. She persevered in prayer in the most distracting circumstances, and wrote an autobiography and letters full of good sense and amused observation on human foibles, including her own.

It was she who said that life on earth was like "a bad night in a bad inn" – as she had reason to know, often arriving cold, sick, old and hungry at a flea-ridden comfortless stable with no fire or food. She knew that mundane tasks done for love of God were as valuable as the most recollected prayers.

A dangerous road in the floods

In the winter of 1582 Fr Jerónimo Gracián, the Provincial of the Carmelites, insisted on going with Teresa, then 66, to see a new convent in Burgos. It was a cold, wet, dangerous three-week journey

The Father Provincial was anxious to go with us so that he might look after my health on the journey, because the weather was so severe, and I was so old and ill, and they apparently think my life of some importance. It was certainly by God's ordinance that he went, for the roads were frequently flooded, and so bad that he and his companions had to go on ahead to find the best paths for us, and help to drag the carriages out of the bogs: it was especially bad between Palencia and Burgos – in fact, it was very rash of us to set out when we did at all.

Sinking in the mud

True, Our Lord had told me that we could safely go, and that I was not to fear, for he would be with us. But I did not tell the Father Provincial this at the time, though it was a comfort to me in the great difficulties and dangers which we met, especially at the ford near Burgos which is known as the Pontoons. Here, in many places, the water had risen so high that it had submerged these pontoons. There was water everywhere, and on either side it was very deep. If any of the carriages heeled slightly, all would be lost.

We had taken a guide we had found at an inn who knew the best way through, but it was certainly a very dangerous one. Then there was the question of lodgings. We could not cover our usual day's mileages on the bad roads. It was quite usual for the carriages to sink into the mud and the animals would then have to be taken out of one carriage to drag out another. The Fathers who went with us had a very bad time, for the drivers were young and rather careless. The fact that the Father Provincial was with us helped us a great deal, for he saw to everything, and nothing seems to upset him. So he made our troubles seem light, though he could do nothing about the Pontoons, which gave him a real fright. When I saw that we were entering a regular sea of water, with no sign of a path or a boat, even I was not without fear, despite all the strength Our Lord had given me. What, then, must have been my companions' state of mind?

Fever and pain

There were eight of us altogether: two were to return with me and five were to remain at Burgos, four choir nuns and one lay sister. I was suffering from a troublesome sore throat which I contracted on the road; I still had a fever and eating caused me great pain. This detracted from my enjoyment of the pleasanter parts of the journey. I am still suffering from this sore throat, though it is the end of June; it is still extremely painful. The nuns were all quite happy; and, once the danger was passed, they enjoyed talking about it. It is a great thing to suffer under obedience, especially for those who practise it as consistently as these nuns.

Christianity round

In the 16th century while Europe was being rent by the dissensions of the Reformation, explorers returned with reports of new worlds. European countries were to embark on a race to colonise vast territories. Christianity was part of European civilisation, but Christian values rarely lay behind settlers' greedy motives. The globalisation of Christianity began with the distressing example of the conquest of America

Two Inca princes stand in formal clothes and head-dresses in the background of this painting of the Corpus Christi procession in Cusco, Peru, by an anonymous 18th-century painter. The floats (from left) are of Sts Sebastian, Christopher and James (vanquishing Moors), devotion to whom was popular in Spain

The conquest of Mexico, Peru and the Caribbean followed rapidly on the discovery of this new world by Columbus in 1492. Cortés conquered the Aztec empire of Mexico with 600 men in 1521; Pizarro with 180 men overthrew the Incas of Peru in 1532. From the first the explorer soldiers behaved very badly. War was a way of life for whole classes of landless men from which the adventurers came. Gold, though, not land, was the first attraction, and greed for it brought out the worst in the *conquistadores*.

Queen Isabella of Castile had from the first strongly opposed the enslavement of the Indians, insisting that they be paid wages. But a system of property rights known as *encomiendas*, which started as the exaction of labour in return for defence and education by the new landowners, soon became degraded to a method of slave-owning. A campaign against this system was the work of the Dominican friars, who arrived on the island of Hispaniola (modern Haiti and the Dominican Republic) in 1510.

One man who had given up his *encomienda* and joined the Dominicans was Bartolome de las Casas (*see panel, right*). He spent his life trying to free the Indians. At first sight his reports sounded like the fantasies of a sadist. But the monstrous behaviour of the Europeans was only too true. Between 1494 and 1508, Las Casas calculated, three million indigenous people had died on the island of Hispaniola.

The Indians seemed noble savages to many of the idealistic friars (Franciscans as well as Dominicans) who set in train a vast programme of conversion, which went in parallel with the soldiers' brutality. The Indians were "of such simplicity and purity of soul that they do not know how to sin", one Franciscan wrote. It was not, of course, that the peoples of central and south America really were sinless noble savages; they knew wars and slavery in their own territories. But how could the indigenous people

believe in the Christianity that the good friars taught if their soldier compatriots brought nothing but murder and slavery? It is surprising that so many Indians, quite apart from baptisms under duress, did become Christians.

The campaign by Las Casas persuaded Charles V to pass the so-called New Laws in 1542, abolishing *encomiendas* and guaranteeing liberty to the Indians. It was a different matter to enforce the laws. Meanwhile, forced labour and Western disease killed the Indians in huge numbers. Their population in Mexico fell from 25 million in 1518 to 2.5 million by 1570; Peru's population fell from 9 million to 600,000 by 1620. African slaves were imported by the settlers to replace American Indian labour.

An extraordinary social experiment, which stands out against this tragically dark background, came in the early 17th century, when Jesuit missionaries set up reserves where Indians could be protected from marauding slave-hunters. But the slavers' attacks forced the Jesuits to seek more distant and secure havens. The most successful settlements known as Reductions were set up around the rivers Paraná and Uruguay (now in Argentina, Paraguay

the globe

The slaughter of the Indians

In *A Short Account of the Destruction* of *the Indies* published in 1542 Bartolomé de las Casas (1484-1576) drew the attention of people in Spain to the monstrous behaviour of the settlers. Here he describes incidents in Yucatan

The wretched Spaniards actively pursued the Indians, both men and women, using wild dogs to track them down and hunt them. One woman, who was not well and so unable to escape, determined that the dogs should not tear her to pieces as they had done her neighbours and, taking a rope, and tying her one-year-old child to her leg, hanged herself from a beam. Yet she was not in time to prevent the dogs from ripping the infant to pieces.

When the Spaniards were in the very act of leaving the province, one of them demanded that the son of a local chief go with him, but the boy declined, adamant that he did not want to leave home. The Spaniard retorted: "You will come with me or I will cut off both your ears." When the boy persisted, repeating that he had no wish to leave home, the Spaniard took out his dagger and lopped off first one of his ears and then the other. When the boy again insisted that he did not want to go with him, he hacked off his nose, laughing out loud as he did so as though he were doing no more than pull his hair playfully.

This was the same fiend who was later to boast to a venerable cleric, without any sign of shame or remorse, that he always laboured long and hard to make the local women pregnant so that they would fetch a higher price as slaves.

These examples should suffice to give some idea of the brutality of the Spanish throughout this territory and of the attitude they take towards a people created in God's image and redeemed by His blood. Yet, as we shall see, worse was to come.

A hunter feeds his dogs with a child, one of the atrocities described by Las Casas, engraved by the Fleming Theodor de Bry

and Uruguay), which by 1722 sheltered in 22 villages more than 140,000 Indians in a "Christian Indian State".

The organisation was frankly Utopian, with families being housed in ideal dwellings, which could not be sold; they were encouraged to cultivate a wide variety of crops and engage in useful trades and even to set up their own defence militia. Spaniards (apart from officials representing the Crown) were prohibited from entering the territory of the Reductions.

The fortunes of the Reductions varied. Sometimes sudden epidemics of common European diseases struck (measles killed 18,773 Guaraní Indians of the Reductions in 1737). But they were at their best truly idealistic Christian settlements.

In 1750, rivalry between Brazil and Spain led to a disastrous treaty imposed by a distant government in Spain requiring the Indians to move overnight to the far bank of the Uruguay. The last straw was a move by the enemies of the Jesuits which succeeded in 1767 in having the entire order expelled from South America. Left to unfriendly European influences the Reductions dwindled and died. One bright spot in the development of South American Christianity went out.

Not all missionary efforts were compromised by colonial exploitation. From the 16th century, Jesuit missionaries tried to follow the cultures of Chinese, Japanese and even Tibetans

Donning different clothes

Some Christians made a brave attempt to respect the cultures of Asia during a series of missionary enterprises in the 16th and 17th centuries. There had long been Christians in India, mostly in the south, following the so-called Syro-Malabarese rite of worship, which derived from early contacts with Syria. But the usual sad story of colonial exploitation – mostly by the Portuguese in the East – gave Christians a bad reputation. Nevertheless there were large-scale conversions, around Goa in India or among the Parava fishermen of the Coromandel coast.

A new initiative began with the energetic figure of the Basque saint Francis Xavier, one of the first companions of Ignatius Loyola, the founder of the Jesuits (*see page 142*). In the years from 1542 to his death, 10 years later, looking longingly towards the coast of China, Xavier worked out a way of presenting Christianity while preserving the best in native cultures.

Another Jesuit, the amazing Matteo Ricci, with his mastery of the art of memory, his fascination with clocks, maps and astronomy and his patient study of Chinese culture, arrived in China in 1582, gained a welcome at the Imperial court and stayed till his death in 1610. Ricci allowed convert officials to continue the purely formal obeisance to ancestors; a century later this was ruled unacceptably superstitious in Rome.

Europe was puzzled, fascinated and nonplussed by eastern civilisations. In 1687 James II entertained a Chinese convert brought to Europe by the Jesuit Philip Couplet; this was Michael Alphonsus Shen Fu-Tsung, who was to enter the Jesuit congregation, but die in 1691 on his way back to China.

There were false dawns. In India, the Mogul ruler Jahangir (reigned 1605-27) had taken Christianity to heart and was known for his devotion to Jesus and the Virgin Mary (who figure in the Koran). In India, the Jesuit Roberto de Nobili lived from 1605 to 1642 as a *sanyassi*, a holy man. The debate about how far Christians can go in Hindu practice still rages 350 years later. In 1626 the first church was built in Tibet. In Japan there were thousands of converts. But here, from 1616, there were the cruellest persecutions; 2,000 converts were crucified or tortured to death. Europeans were excluded for 300 years; but Christianity survived. The biggest concentration was, by a twist of fate, at Nagasaki.

Godfrey Kneller thought this portrait the finest he ever painted. It is of Michael Alphonsus Fu-Tsung, a convert brought to England by the missionary Philip Couplet in 1687. James II, who referred to him as a "little blinking fellow", hung the picture at Windsor

Treasures from the Holy Mountain

By the 18th century, Orthodoxy seemed to be in a rut, under pressure from Islam and the Enlightenment rationalists. One man, Nicodemus of the Holy Mountain, gave it a new spiritual impetus by rediscovering its past

By the end of the 18th century the Orthodox churches of south-eastern Europe and the lands bordering the Eastern Mediterranean had lived for more than 300 years under rule by Islamic Turkey. The Ottoman Yoke, as it was called, was in fact reasonably tolerant, although Christians were regarded as second-class citizens and were subject to some restrictions. This had led to a serious weakening of the inner vitality of the Orthodox churches, which had battened down their ecclesiastical hatches to protect the Christian treasure.

Now the ideas of the secularist Enlightenment were posing a new threat. So it was of the greatest importance when in the 1780s a spiritual revival began on Mount Athos in what is now northern Greece. This owed everything to a monk, St Nicodemus of the Holy Mountain, who edited writings about the theory and practice of prayer dating from the 4th to the 15th century and himself wrote books on spirituality that were widely circulated.

Contemplative life

Nicodemus had been born Nicholas Kalliboutzes on the island of Naxos in 1749. He was educated at the leading school of Orthodox culture in Smyrna, now in Turkey. On his return to Naxos he became secretary to the local bishop. Drawn to a contemplative life in 1775 he entered a monastic community on Mount Athos, taking the new name Nicodemus.

Among his visitors was the Bishop of Corinth, Macarius Notaras, who brought a large collection of spiritual writings which Nicodemus was to turn into a 1,207-page volume entitled *Philokalia* ("Love for what is good"). It was described as instruction on pure prayer and the ascetic means to achieve this. It included guidance on the ancient Jesus Prayer – "Lord Jesus Christ, Son of God, have mercy on me" – which was to be repeated many times with the aid of a prayer rope or rosary. This was intended to lead to interior prayer, or prayer of the heart, which has a long history in Orthodoxy. It became a popular devotion in Greece and spread to Western Europe.

Source of guidance

Nicodemus divided his day between prayer and intellectual work, examining, copying and editing ancient manuscripts. *The Standards of Christian Behaviour*, originally assembled by Macarius, became the most widely used source of guidance for Church life in the Greek-speaking Orthodox world. *On Frequent Communion*, again basically Macarius's work, used the Bible and teachings of the Fathers, and led to the rediscovery of the central place of the Eucharist in the life of the Church.

Like most Orthodox theologians of his time, Nicodemus was fiercely anti-Roman Catholic, but he was open to Western spirituality when he saw that it had valuable insights. Two other books by him – *Unseen Warfare* and *Spiritual Exercises* – were slight adaptations of the work of Italian Catholic authors.

Nicodemus, who never left Mount Athos, died in 1809. He and Macarius were declared saints.

Orthodoxy expressed itself both in the cathedral of the Transfiguration (1744) on Kizhi island, Lake Onega, Russia, and in the icon of the Trinity (*above left*) by Andrei Rublev from about 1411

Ethiopia on its own

The mountainous African empire of Ethiopia boasted an ancient civilisation. This became Christian in the early centuries, but cut off from outside influences, developed many peculiarities. In the 18th century, travellers' tales of Ethiopia's outlandish customs began to reach Europe

On one day 2,357 priests were ordained. Sometimes babes in arms were made deacons

The Ethiopian Church presented a strange face to the world of the Enlightenment in the 18th century. Its peculiar customs had developed during long periods of isolation since its foundation at least as early as the 4th century. Western Europe was fascinated by travellers' tales of this ancient black civilisation in the almost impenetrable highlands of eastern Africa. The imperial line itself was said to have descended from the union of an Ethiopian queen and Solomon, who entrusted their son with the care of the Ark of the Covenant. Copies of the Ark were paraded on holy days; the original was said to be kept in one of the country's half-dozen churches hewn from living rock. Worship was often accompanied by drums, dancing, ululation and the carrying of umbrellas.

Among the peculiarities of the Church were a number of Jewish influences probably attributable to a common Semitic heritage, notably the keeping of the Sabbath as well as Sundays, and the Mosaic laws as to clean and unclean food. Boys were baptised on the 40th day, girls on the 80th.

Because the bishop, or *abuna* ("Our Father"), might visit the people only at long intervals he often ordained many priests at once. A 16th-century European witness, Francisco Alvarez, saw an *abuna* lay hands on 2,357 candidates in one day to make them priests. Sometimes babes in arms were ordained deacons.

The Ethiopic scriptures contain a number of apocryphal books. The liturgy uses a classical language, Ge'ez, which is not understood by most in the congregation. There are two types of clergy: the priests, who administer the sacraments; and the rather more educated clerks, who are in charge of teaching and the chant. Numerous fasts are held – Lent lasts an extra 10 days – and Epiphany is celebrated by ritual bathing, once led by the king or Negus.

All this exercised a strong appeal to the imagination of the Europe of Voltaire. Samuel Johnson's *Rasselas* was not the only work to take its inspiration from this ancient civilisation. There is a mention of missionary work in Ethiopia at the time of the Apostles (Acts 7: 26-40), but the Church first seems to have taken root in about 326, when St Frumentius became its first missionary. The story goes that Frumentius and his cousin Edesius were captured as children when they were on a voyage from Egypt to India and were subsequently raised by the Negus of Ethiopia. When he died, he entrusted his children to them, and the pair used their influence to begin evangelising the country.

In 326, Frumentius returned to the Egyptian capital, Alexandria, and asked its Patriarch, Athanasius (*see page 35*), to find a suitable head of the new church. Athanasius recognised that he already had the ideal man and consecrated Frumentius. A cathedral was built at the ancient capital of Axum, in northern Ethiopia, and this became Frumentius's see.

The Ethiopian liturgy and bible were in consequence heavily influenced by Alexandrine practice. Remarkably, throughout the centuries, the Ethiopian *abuna* continued always to be chosen by the Patriarch of Alexandria from among the Egyptian Coptic clergy. Few of these Arabic-speaking bishops ever learnt the Ethiopian tongue, Amharic.

The Papacy also made sporadic efforts to bring under its wing the Ethiopian Church (which, because of its links with Egypt, adhered, at least theoretically, to a Monophysite notion of the nature of Christ). In 1441 Ethiopian delegates to the Council of Florence accepted union with Rome. But the agreement was not ratified back in Ethiopia.

In the early 17th century, under the influence of Portuguese Jesuits, Roman Catholicism became the official religion, and a Catholic Patriarch was dispatched from Rome. But there was widespread resentment among the Ethiopian people at unfamiliar practices, and on the abdication of the Emperor Susenyos in 1632 all the Jesuits were expelled. Subsequent missions by Franciscans only met with their martyrdom.

The 13th-century church of St George at Lalibela was cut out of the surrounding rock so that it sits in a deep trench. Its hollowed-out interior is cross-shaped

PHOTOGRAPHER: THOMAS PAKENHAM

Forging a Protestant culture

In England, the battles of the Reformation continued into the 17th century. Radical Protestants pressed the king to 'purify' the Church. These Puritans allied themselves to political revolutionaries who won a civil war and beheaded the king. It took a new settlement in the 1660s to consolidate the practice of the Church of England through the Book of Common Prayer

When King James VI of Scotland was on his way to London in 1603 to reign as James I of England, he was presented with the Millenary Petition – so called because it was said to represent the views of 1,000 Puritan ministers. They asked the new king to relieve them from their "common burden of human rites and ceremonies". By this they meant such things as the use of the sign of the cross at baptism, of the ring at marriage, bowing at the name of Jesus, and the wearing of white surplices by the clergy when conducting worship. They thought it unwise to disclose at this point that they also wished to be rid of bishops and to introduce a presbyterian system of church government.

They got little change out of King James. He held a conference at Hampton Court in 1604, after which he granted a few minor concessions in worship, but he upheld the Book of Common Prayer. Later he linked the idea of the office of bishop as coming from the Apostles and the principle of the Divine Right of Kings. "No bishop, no king" was the watchword attributed to him.

The Puritans did no better during the early years of Charles I's reign (from 1625). He was a devout High Churchman, and in William Laud he had an Archbishop of Canterbury who was implacably opposed to Puritanism. But the strength of Puritan feeling in the country was to lead to the beheading of King Charles, and of Archbishop Laud before him.

With the establishment of the Commonwealth under Oliver Cromwell, the Puritans came into their own. In 1644, five years before the king's execution, they had got Parliament to ban the use of the Book of Common Prayer and substitute for it the Directory, an ultra-Protestant service book. During the Commonwealth, bishops and the controlling bodies of cathedrals (deans and chapters) were removed. A mixed bag of approved ministers – some ordained, some not – were installed in the parishes.

With the Restoration of the monarchy in 1660 a declaration by the new king Charles II of "a liberty to tender consciences" failed to allay the fears of the Puritans. A Puritan delegation urged him, among other things, to forbid his chaplains to wear surplices.

On his return to England the Puritans tendered him an Address in which they said they would accept a lawful liturgy provided that it be "agreeable to the Word of God, neither too tedious in the whole, nor composed of too short prayers, unmeet repetitions or responsories".

In October 1660 the king announced the setting up of a commission of "learned divines of both persuasions" to revise the Prayer Book. Several bishops were appointed by the Convocations of Canterbury and York to the commission. It carried out its revision of the 1552 Book very thoroughly and remarkably quickly. The Puritans were firmly put in their place in a preface which described them as "men of factious, peevish and perverse spirits".

The new book was debated in the Privy Council, then sent by the king to the House of Lords. On May 19 1662 the new Book of Common Prayer was given the Royal Assent and attached to a new Act of Uniformity. It has remained unchanged and entered deeply into the religious culture of the English nation, though the second half of the 20th century saw the authorisation of an Alternative Service Book for optional use.

According to George Fox (*above*), the inner light gave anyone authority to preach. For the first time women spoke publicly

George Fox – blinded by the inner light

One day in 1651 George Fox saw the triple spires of Lichfield cathedral in the distance. He left his shoes with shepherds and walked barefoot into the town crying: "Woe to the bloody city of Lichfield."

In his *Journal*, Fox (1624-91) gives no reason for his action that day beyond the prompting of an inward light. This was his great principle: to act "in the light of the Lord Jesus Christ, and by his immediate Spirit and powers, as did the holy men of God by whom the Holy Scriptures were written".

This was a large claim, but under its force Fox consolidated a Society of Friends as it was later called, going in his own time by the name given by its detractors as Quakers. Fox himself had much in common with the radical Puritan and independent sects of his time when Ranters, Levellers, Seekers and Muggletonians competed for allegiances.

It was easy to tell what Fox was against: the priesthood, parish churches, tithes, the swearing of oaths, the authority of magistrates (he would keep his hat on in their presence). In 1670 Fox declared that "All bloody principles and practices we do utterly deny, with all outward wars and strife and fightings with outward weapons, for any end or under any pretence whatsoever."

Fox was imprisoned eight times between 1649 and 1673. In between he went on foot for hundreds of miles, preaching. He took the truth of the Bible as read, but saw the effective power of Christ not on Calvary but within himself. Since the inner light had the highest authority, anyone might preach, including women. Some Quakers claimed to work miracles; others undertook long fasts. The Quakers had a strong appeal to plain, good-hearted people who had tired of wrangling between rival theologies.

In 1671 Fox visited north America where his followers soon established a lasting influence.

A woman speaking at a Quaker meeting by Egbert van Heemskerk the Younger (1645-1705)

Bunyan on trial

In 1660 John Bunyan appeared before a Justice at Bedford charged with preaching unlawfully.

Foster [*prosecuting counsel*]: Which of the Scriptures do you understand literally?

Bunyan: "He that believes shall be saved"; that whosoever believeth in Christ, shall, according to the plain and simple words of the text, be saved.

Foster: He said I did not understand Scriptures, for how (said he) can you understand them, when you know not the original Greek &c.

Bunyan: I said, that if that was his opinion then but a very few of the poorest sort should be saved. This is harsh, yet the Scripture saith, That God hides his things from the wise and prudent (that is from the learned of the world) and reveals them to babes and sucklings.

Foster: He told me that I made people neglect their calling; that God had commanded people to work six days, and serve him on the seventh.

Bunyan: I told him, that it was the duty of people (both rich and poor) to look out for their souls on them days.

Foster: Will you promise that you will not call the people together any more? Then you may be released, and go home.

Bunyan: I durst not leave off that work which God had called me to.

Bunyan was committed to prison to await trial at the quarter sessions.

The diary of a country parson

James Woodforde (1740-1803) was the Rector of Weston Longville, Norfolk, for the last 27 years of his life. He kept a diary for 44 years giving a rounded picture of a country parson's life: his duties and kindnesses and the vast dinners people of the time habitually ate

1787 June 9 I went and read Prayers again this morning to Mrs Leggatt and administered also the Holy Sacrament to her – she was very weak indeed and but just alive. She was sensible and showed marks of great satisfaction after receiving the H. Sacrament. She never received it before. Pray God bless her.

1793 Sept 26 Thursday We were sorry to see on this Days Paper from Bath that our very valuable and worthy Friend the Revd Mr DuQuesne of Tuddenham was no more. It is a very great Loss to us, but I hope to him, Gain. Pray God he may be eternally happy. Dinner today boiled Leg of Mutton & a rosted Rabbit.

1794 Sept 15 Thursday Took a ride this morning in my little Curricle to Mr Mellish's at East Tuddenham, to make him a Visit after his return from London on Friday last, after the very late melancholy Event in his Family, the Death of his Mother, who was taken off very soon indeed, by a very violent Fever. She is much regretted by all that knew her.

We never saw her but twice, once at Mr Mellish's & once at my own house and that not above two Months ago, and then she appeared as well & in as good Spirits as I ever saw any Person. Pray God! she may be happier and send Comfort to her much distressed Family. As so good a Parent must occasion on her decease such sorrow as is not to be described or felt but by those that have experienced it – The Loss of my dear Parents I feel to this Moment and never can forget it during Life.

I stayed with Mr Mellish about an Hour, and then returned home to dinner. I found him very low. Mr Jeans had been with him this Morning before. At Harwich all Day, having Masons white-washing my Study Ceiling &c. &c. Dinner to day, Neck of Pork rosted &c. Mr Collinson sent us 2 brace of Partridges this Aft.

A bishop in a wig

Richard Challoner demonstrated how Roman Catholics could be good citizens

Richard Challoner (1691-1781) was consecrated a bishop in Hammersmith in 1741, in charge of 25,000 Roman Catholics in the London area, cared for by about 100 priests. No English priest had been executed since John Southworth in 1654. But the Catholics still found themselves under civil disabilities. Any common informer could gain a reward for denouncing a priest until the judge Lord Mansfield put a stop to it in 1771 by requiring evidence of ordination.

Challoner, whose mother was a servant in a great Catholic household, presented a very English exterior to the world. In church he wore his mitre over his wig; in the street he wore a sober coat and breeches. He lived in a plain brick house, he said Mass in hired rooms of public houses or among the garrets of the poor. He felt more at home among tradesmen such as his friend William Mawhood, a draper, than in the baroque embassy chapels where Catholics could worship unharried by the law.

He produced a popular prayerbook called *The Garden of the Soul* that was used for two centuries, and revised the Douai translation of the Bible. Two saints he followed were Francis of Sales and Vincent de Paul, both men active among lay people.

In 1778 a Relief Act put Roman Catholics in the same category as dissenters. George III was prayed for in the Canon of the Mass. It came, then, as a blow to Challoner, 40 years a bishop, 64 years a priest, when in 1780 the Gordon riots broke out in London. Catholic chapels were wrecked, mobs stormed prisons and rampaged drunk on the 120,000 gallons of gin from Langdale's burning distillery. It shocked the old man who had long seen Catholics working peaceably alongside their fellow citizens. Within six months he was dead of a stroke.

Parson and parish

The Church of England in the 18th century superimposed its own measured way of life on its medieval foundations. If the university-educated clergy lived like gentlemen it did not mean they neglected the bodily and spiritual needs of their parishioners

The Church of England of the 18th century left its mark on hundreds of parish churches such as St James, Tong, near Bradford (*pictured left*). On either side of the medieval east window can be seen the usual boards bearing the Ten Commandments, the Creed and the Lord's Prayer to instruct worshippers. The congregation sat in new box pews within earshot of the triple-decker pulpit (dated 1727), with reading desk and clerk's stall, from which the responses to the service given in the Book of Common Prayer were given. On the left-hand wall may be seen a hatchment – a coat of arms put up after the death of a prominent parishioner. The altar is fenced off by a rail, in accordance with the instructions of Archbishop Laud in the reign of Charles I. In the 18th century, though, the altar would have had no cross, candles or decorated frontal, which came with 19th-century ritualism.

Such trappings as St James's should not conceal the problems of the Georgian Church. The Reformation battles had over 150 years left it institutionally exhausted, and exclusion of the Puritans deprived it of a rich spirituality. Its leaders came to be too closely identified with the wealthy. The clergy, educated at the ancient universities and married, expected incomes that could often come only by a priest taking on several parishes.

Even so, the Church was by no means ineffective in the parishes. Every parish church had at least one service, with a lengthy sermon, on Sunday. The sick were visited and the poor cared for through charities for bread and clothing. Church courts upheld morality with some severity (public adulterers sometimes standing in a shroud at the church door to do penance).

Parsons, then, could take on the welfare of their parishes. Not all were equally diligent, but the evidence of

Bishops' Visitations indicates a generally high standard. In the language of the time, the Vicar of St Andrew's Plymouth, Zachary Madge, was praised by Samuel Johnson, the dictionary-maker and devout High Churchman: "Though studious, he was popular; though argumentative, he was modest; though inflexible he was candid; and though metaphysical, he was orthodox."

Had Johnson visited Stanhope, in remote north-west Durham he would have found in its Rector, Joseph Butler, not only a dedicated pastor but a philosopher of European standing. He became Bishop of Durham, and his book *The Analogy of Religion* (1736) had a lasting influence.

Of a different sort, but no less influential, was William Law's *A Serious Call to a Devout and Holy Life* (1728). Its author lost his Cambridge Fellowship when, because of his Stuart sympathies, he refused to take the Oath of Allegiance to George I. He was essentially a mystic who had been influenced by continental spiritual writers of the 14th and 15th centuries. Dr Johnson said that his own conversion came through reading *A Serious Call*, and both John and Charles Wesley (*see page 154*) acknowledged their debt to Law.

Robert Raikes (1736-1811) was different again. A printer and editor of the *Gloucester Journal*, he was concerned about the neglect of poor children in the town, and in 1780 started a Sunday School to teach reading, writing and knowledge of the Bible. This proved to be so successful that the idea was taken up by Hannah More, a writer and philanthropist. Sunday Schools soon became an important feature of English life.

Much earlier in the century the choirs of Worcester, Hereford and Gloucester cathedrals had come together to inaugurate a Three Choirs Festival, while in London a German composer named George Frideric Handel was a regular attender at the newly built St George's Church in Hanover Square. His oratorio *Messiah* was first performed in 1741.

St James, Tong, Yorkshire, is a well preserved medieval church with Georgian fittings. The centre of attention would be the pulpit from which the parson preached

Stupendous Bach

While the Church of England was developing its steady 18th-century form, in Germany the Lutheran Church benefited from the great gifts of Johann Sebastian Bach (1685-1750)

Richard Wagner judged Bach "The most stupendous miracle in all music". It is above all a Christian miracle. Bach inscribed the scores of his religious music with the letters JJ (*Jesu, juva* – Jesus help) at the beginning, and SDG (*Soli Deo Gloria* – to God alone the glory) at the end.

Bach saw himself not as a supreme genius, but rather as one of God's craftsmen. He produced masterpiece after masterpiece in the face of almost complete indifference.

In his first five years as Cantor at St Thomas School in Leipzig (a

position he held from 1723 until his death), Bach wrote not merely the *St John Passion*, the *St Matthew Passion* and the *Magnificat*, but also produced three complete cycles (60 hours) of cantatas. This phenomenal labour was accomplished in addition to his teaching duties and the cares of parenthood; from his two marriages Bach fathered 20 children.

The two settings of the Passion combine deep religious feeling and intense drama, held together with gigantic intellectual control; together with the *Mass in B minor* they are Bach's greatest achievements.

Few of his compositions were published in his lifetime. The first public performance after his death of the *St Matthew Passion* did not occur until 1829, when Mendelssohn conducted it in Berlin. The cantatas, 20 or 25 minutes long, were mostly written for Sunday services that began at 7am and lasted four hours. The Cantor complained about the inadequacy of his singers; it is impossible, though, not to feel sympathy for boys required to sing such profound and difficult music at that hour.

Part of Bach's score for his wonderful St Matthew Passion

For most of the 18th century the extraordinary John Wesley rode from town to town stirring audiences to faith. He meant to strengthen the Church of England; instead he founded a new denomination, Methodism

Reading in the saddle

John Wesley (1703-91), famed after his death as the founder of Methodism, was an astonishing figure in his life. Methodism was to become a separate religious denomination, but in 1790, towards the end of his life, Wesley felt able to say: "I live and die a member of the Church of England."

At his death Wesley left 70,000 Methodists in Britain and Ireland; there were 60,000 more in America. His achievement on a human level was extraordinary: here was a man who "first began to feel old" at 85, who travelled 225,000 miles on horseback, preaching 40,000 sermons, some to crowds of 20,000 people.

He always got up at four in the morning, and never lost a night's sleep, despite the dissensions of colleagues, his troubled marriage and the opposition of authorities. Most of the many books he devoured, he read in the sad-

dle, as he rode with a slack rein towards his next public meeting.

Wesley was educated at Christ Church, Oxford, and ordained in 1726. He assisted his father (a former nonconformist), the Rector of Epworth, Lincolnshire, before joining his brother Charles in Oxford in a group nicknamed the Holy Club, which took Holy Communion frequently and fasted on Wednesdays and Fridays. Its stress on methodical study and prayer won it another name – Methodism.

Wesley was open to eclectic influences, from the Moravian sect as refounded by Count Zinzendorf (later to plague him by competing for converts) to the zealous idealism of St Ignatius Loyola (c1491-1556), whom he described as "surely one of the greatest men that ever was engaged in the support of so bad a cause".

In 1735 Wesley went off to Georgia in North America, but his mission there became complicated by misunderstandings on every side (he barred from Holy Communion a woman whom he had courted and who had married another man) and he returned to England. He was already convinced that "every part of my life (not some only) must either be sacrificed to God, or myself – that is, in effect, to the devil". On May 25 1738 he underwent a conversion at a meeting, largely of Moravians, in Aldersgate Street, London, at which was read Luther's commentary on St Paul's Epistle to the Romans, with its doctrine of justification by faith.

Under the influence of George Whitefield (see opposite), Wesley began in 1739 to preach to those who did not go to the parish church. He found a hunger among them for instruction and a holy life. "God deliver me," he would say, "from a half Christian." He published in 1743 Rules for societies formed in each area, and he recruited itinerant preachers to visit and revisit localities. Many Methodist preachers were humble men of little education, scorning, like those in the tradition of Bunyan, the learning of the universities.

Though Wesley encouraged his people to go to the parish church, many focused their new Christian life on regular Methodist meetings. Church of England authority distrusted Wesley's confidence that he was doing God's work. Bishop Joseph Butler admonished him with: "Sir, the pretending to extraordinary revelations and gifts of the Holy Ghost is a horrid thing, a very horrid thing." Anglican pulpits became closed to Wesley, and if he wanted his helpers to be ordained, no bishop would do so. In fact he let lay preachers behave as ministers. But by 1784, when he wanted to send more preachers to America, he resorted to himself commissioning them as ministers.

Wesley never seemed to doubt his authority to act in an increasingly independent way. Nor did he hesitate to expel members who "walked disorderly"; once, on visiting the society at Gateshead, he felt obliged to halve its numbers from 800 to 400 by expulsions. Doctrinally, Wesley resisted the Calvinism of Whitefield and others; in Britain, a Calvinist Methodist sector split off, with much support in Wales.

An oddity about early Methodism was the frequency of abnormal manifestations. Again and again in Wesley's lengthy journals there are notes of meetings where "men, women and children wept and groaned and trembled exceedingly", or "great indeed was the shaking among them; lamentation and great mourning were heard". He saw these as the work of God, though not essential to conversion.

Wesley brought to Christianity swathes of the people left beyond the reach of the Established Church, either in isolated countryside or the new industrial urban settlements. Perhaps this Christianisation of the proletariat helped keep Britain from revolution in the 19th century. Methodist influences later prevented the Labour Party from being a Marxist party. Neither these things nor the spread of Methodist churches around the world were in Wesley's mind when he resolved to spread the good news of salvation by faith.

Detail of a painting of John Wesley preaching from his father's tombstone. His father, Samuel, was rector at Epworth in Lincolnshire, and from 1727 to 1729 Wesley acted as his curate before becoming a priest. After his father died in 1735 he and his brother Charles went to preach in the American colonies

America's great awakening

The Puritans prospered in 18th-century New England. Suddenly their communities were struck by enthusiastic prayer meetings where great crowds shrieked and fell into convulsion accompanied by feelings of conversion

The Puritan churches of New England, planted in the 17th century by the Pilgrim fathers and other refugees, experienced in the 1730s an intense revival later known as The Great Awakening. This was stimulated by two remarkable men.

Jonathan Edwards, a Puritan pastor's son, was born in Connecticut in 1703. After studying at the infant Yale University he became in 1727 assistant minister to his grandfather at the Congregational Church in Northampton, Massachusetts. In 1734 his sermons suddenly began to evoke a response from the congregation.

Edwards, surprised, described it as "an extraordinary dispensation of Providence". He was grateful, he said, that there had been no "emotional excesses". His sermons were in fact intellectually demanding, teaching an unbending Calvinism of Predestination and Election. This had its other side – damnation for those not Elected to salvation – even if Edwards declared God's love for all.

The revival had by 1738 subsided, but two years later a preacher from England rekindled it. George Whitefield was born in Gloucester in 1714. He went to Oxford, was influenced by the Wesleys (*see opposite*) and ordained in the Church of England. He followed the Wesleys to Georgia but returned to begin open-air meetings in England, South Wales and Scotland. Huge crowds gathered – 50,000 in London – people fainted and were convulsed with "violent agonies".

Whitefield's six further visits to America were sensational, his sermons often provoking screeching in the crowds. In his *Treatise on Religious Affections*, Jonathan Edwards, who shared in the renewed Awakening, made a deep examination of religious experience. "Gracious and holy affections," he wrote, "have their exercise and fruit in Christian practice."

After 23 years, Edwards was dismissed by his own congregation for advocating stricter standards for admission to Holy Communion. He became pastor of two communities, one Indian one white, in New Hampshire. In 1757 he was appointed President of the College of New Jersey, later Princeton University. But within three months he was dead of smallpox, contracted through vaccination.

George Whitefield was still on the road. He preached over 18,000 sermons before, in 1770, dying in Exeter, New Hampshire, after delivering a two-hour sermon.

The artist, Edward Hicks, shows himself as a little boy at the knee of Elizabeth Twining reading her Bible, in this painting *The Residence of David Twining in 1785* from the Carnegie Museum in Pennsylvania. It was in this atmosphere that American Christianity flourished. Hicks went on to start a Quaker sect of his own

CHAPTER SIX

AD 1800-2000

From here to eternity

As the 19th century wore on, it must have seemed to many British Victorians that the nation had never been so Christian: new churches were built, clergymen ordained, children taught at Sunday school, hymns lustily sung, missionaries dispatched abroad, the evils of the industrial revolution repulsed by laws and charity.

Yet doubt crept in. Darwin seemed to say that the Bible lied, because species did not originate from a simultaneous creation. Even bishops reinterpreted biblical teaching through German methods of textual criticism. Worship in parish churches developed a new ritualism, with vestments and lighted candles, and the established Church of England was challenged by the re-establishment of a Roman Catholic hierarchy. Abroad revolution followed revolution, with churches burnt by the mob.

In the 20th century the two monstrous totalitarian enemies of God – Stalinism and Naziism – left millions with the choice of compromise or death. By the time these political Leviathans collapsed, the churches had set about re-adjusting their own relations with the modern world. . Liberation theology proposed one way of approaching the poor; Mother Teresa another.

We are too close to the events of this century to see how they will mould the future. If the celebration of the Millennium demands a re-examination of the origins of Christianity, it also invites the consideration that one day history will come to an end.

Victorians in turmoil

The Victorians were full of energy and dealt with unprecedented forces, from the industrial revolution to Darwinian doubt. It was an age of church building and missionaries but also of new uncertainties about biblical truth. One man who rose to the intellectual challenge of the age – both as a Protestant and a Catholic – was John Henry Newman

Newman the thinker

A key to Newman's thought is his *Essay on the Development of Christian Doctrine* (1845), which he wrote at the time he was moving into the Roman Catholic Church. It explained that teachings such as the Trinity, while implicit in Scripture, are "developed" by Church authority through Christian history.

Earlier, Newman had sought doctrinal truth by studying what the Christians of antiquity believed. He appealed to a standard of "what had always been believed, everywhere and by everyone" formulated by Vincent of Lérins. Newman was then seeking ammunition against liberals who devalued doctrine. The result of his research was *The Arians of the Fourth Century* (1833), which confirmed his admiration for Athanasius (*see page 35*).

Still an Anglican, Newman wrote his *Lectures on Justification* (1838). This cuts through much bickering of the Reformation era. It is still of the greatest help in attempts to reconcile Catholic and Protestant explanations of Redemption. He ▶ *page 158*

John Henry Newman (1801-90) spent half his life in the Church of England and half his life as a Roman Catholic. His influence on both churches was profound. He was one of the great Victorians. Newman caused a storm in 1841 by arguing that the 39 Articles, the supposed bulwark of the Church of England's Protestantism, could be interpreted in a Catholic sense. His claims came in a pamphlet that was the 90th in a series of "Tracts for the Times" – hence the name "Tractarian" for his associates.

The Tracts had begun after Newman, recovering from an illness in Sicily in 1833, launched a campaign of spiritual renewal that became known as the Oxford Movement. Allies included John Keble (1792-1866) and the Hebrew scholar E B Pusey (1800-82), both of whom remained Anglicans. Among its effects was a move in the Church of England towards ritualism (*see page 161*).

The row over Tract 90 led Newman to retire from Oxford (where he was Vicar of St Mary's, the University church) to the nearby hamlet of Littlemore, where he and some followers lived, prayed and studied in some converted stables. There, on October 9 1845, he was formally received into the Roman Catholic Church.

Newman had been born in London. In 1816, after the failure of his father's bank, he was converted to Evangelical Calvinism. He went to Trinity College, Oxford, and then, as a Fellow of Oriel (from 1822), encountered the High Church tradition in the Church of England, defending it against liberalism and the idea that one religion is as good as another. As Vicar of St Mary's, from 1828, his understated, unemotional preaching cast a kind of enchantment on undergraduates.

After becoming a Roman Catholic he introduced into England a religious institute, the Oratory, founded in 16th-century Rome by St Philip Neri. Newman established a house in Birmingham. There, apart from his writing, he worked with the poor, even amid cholera.

Few of Newman's projects seemed to prosper. For a time it was thought he might make a new translation of the Bible; in 1853 he was sued successfully for libel by an apostate Italian priest; he spent frustrating years (1851-58) trying to set up a Catholic university in Dublin; he failed to open an Oratory in Oxford. He was treated with suspicion for refusing to support Pope Pius IX's claims to temporal power. But in 1864 he was provoked, by being represented as a liar by Charles Kingsley, into writing the *Apologia Pro Vita Sua*, which has been called the greatest of English spiritual autobiographies after Bunyan's.

His differences with the English establishment and with the authorities in Rome were forgotten when he was made an honorary Fellow of Trinity (1877) and a Cardinal (1879). "Whether Rome canonises him or not," wrote the *Times* in his obituary, "he will be canonised in the thoughts of pious people of many creeds in England."

FATHERS OF THE BIRMINGHAM ORATORY

Newman, 1845, in an Anglican clergyman's white stock, by the leading Victorian miniaturist Sir William Ross. Newman's sittings interrupted his work on his Essay on Development

continued to ponder the position of the Church of England within the universal Church. At first he thought it one of the three "branches" of the Church: the corrupt Roman Catholics, the Orthodox and the reformed Anglicans. Later he was convinced that the Church of England was in the same isolated position as the Donatists in St Augustine's day (*see page 38*).

In his preface to *The Via Media* ("The Middle Way"), a collection of his Anglican writings, he argued for a conception of the Church in which the intellectual or prophetical office of the theologian and the worshipping office of the priesthood and people are to be held in creative tension with the regal authority of the pope and curia. These themes were echoed at the Second Vatican Council (*see page 172*).

Newman was unusual among Roman Catholics in not coming to philosophy armed with the methods of Scholasticism, as represented by Thomas Aquinas (*see page 100*). From Bishop Joseph Butler (1692-1752) he drew two powerful ideas: first, the principle of analogy between realities in different fields, and second the role of convergence of probabilities in forming certainty in belief. Newman's philosophy puzzled his critics in Rome, for they could hardly get a hold on it.

In old age, he wrote what some think his finest philosophical study, his *Essay in Aid of a Grammar of Assent* (1870), exploring how the rational mind acts with faith. He argued that people's beliefs might be rational without being susceptible to reductionist logic. In a way the *Grammar* anticipated Wittgenstein and foreshadowed attempts by modern writers to show the rationality – the internal grammars – of subjects other than empirical science and formal logic.

The same year, 1870, saw the definition by the First Vatican Council of the infallibility of the Pope in making solemn pronouncements on matters of faith or morals. Newman believed in the doctrine but thought it inopportune to define it, as he worried about the intellectual difficulties which it was causing other Catholics. Cardinal Manning, the Archbishop of Westminster, who had long been ill at ease with Newman, had sought the declaration.

Newman's philosophy puzzled critics in Rome who could not get a hold on it

Yet it was he who prevented Rome from censuring Newman's moderate defence of infallibility against Gladstone's criticisms in his *Letter to the Duke of Norfolk* (1875).

People who have never read a line of Newman's theological works have sung his hymn, "Lead kindly light", and know his poem *The Dream of Gerontius*, set to music by Edward Elgar and the source of the hymn, "Praise to the Holiest in the height". The publication of his correspondence in 31 volumes, not yet quite complete, shows him as one of the great letter-writers of the 19th century.

Darwin, caricatured in the *London Sketch Book* (1874), showed Victorians they were made in the image of apes

Darwin's origin of doubt

People thought Darwin disproved Christianity not because evolution replaced God but because it seemed to contradict the Bible

Darwin's *Origin of Species* came out in 1859. At that time he still believed in God, but was not a Christian. Within a decade many people came to doubt Christianity somehow "because of Darwin". As a young man Charles Darwin (1809-92) had been invited by his father to take holy orders, since he seemed no great scholar. Charles liked the idea of being a country clergyman, but scrupled to subscribe to all the teachings of the Church of England. After five years spent as a naturalist on board the *Beagle*, he had lost his belief in the special revelation of the Bible. But his doubts had more to do with historical criticism of the Bible than with ideas on natural selection.

Yet to the layman it seemed that Genesis and geology had contradictory explanations of the early days of the Earth. Some scientists, such as TH Huxley or John Tyndall, opposed religion; many did not. "It is very unfair," wrote Professor William Flower of the Natural History Museum, "that, because Huxley and Tyndall happen to be scientific men of the first order, and happen also to be opposed in some sense to the truths of religion, scientific men generally should be ticketed as though they belonged to the same school of thought."

Scientists had, of course, had plenty of time to adjust their minds to the question of whether Genesis was intended by its author as an empirically scientific description of the origins of creatures. Unsettlement of mind was far more prevalent among non-scientists, who had never considered the question until one day they were shaken by something they saw in a newspaper. These people often took the anti-religious assertions of TH Huxley on trust.

In 1860 there was a debate on evolution at Oxford; Huxley was opposed by Bishop Samuel Wilberforce. Huxley was supposed to have declared that he "would rather be descended from an ape than a bishop". He insisted later that he had said no such thing. In fact the quite cogent arguments of Wilberforce were countered more effectively by JD Hooker, the president of the British Association, a much less well-known figure.

Evolution and belief in God might not be incompatible. But because some churchmen denied Darwin's theories solely on the authority of theology many were driven to feel that the apes had trounced the clergymen.

It was a rehearsal of rationalistic conflicts to come in the 19th century. In 1864 Bishop JW Colenso of Natal was deposed by a synod of Anglican bishops in South Africa for denying the truth of the first five books of the Bible. In 1863 Ernest Renan's *Life of Jesus* provoked the idea that the Jesus of the New Testament was different from the "historical" Jesus.

So it was that Victorian conformity came to be swamped by a rising tide of doubt.

The Empire at prayer

David Livingstone thought it natural that commerce and Christianity should march together into Africa. HM Stanley appealed through *The Daily Telegraph* for missionaries to Uganda

The talents and forcefulness of the Victorians found expression in heroic missionary work, which, by the end of the century, had taken the Christian faith to every part of the earth.

On December 4 1857 Dr David Livingstone spoke at a crowded meeting in Senate House, Cambridge, about his explorations in Central Africa. Seeing himself as a pioneer missionary, rather than a mere explorer, he challenged the Church of England and universities, to plant a mission in Central Africa. His closing words were, "I go back to Africa to try to make an open path for commerce and Christianity. Do you carry on the work, which I have begun? I leave it with you."

The immediate response was the foundation of the Universities' Mission to Central Africa. In 1860 the first missionaries sailed from Plymouth and 15 months later their leader, 36-year-old Bishop Charles Mackenzie, died of fever in what is now Malawi. The following year two other members of the Mission died, but all were replaced. From headquarters at Zanzibar, mission stations were gradually established throughout the vast region.

Meanwhile HM Stanley had gone to Uganda from where, finding that Islam had preceded him, he wrote a letter to *The Daily Telegraph* appealing for Christian missionaries. Seven months later volunteers landed at Zanzibar and in June 1877 reached Kampala. They were sent by the Church Missionary Society, founded by Anglican Evangelicals in 1799. During the second half of the 19th century the society recruited hundreds of missionaries to Africa, India, Ceylon, China, Japan and the Middle East.

Missionary work at this period was carried out by dedicated individuals and societies, not by the Churches themselves. Another Anglican agency, the Society for the Propagation of the Gospel, had been founded by the Rev Thomas Bray as early as 1701 to provide a ministry to English settlers in North America and its work spread to the West Indies, South India, the west coast of Africa and Australia. In the 19th century it took the Gospel as far as Burma, Japan, China and Korea.

Cricketing missionary
The China Inland Mission, founded in 1865, made remarkable progress in all the enormous inland provinces. Among its missionaries was CT Studd, said to be England's best cricketer. After being invalided home, he took on missionary work in India and the Congo.

In the Roman Catholic Church self-sacrificing missionary work was carried out by religious orders. A specialised association for priests, the Mill Hill Missionaries, was founded in London in 1866, with a training house for missionaries throughout the Empire.

The 1890s saw a slogan coined: "The Evangelisation of the World in this Generation." But there were to be unforeseen problems for the Church when the colonial era ended.

"The Rev and Mrs Townsend arrive at Ijaye, Nigeria, to do the Lord's work among the benighted heathen who are amazed..." from *Missionary Scenes* by an unknown artist, published in Basle around 1850

Divine sparks in the urban smoke

In the mid 19th century the Church of England expanded with the growing population. This meant adaptation, for the labouring classes lived far from the old parishes

W ith the smoke and throb of Victorian industry the expanding new cities threatened to lose touch with the Church of England. Partly this was just bricks and mortar: people lived in new areas with no parish church. In response the Church of England built 1,727 new churches and rebuilt 7,144 old churches between 1840 and 1876. To keep up with the expanding population (nearly three million increase per decade) it had to find 70 new parishes and 97 new clergy a year. In parallel there was a great expansion of nonconformist chapels (which always attracted worshippers where no Anglican church was near), and of Roman Catholic churches, which had to keep pace with Irish immigration too.

The Church of England rapidly broke free from its country-squire and parson image. The proportion of magistrates who were clergymen was in 1816 37 per cent, in 1837 27 per cent and in 1857 21 per cent. In urban parishes far more curates were needed to help rectors and vicars. (The new diocese of Ripon, with Leeds and Bradford still in it, had 297 incumbents and 76 curates at its creation in 1836, and 462 incumbents with 245 curates by 1872.) A charitable body quaintly named

the Additional Curates Society proved itself more useful than it sounded.

The increase in Church of England clergy lagged behind the bulge in population. In 1841 there were 14,613. Ten years later they had increased by more than 3,000 to 17,621 (partly with the impetus of the Oxford Movement). Thereafter the increase each decade was between 1,000 and 1,500, so that by 1891 there were 24,232. But of the new clergy a greater proportion than before entered active parish life; there was a smaller admixture of schoolmasters, University Fellows and secluded scholars.

Outside church, on the matter of Sunday working and shop-opening, neither bishops nor MPs always walked in step with the people. On July 1 1855 there was a meeting

"Temples of Industry and Divinity", Bradford, Yorkshire, from the Illustrated London News, June 14 1882

MARY EVANS PICTURE LIBRARY

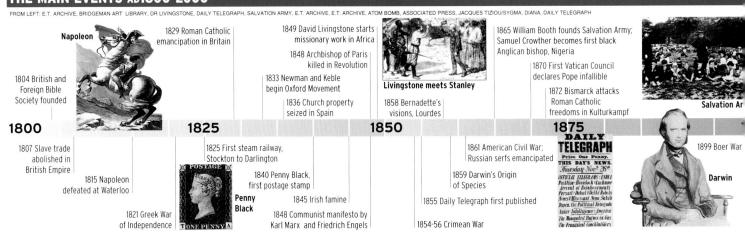

THE MAIN EVENTS AD1800-2000

FROM LEFT: E.T. ARCHIVE, BRIDGEMAN ART LIBRARY, DR LIVINGSTONE, DAILY TELEGRAPH, SALVATION ARMY, E.T. ARCHIVE, E.T. ARCHIVE, ATOM BOMB, ASSOCIATED PRESS, JACQUES TIZIOU/SYGMA, DIANA, DAILY TELEGRAPH

Napoleon

1804 British and Foreign Bible Society founded

1829 Roman Catholic emancipation in Britain

1849 David Livingstone starts missionary work in Africa

1848 Archbishop of Paris killed in Revolution

1833 Newman and Keble begin Oxford Movement

1836 Church property seized in Spain

Livingstone meets Stanley

1858 Bernadette's visions, Lourdes

1865 William Booth founds Salvation Army; Samuel Crowther becomes first black Anglican bishop, Nigeria

1870 First Vatican Council declares Pope infallible

1872 Bismarck attacks Roman Catholic freedoms in Kulturkampf

Salvation Ar

1800

1807 Slave trade abolished in British Empire

1815 Napoleon defeated at Waterloo

1821 Greek War of Independence

1825

1825 First steam railway, Stockton to Darlington

1840 Penny Black, first postage stamp

Penny Black

POSTAGE
ONE PENNY

1845 Irish famine

1848 Communist manifesto by Karl Marx and Friedrich Engels

1850

1861 American Civil War; Russian serfs emancipated

1859 Darwin's Origin of Species

1855 Daily Telegraph first published

1854-56 Crimean War

1875

DAILY TELEGRAPH
Price One Penny.
THIS DAY'S NEWS.
Thursday Nov 26

1899 Boer War

Darwin

Riots over lighted candles

Some of the best clergymen in poor parishes were given to more elaborate ritual than the Victorian Church had seen. This might be no more than the wearing of a chasuble, but it brought riots against 'popery'

The fine Hawksmoor church of St George in the East (since bombed, but retaining some of its glory) became the scene in 1859 of a huge row over ritual. Violence broke out.

The church could hold 2,000; its parish numbered 30,000. In the 733 houses in the streets next to it, 154 brothels traded, for this was close to the docks of Wapping at the height of its maritime bustle. At Communion services at St George's, the Rector, Bryan King, wore a chasuble (the ancient Roman vestment used by priests until the reign of Edward VI, 1537-53) and candles were lit ritually on the altar. This did not shock the congregation (many had little previous experience of churches) but it outraged evangelicals suspicious of popery.

It so happened that a clergyman, Hugh Allen, inimical to the Rector, was elected to preach under an old system by which churchwardens chose a "lecturer" for periodical sermons. He arrived each Sunday afternoon to preach before the Rector's service.

Ritualists and anti-ritualists demonstrated. During King's service, Allen's supporters coughed, groaned and banged pew doors. There were cushions thrown, and fireworks. Choirboys were spat on, clergy kicked. The police felt powerless to intervene. Some 60 or 70 gentlemen, rallied by Tom Hughes the amateur boxer, therefore turned out to defend the Rector. The church became the place to go for those who liked their Sunday entertainment rowdy.

Bishop Tait of London closed the church from September 19 to November 5 1859, when it re-opened with the aid of 50 policemen. They were withdrawn the following January and

the riots got worse. A debate was held in the House of Lords over whether chasubles were illegal.

At last the Bishop persuaded the Rector to take a holiday. It was not, however, the end of dissension. AW Mackonochie, King's curate at St George's, became curate-in-charge of St Alban, Holborn, where he was repeatedly prosecuted.

New ritualism

Ritualists gradually had their way where parishes supported them; these were often poor neighbourhoods where the clergyman was respected for his goodness. In the popular mind "High Church" came to be associated not with the Church Established but with incense and bells. The Blessed Sacrament was reserved where once clergymen feared the law.

Such bitter wrangles seem hard to credit now. A new appreciation of liturgy brought in by the Oxford Movement transformed the appearance of churches during the 19th century. At the beginning of Victoria's reign it was not uncommon to find pews in the chancel; these faced the pulpit, with their backs to the altar. And by the end of the century the poor were seldom crowded out of the paid pews onto benches and stools round the walls.

The historian Owen Chadwick has compiled a list of the first appearance of familiar items: the dog collar (replacing the white cravat or tie) was adopted, strangely enough, from the Roman Catholics, in the second half of the 19th century; collection bags or plates came in from 1868, after the abolition of compulsory church rates; hymn numbers on boards were an innovation of the 1890s.

---

of 150,000 people in Hyde Park protesting against a Bill to close shops on Sundays; 49 policemen were injured in tussles with the crowd. The next Sunday the mob broke the windows of the Archbishop of York's house.

It was not a simple matter of sabbatarianism. Those interested in the welfare of the working class wanted them to have a day off; those who had a day off on Sunday liked to shop or enjoy a drink in a public house.

Seven years earlier revolutions had torn Europe and its churches. In Britain no such revolution came. By 1888 three children out of four in England and Wales from all classes went to Sunday schools. The influence of the Sunday school movement was stronger than that of Marx would ever be.

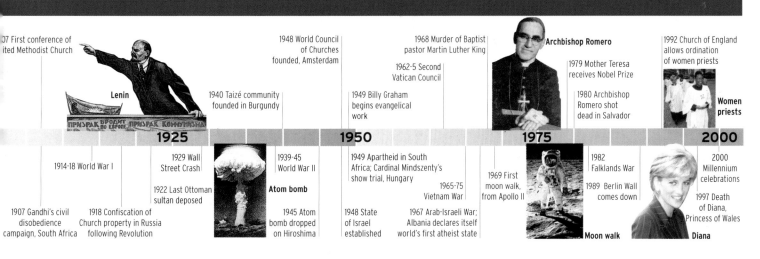

07 First conference of ited Methodist Church

Lenin

1914-18 World War I

1907 Gandhi's civil disobedience campaign, South Africa

1918 Confiscation of Church property in Russia following Revolution

1929 Wall Street Crash

1922 Last Ottoman sultan deposed

1925

1940 Taizé community founded in Burgundy

Atom bomb

1939-45 World War II

1945 Atom bomb dropped on Hiroshima

1948 World Council of Churches founded, Amsterdam

1950

1949 Billy Graham begins evangelical work

1949 Apartheid in South Africa; Cardinal Mindszenty's show trial, Hungary

1948 State of Israel established

1965-75 Vietnam War

1967 Arab-Israeli War; Albania declares itself world's first atheist state

1968 Murder of Baptist pastor Martin Luther King

1962-5 Second Vatican Council

1969 First moon walk, from Apollo II

Archbishop Romero

1979 Mother Teresa receives Nobel Prize

1980 Archbishop Romero shot dead in Salvador

1975

1982 Falklands War

1989 Berlin Wall comes down

Moon walk

1992 Church of England allows ordination of women priests

Women priests

2000

2000 Millennium celebrations

1997 Death of Diana, Princess of Wales

Diana

W. Tyndale -88

Going to church

Anglican church-going reached its height in the second half of the 19th century. Communion services were held each week, instead of monthly or quarterly as it was 100 years earlier. The sermon was important, if not so central as in the Presbyterian established Church of Scotland or in nonconformist churches. What stayed in the memory was hymn-singing

The Victorians did go to church. The numbers are not easy to ascertain; surveys were often impressionistic or unrepresentative. In some towns one in three went; even in the less enthusiastic working-class south London of the 1890s it was one in six. Churchgoing suggests hymn-singing. It was not always so. Hymn-singing of the popular kind started in England during the 18th century and was associated with an Evangelical revival in which Isaac Watts ("When I survey the wondrous Cross") and A M Toplady ("Rock of ages") were notable hymn writers. Charles Wesley, whose brother John founded the Methodist movement (*see page 154*), wrote 6,500 hymns. Of these "Hark! the herald angels sing" and "Love divine, all

loves excelling" are perhaps best known.

At first the Church of England asserted that, since there were no hymns in the Book of Common Prayer, their use in church was illegal. In 1820, however, the Archbishop of York authorised the use of a small hymn book produced for a Sheffield parish by its vicar. Reginald Heber ("From Greenland's icy mountains"), later Bishop of Calcutta, began writing and collecting hymns, a book of which was published shortly after his death in 1826.

The Oxford Movement produced translations of old Latin hymns, such as "Jesu, the very thought of thee" and "O what their joy and their glory must be" (both 12th century). German hymns were also imported.

Hymns Ancient and Modern, the first comprehensive collection, appeared in 1861. It matched hymns to the seasons of the Christian year and proved so popular that supplements were quickly called for. By the end of the century this collection, or *The Hymnal Companion to the Book of Common Prayer* (Evangelical) or *Church Hymns* (published by the Society for the Promotion of Christian Knowledge) were used in most Anglican churches.

The English Hymnal, of high-church sympathy, was prepared for publication in 1904. *The Methodist Hymn-book* was indispensable to a church "born in song". Demand for popular hymns spread to the Roman Catholic Church, which made use of the *Westminster Hymnal* (1912). By then 40,000 hymns were in common use, but neither they nor their tunes were of equal value.

The altar, not the pulpit, had become the focal point of Anglican churches by the mid 19th century. In this detail of *The Sermon* by Walter Frederick Roofe Tyndale (1888) the gallery as well as the nave is full. An unfeigned taste for hearing sermons was still surprisingly common

Catholic emancipation

In Wiseman and Manning, English Roman Catholics gained vigorous leaders for a community transformed by immigration from Ireland, and by converts from the Oxford Movement

In 1829, the year the Emancipation Act allowed Roman Catholics to sit in the Commons, there was a community of about 200,000 Catholics surviving from before the Reformation in the 16th century.

But Irish immigration, which had been a trickle in the 1790s, became a river by the 1830s, and a flood in the 1840s. That decade saw a million Irish die after the failure of the potato crop in 1846, and another million emigrate, mostly to North America. In England and Wales the Irish-born population rose from 291,000 in 1841 to 520,000 in 1851. Almost all were Catholics. The largest concentrations settled in the poorest parts of Liverpool and London. (The Roman Catholic Church in Scotland, where Glasgow drew the highest numbers, came under separate authorities from those in England.)

Rome doubled the bishops in England from four to eight in 1840, and in 1850 re-established a hierarchy in England and Wales with 12 bishops in territorial dioceses under the Archbishop of Westminster. A reaction of horror at this "Papal Aggression", whipped up by *Punch* and the *Times*, changed into an attitude of respect by the time the first Archbishop of Westminster died 15 years later; his *Daily Telegraph* and *Times* obituaries were heartfelt in their language.

This first Cardinal Archbishop was Nicholas Wiseman (1802-65). Born to an Irish merchant family living in Seville, he was educated at the English northern Catholic school of Ushaw College, founded by teachers who had fled Douai in the French Revolution. Wiseman trained for the priesthood at the English College in Rome, and became a celebrated scholar of the ancient oriental language of Syriac.

Wiseman sensed the boom in English Catholicism. He visited England to lecture to Protestant audiences with some success. In 1840, still in his 30s, he was consecrated Bishop and made President of Oscott Seminary, near Birmingham, recently rebuilt by that genius of the Gothic Revival, Augustus Pugin. Oscott was a quick journey on the new railway from Oxford, the centre of the Oxford Movement whose genius, John Henry Newman (*see page 156*), became a Roman Catholic in 1845. Wiseman's sympathy for Newman and his fellow-converts brought a new intellectual strength to English Catholicism.

Favoured converts

From 1847, Wiseman's base was London. The Catholic Church in England grew under a body of decrees laid down by Wiseman at the Synods of Westminster, while converts rose to a disproportionate influence. Chief of these was Henry Edward Manning (1808-92), former Archdeacon of Chichester. Ordained a priest within weeks of his reception into the Church, he trained in Rome and founded a congregation of secular priests, the Oblates of St Charles Borromeo, who were Roman down to their stockings and shoe-buckles. Manning succeeded Wiseman as Archbishop of Westminster in 1865, becoming a Cardinal in 1875.

Manning's claim to fame is three-fold. First, he was convinced of the Holy Spirit's abiding presence in the Church, and this led him to fight for the declaration of the doctrine of papal infallibility, which was defined by the First Vatican Council in 1870.

Secondly, his love of his largely Irish flock made him a passionate pastor to them. He spent the money for a new cathedral on poor schools for them and did all he could for their temporal as well as their spiritual welfare.

Thirdly, he became the patron of every movement to improve the condition of the English poor, through housing reform, trade unions and prevention of cruelty to children. His settlement of the Dock Strike of 1889 was marked by a trade union banner with his portrait. In 1892 vast crowds of non-Catholics honoured his funeral.

"The Thin End of the Wedge" was the caption for this cartoon by John Leech in *Punch* in 1850. Wiseman is the look-out while the Pope tries to break in with a wedge marked "Roman Archbishopric of Westminster"

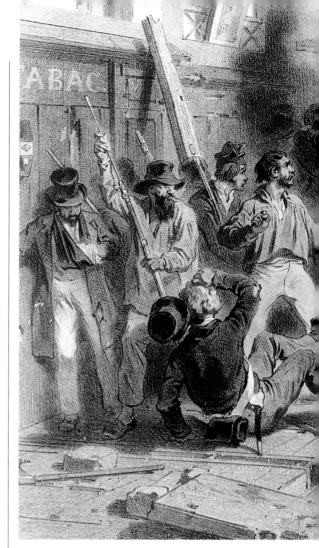

Bishops

Britain escaped revolution in the 19th century. On the Continent with the coups and fighting in the streets went an underlying anti-clericalism which made monasteries and clergy the first target of liberal governments

In England in 1831, during the period of agitation for parliamentary reform, the Bishop of Bristol's palace was burnt down, and stones were thrown at other bishops in the street. But there was no revolution or lasting hatred of the clergy. In continental Europe it was different.

Three Archbishops of Paris in a row died violently. The first, Denis Auguste Affre, visited the barricades during the revolution of 1848 to appeal for peace. Shots were heard, and the insurgents, thinking they were being ambushed, fired on the Archbishop's escort. He fell, mortally wounded. Vast crowds of all sympathies attended his funeral. His successor was merely murdered by a lunatic, but in 1871, Archbishop Georges Darboy was shot without trial by firing squad in the Paris Commune.

and barricades

The classical development of anti-clericalism, though, was in Spain. At the beginning of the 19th century, Spanish churchmen were at one with national opposition to Napoleon's invasion. One of the men being shot by French soldiers in Goya's painting *Tres de Mayo* is a friar. Napoleon's brother Joseph, put on the Spanish throne in 1808, set about suppressing all monasteries and convents, confiscating their property. The next administration confirmed the uncompleted suppressions. More expropriations came after the revolt against Ferdinand VII in 1820. A pattern of anti-clerical murders developed: 24 priests and monks taken from Manresa and murdered in the countryside on November 17 1822; 51 people people including priests and monks bayoneted and thrown into the sea at Corunna on July 24 1823. These were symptoms of how the liberals saw the Church: the enemy, as part of the old order.

The rest of the century in Spain saw a cycle of secularising governments, traditionalist repression, coups. In the 1830s, traditionalist Carlism was the enemy. In the summer of 1834 an absurd story spread that an outbreak of cholera was in fact the poisoning of wells by monks. In Madrid, with the cry "Death to the friars!" the houses of the Jesuits, Dominicans, Mercedarians and Franciscans were sacked and the priests hunted and killed.

But the worst outbreak of anti-clerical violence was in Barcelona in the summer of 1835. While monasteries were burnt and the corpses of monks mutilated in the city (in the throes of a separatist struggle against central government), in Madrid itself a new liberal government came in, and dissolved 900 religious houses.

In 1851 a concordat between the Vatican and Spain stipulated that the state should pay priests' stipends in compensation for its expropriation of Church property. Very soon the reason for this payment was forgotten, and clergy stipends were seen as a privilege afforded by the state to the priests. In any case a revolution changed things in 1855. A new Ley de Desamortización expropriated any property still remaining to the religious orders or newly acquired by them. After more years of turmoil the First Republic was declared in 1873; it was celebrated in Cadiz by the municipal council turning the Franciscan church and friary into a Federal Club for Workers.

Spain, so long isolated from the world (*see page 122*) embraced Anarchism and Socialism with surprising fervour, while in the newly industrialised cities capitalists imposed terrible conditions on workers, making use when they could of the brutal habits of the police and army. This cycle of repression, revolution, coups, corruption, polarisation and anti-clericalism prepared the ground for the Spanish Civil War of 1936-39 with a million deaths (in a country of 25 million). All along, the great majority of the people still went to church and prayed before their favourite statues. For an often desperately poor population, in city and country, the parish church might be the only place they could go where there was space, beauty and calm. To burn a church was thus in part a crime against the people.

Denis Auguste Affre, Archbishop of Paris, is fatally wounded at the barricade of the Faubourg Sainte-Antoine during the street fighting in the revolution of 1848. This lithograph by A. Bayot comes from *Paris dans sa splendeur*, June 25 1848

Justice for the workers

Whole cities dependent on factories gave rise to kinds of poverty and injustice that the Church had never dealt with before. It made a stir when a pope set out some fundamental principles

Struggles between State and Church developed in both Germany and France in the late 19th century. In Prussia the Kulturkampf ("struggle of civilisations") encouraged by Bismarck in the 1870s was given teeth by one of his ministers, Adalbert Falk, whose laws expelled all members of religious orders (including the nuns drowned on the ship *Deutschland*, celebrated by Gerard Manley Hopkins' poem). A thousand priests were imprisoned or exiled; a million Catholics left without the sacraments. Switzerland too imitated the Kulturkampf.

In France during the 1880s a republican government also adopted some features of the Kulturkampf, restricting religious orders and religious education, even encouraging Sunday working. In response Pope Leo XIII wrote in 1885 an encyclical letter *Immmortali Dei* ("Of the Immortal God") arguing that Church and State are both fully competent societies in their own realms. But it came as an utter surprise when he published an encyclical on social teaching, *Rerum Novarum* ("Of New Matters"), in 1891. The terrible position of the poor in cities transformed by the industrial revolution had caught the Pope's attention, in part through briefings by the socially conscious Cardinal Manning (*see page 164*). Manning had, in 1887, published an article in a periodical explaining that natural rights to life and food prevailed over the right to private property, so that for a starving man to take food for himself and his family was not theft.

For a starving man to take food for himself and his family was not theft

Pope Leo XIII also asserted the limitations of private property. Workers' material and spiritual rights must be respected; a living wage and time to worship must be granted. They had a right of association (into unions), and a right to strike (which was not absolute). Two inhuman political systems were condemned: atheistic or totalitarian socialism, and economic liberalism of the "Manchester school" which allowed markets to operate unchecked while letting workers starve or suffer.

The encyclical could not prevent directly the injustices it denounced. The Pope in effect invited political action to ensure that the State performed its duty to defend the workers. Naturally many Protestants thought the Pope too cautious or paternalistic. Prussian mill-owners or Salford Marxists would of course ignore him.

But a new impetus was given to the setting up of explicitly Christian Democratic parties, or the introduction of Christian moral principles into established parties. Future popes developed Leo's social teaching. Undoubtedly it had a far-reaching influence on the politics of Australia, Canada, Germany, France and Italy.

Darkest England

In England, socialists often disbelieved Christianity; Christians were not sure if they could be socialists. BF Westcott, Bishop of Durham 1890-1901, was the first President of the Christian Social Union, founded in 1889. But Herbert Hensley Henson, eventually Bishop of Durham too, believed the market should control wages; he mocked the Christian Socialists.

Most of the early leaders of the Labour movement were influenced by Christianity. "I claim for Socialism that it is the embodiment of Christianity in our industrial system," Keir Hardie, Labour's first candidate for Parliament, wrote in 1894. Cardinal Manning's intervention in the dock strike at the Port of London in 1889 was well known; but Catholics were quickly made aware they could not be Marxist socialists.

Christians also intervened directly. Roman Catholic priests exhausted themselves helping desperately poor Irish families living in cellars, vulnerable to cholera. Father James Nugent (1822-1905), an indefatigable worker, estimated there were 23,000 homeless children in Liverpool alone. Dr J T Barnardo (1845-1905), an Irish revivalist Christian, worked from 1867 for homeless children in London.

And who can fail to be astonished by the story of the Salvation Army? It developed from the street evangelisation of William Booth (1829-1912), who had been a Methodist. By the 1880s it helped drunks, dossers, homeless children, prostitutes. Booth wrote *In Darkest England* (with the help of the reforming journalist W T Stead, who with Booth's son exposed the sale of children for prostitution). The Salvation Army's work continues.

East London children, some barefoot, queue for their Farthing Breakfasts provided by the Salvation Army

THE SALVATION ARMY

The evil of Stalin and Hitler

Soviet Communism and German Nazism strove to replace rival systems such as Christianity with their own totalitarian ideology. Cruelty and death awaited any opponents. The alternatives seemed to be compromise or extinction

The evils of Stalinism and Nazism are now known in horrible detail. When these totalitarian systems were in power, no one could predict whether they would triumph and exterminate Christianity. The Church in Russia experienced during the 20th century the most savage and sustained persecution known to history. Statistics of the Russian Orthodox Church in 1914 and 1939 speak for themselves. Bishops in diocesan service in 1914: 163 (1939: 4); parish clergy 51,105 (some 100s); churches 54,174 (some 100s); monasteries and convents 1,025 (0); monks and nuns 94,629 (not known); theological seminaries 57 (0); parish schools 37,528 (0). The other churches, not least the Baptist, had a similar experience.

For a short time Lenin had followed Marx in believing that religious persecution was unnecessary, since religion would fade away once the proletariat was liberated from its economic shackles. Nonetheless in the year following the Revolution of 1917, the new Communist government adopted a constitution which separated Church from State and opened the way to religious repression.

Civil war delayed the implementation of this policy until 1921. Even so, in the space of three years, 28 bishops and more than 1,200 priests of the Orthodox Church had been killed. When the war ended there was a determined assault on the Church, in which its land and treasures were seized. The Patriarch, Tikhon, was imprisoned; after a year he was released and in a statement disavowed his opposition to the Soviet system. He died in 1925.

Meanwhile the death of Lenin in 1924 let Stalin gain power. The election of a new Patriarch was forbidden, and Metropolitan Peter who was appointed to hold the fort was soon imprisoned. So also was his successor, Metropolitan Sergii, who on his release in 1927 issued a pastoral letter urging collaboration with the State. Sergii's pastoral letter caused division in the Church and highlighted a dilemma that faced all the Russian churches for the next 60 years: is the Christian cause best served by opposition and possible martyrdom, or by compromise with an evil power, allowing the possibility of renewed witness once its days are ended? With many heroic exceptions, the Orthodox Church chose the second course. It was persuaded partly by its long view of history and also by its experience, going back to the 4th century, of working in partnership with the State.

During the 1930s, however, it had little choice. Foll-

Demolition of the Simonov Monastery, Moscow, in 1927 during a wave of destruction under Yaroslavsky, the Commissar of Anti-Religious Affairs. Nationalisation of Church property in Russia begun in 1918, immediately after the Revolution, but civil war delayed implementation until the 1920s. Church marble was used in the building of Moscow's metro

A modern martyr
Polish Franciscan friar Maximilian Kolbe who voluntarily asked an SS officer in a concentration camp to let him die in the place of another prisoner, Franciszek Gajowniczek. The request was granted and in 1982 he was declared a saint as a martyr

owing the promulgation of a new law governing Church-State relations in 1929, Stalin launched a five-year campaign of violence against the Church. Even in 1934, when the terror showed signs of easing, four bishops were shot. At this time hermits and wandering monks helped keep the faith alive. They were joined by many bishops and priests who conducted acts of worship in secret. Icons in the homes of the people also became a focus of family worship – the father acting in place of the priest.

The systematic terror against the Church – arrests, torture, imprisonment, forced labour, execution – was renewed between 1936 and 1938. The number of Christians who died certainly ran to many millions. There was no relief until the Germans invaded Russia in 1941, when Stalin, seeking national unity, decided to reverse his religious policy. In 1943 the Administrator of the Patriarchate and two other bishops were called to the Kremlin. Stalin promised greater freedom in return for support.

A large number of churches and monasteries were re-opened. Bishops and priests came out of hiding. The government even provided resources to enable the Church to find its feet again. It became a time of religious revival; the detente between State and Church continued until 1955. Church authorities expressed their gratitude by becoming instruments of Soviet foreign policy during the Cold War. State-approved Church leaders were allowed to travel to assure the West that repression was ended and all was well.

The number of Christians who died certainly ran to many millions

But this line became even less credible in 1953 when Stalin was succeeded by Khrushchev who launched an anti-religious campaign lasting until 1965. If not as bad as the campaign of the 1930s, this meant wholesale closure of churches and monasteries. Some bishops were sent to prison, priests were also imprisoned or sent to mental hospitals and the Church's work among the young was severely restricted. The bishops for the most part seemed to accept the new policy. But from 1965 some of them began to protest, and by the 1970s dissident movements were emerging.

A dramatic change came with Gorbachev's attempt to reform the Soviet system, with the aid of the Russian people including religious believers. It was in time for there to be a great millennium celebration in 1988 to mark the first acceptance of Christianity in Kiev. Two years later the government replaced Stalin's law of 1929 with a new law guaranteeing freedom for all religions. Churches and monasteries were handed back in large numbers. Once again the Orthodox Church had outlived its enemies.

From 1945 the Russian experience was shared in varying degrees by all the churches of the Eastern European countries which formed the Soviet bloc. They, too, suffered persecution and were faced with the same hard choices. And they produced their saints and martyrs who testified to the ultimate indestructibility of faith.

The Nazi-sponsored Church

For Hitler, the Nazi ideology was a religion. But he sought at first to use the Protestant Church as an instrument of policy, and he sponsored a German Christian Church Movement, which expressed a synthesis of Nazism and Christianity.

In September 1933 at a synod of the Church in Prussia a large Nazi presence secured the replacement of 10 general superintendents of the Church by 10 German Christian Bishops. More than half of the Protestant regional churches subsequently accepted the new movement's ultra-liberal theological opinions. These opinions included the anti-Semitic tenets of Hitler's Aryan doctrine. The Old Testament and the writings of St Paul were to be ▶

rejected, and pastors of Jewish descent excluded. Immediately a number of churchmen saw the great danger facing the Church. Among them was Martin Niemöller, a famous U-boat captain in the 1914-18 war. He now convened a meeting of pastors which formed the Pastors' Emergency League. It issued a protest against the government's policy and the compliance of the Church's leadership.

Soon the League had 3,000 members. At an historic meeting in Barmen in 1934 it drew up a declaration defining the belief and mission of a Confessing Church that would acknowledge only God's revelation in Jesus Christ and would preach only the Gospel of the free Grace of God.

The attraction of 4,000 more members to the Confessing Church convinced Hitler that Church activities everywhere must now be reduced to worship and devotion. Its youth movement was eventually absorbed into the Hitler Youth and by the end of 1936 the Confessing Church had become subject to constant persecution. Niemöller was in prison. During 1937 there were many arrests and imprisonments. Pope Pius XI issued an encyclical, *Mit Brennender Sorge* ("With burning sorrow"), condemning the attacks on the Church. This was read from every Catholic pulpit on Palm Sunday. The Bishop of Munster gave a public address on the same theme, and among others who spoke out was Cardinal Faulhaker. But in 1938 the clergy were required to take an oath of allegiance; continuous persecution had worn down much of the resistance.

When the Dutch bishops protested, the Nazis increased deportations

On the outbreak of war in 1939 the Confessing Church was driven underground. The brutal repression exercised by the Gestapo in wartime Germany made open opposition impossible, except for those who felt called to martyrdom. Among those who paid this price was a brilliant theologian, Dietrich Bonhoeffer, who ran a training college for Confessing Church pastors until it was discovered by the authorities and closed. He then contrived to get a post in Army Intelligence and used his position to travel to Sweden in 1942 to hold a secret meeting with Bishop George Bell of Chichester in the hope that he might persuade the British government to declare its support for those in Germany who were planning to overthrow Hitler.

This proved to be impossible and in May of the following year Bonhoeffer was arrested, imprisoned, then hanged in 1945, shortly before the American army occupied that part of Germany. His final words were, "This is the end; for me the beginning of life."

Four years earlier a Franciscan friar, Father Maximilian Kolbe, was arrested in German-occupied Poland and sent to the death camp at Auschwitz. His life had been spent in the cause of traditional Catholic education and he published a successful magazine, also on traditional lines. In Auschwitz he ministered to his fellow prisoners until, in August 1941, he volunteered to take the place of a young married man who had been chosen for death by starvation. He survived for nearly a fortnight and was then given a lethal injection. In 1982 he was canonised; the man for whom he gave his life attended the ceremony in Rome.

The heroism of Maximilian Kolbe, Dietrich Bonhoeffer and others has inevitably led to questions about the attitude of Pope Pius XII to the Nazi atrocities, in particular the mass killing of Jews. Should he not have spoken out specifically in their defence? Yet he saw that when the Dutch Roman Catholic bishops protested against the deportation of Jews from Holland to Nazi death camps, not only were there reprisals against the Catholic community, but also additional deportations were put into effect of Jews who had become Christians. If Pius XII believed that he could achieve more by behind-the-scenes influence, most people today are left with the impression that he did not do enough publicly.

A religion for Latin America

A television, family photos and religious pictures decorate one corner of a tin-roofed shack in Mexico. Latin American religion means predominantly a religion for the poor

Latin America did not suffer the simple Cold War division between democracies and Communist countries which split Europe after the Second World War. If each nation had its complex history, all Latin American societies were implicitly built on the assumption that th majority were Roman Catholics. But a survey 1953 found that although 90 per cent were baptised, only 15 per cent practised their religic

Mexico had seen a state persecution in the 1920s that by 1933 left only 200 priests wher there had once been 7,000. Argentina had the political experiment of Juan Domingo Perón

communicated in 1955) and his wife Eva. In
caragua a revolutionary Sandinista government
luded two Catholic priests but was rejected by
ters. In Cuba the Pope was welcomed after
ore than 30 years of Castro's Communist rule.
Meanwhile the poor worshipped as best they
uld. The picture above shows one form of
votion in a Mexican shack. And in the late
60s a revolutionary kind of Christianity
empted to appeal to the neglected poor. It
nt by the name of Liberation Theology. This
stem fused two elements: the struggle of the
or and theories that clergymen brought back

from European universities. Academics in
Münster and then in Belgian Catholic university
faculties evolved a theology of revolution to seek
a world without servitude, an idea taken up at a
congress of Latin American Roman Catholic
Bishops at Medellin, Colombia, in 1968.

Using Marxist methodology, priests began
building up "basic communities" which promised
development determined by "*praxis*" – practical
action – of struggling poor people. The theory
was outlined by Gustavo Gutierrez, a Peruvian,
in his book *Liberation Theology* (1971).

Certainly many priests working among the

downtrodden knew something had to be done.
Civil wars raged in Nicaragua and El Salvador;
thousands went missing in Guatemala and
Argentina; Maoist guerrillas terrorised Peru.

But the Marxist language and the reduction
of all spirituality to social reform alarmed
Church leaders. In 1984 Rome issued a negative
critique of liberation theology. It was followed
in 1986 by a series of positive proposals, which
gained less publicity. Some radical theologians,
notably Father Leonardo Boff, a Brazilian
Franciscan, left the active ministry. Others
adjusted their behaviour.

Updating the Church

In the rebellious Sixties the Second Vatican Council changed the face of the Roman Catholic Church. It meant much more than the Pope giving up being carried about in a chair

There is no doubt that the Second Vatican Council (1962-65) turned the Roman Catholic Church upside down. It also encouraged other Christians to emulate its spirit of *aggiornamento* – an Italian term for bringing things up to date, or adapting to the modern world.

This universal council of bishops was the first since the Vatican Council of 1869-70 had broken up at the outbreak of the Franco-Prussian war. And the next most recent precedent was the Council of Trent, with its reforming, organising measures, in the middle of the 16th century. The new council in the rebellious Sixties was a leap into the unknown.

It was the work of Pope John XXIII, elected as a compromise caretaker pope at the age of 76 in 1958. Of Italian peasant background – not a novelty in itself – he was an experienced diplomatist who had expected to retire as Archbishop of Venice. As Pope he lived to see the new council open in 1962, and the "windows opened", as he put it, to let in, as he hoped, the light and breath of the Holy Spirit.

The council continued under his less jolly successor Paul VI. For many, its most obvious result was the rewriting of the Mass, now celebrated in the language of each country, instead of Latin. Technically, Mass was already said in more than a dozen languages (Syriac, Ge'ez, Greek) for Catholics who were not of the Roman rite but were in communion with the Pope. And the Council directed that the rewritten *Missa Normativa*, still in Latin, be made familiar to all the faithful.

For all that, the *de facto* dropping of Latin was the visible change that symbolised the council. Yet the deepest achievement of "Vatican Two", as it became known, was to recognise that the Church was made up of all baptised people. The Council moreover explained that everyone was called to holiness. Since most people are lay people, they were to achieve this holiness not by apeing the clergy but through their ordinary secular work. In this way the Church, through its members, was to bring the world to God. Theologically, since members of the Church are members of the mystical Body of Christ (as St Paul called it), this activity by lay people would help accomplish the intervention into history of Jesus Christ, God made man. (The one baptism that Catholics and Protestants received made their divisions the more scandalous; the council encouraged Christian unity through a movement called ecumenism.)

This sublime and universal call to evangelism was not,

The Second Vatican Council encouraged Christian reunion. Above: Patriarch Athenagoras of Constantinople, the Orthodox leader, meets Pope Paul VI at St Peter's basilica on a three-day visit to Rome in October 1967.
Right: Vatican II began in October 1962 with 2,500 bishops from all over the world. It was initiated by Pope John XXIII, who was unhappy about stagnation in the Church. He hoped to bring it into closer contact with the modern world

however, communicated very clearly to churchgoers, concealed as it was beneath the jolting changes in worship and the multitude of sometimes hair-raising innovations justified by the "spirit" of Vatican II. Guitars in church, lipstick-wearing nuns on motor scooters, the binning of clerical dress by priests, the ripping out of altars – everything, from the introduction of stacking-chairs to the abandonment by hundreds of priests of their calling, was attributed to the Council.

At the heart of the Council's published conclusions were three Dogmatic Constitutions, as they were called. The Dogmatic Constitution on the Church (*Lumen Gentium*, "Light of the people") outlined the universal call to holiness. The Church, it said, owed everything to the foundations laid by Christ (prepared for by the Old Testament history of the Jewish people). The developed Church was to be ruled by the bishops as a college under the primacy of the Pope. (This was, after all, a Roman Catholic analysis.) The Dogmatic Constitution on the Liturgy (*Sacrosanctum Concilium*, "The holy council") saw the task of worship as no less than the bringing of the redemptive action

> **Everything from nuns wearing lipstick to priests giving up their calling was blamed on the Council**

of Christ to the people he has saved. In Catholic theology this is done through the sacraments, principally through the Mass as the sacrificial celebration of the Eucharist. The liturgy should possess a noble simplicity, the document added, and be open to the active participation of the laity. The third Dogmatic Constitution, on Scripture (*Dei Verbum*, "The word of God"), said that the Bible should be understood with the insights passed on as a developing tradition by the Church. The Council encouraged study of the Scriptures and the commentaries of the early Fathers of the Church upon them.

Among other documents, a Pastoral Constitution (*Gaudium et Spes*, "Joy and hope") encouraged openness to the modern world, and a Decree on Religious Freedom (*Dignitatis Humanae* "Of human dignity") condemned both the persecution of Christians and the forcible coercion of non-Christians (such as forced baptisms).

At the same time as Vatican II, theologians came to the fore who spoke vehemently against the old order of the Church, often describing its "fortress mentality". There were calls for married men to be made priests, and also for the ordination of women. But the most obvious pressure was for great changes in moral standards, notably sexual ones. It was said that sexual acts outside marriage might not be wrong, that homosexual people should be encouraged to form stable sexual relationships. The most widely canvassed proposal was that contraception might be a good thing. It came to many as an unacceptable surprise that Pope Paul VI in 1968 published an encyclical letter *Humanae Vitae* ("Of human life"), reasserting the Church's prohibition of artificial contraception.

Since Vatican II, mainstream Catholic theology has tended to become polarised. Two main groups rallied to rival theological journals: liberals to *Concilium* and the traditionally minded to *Communio*. Meanwhile the wilder fringe have had their mandate to teach theology in the name of the Roman Catholic Church withdrawn. The best known of these is Hans Küng.

It is notable that Pope John Paul II (elected 1978) had been the man chosen by his fellow Polish bishops to draw up a programme for the implementation of Vatican II in that country. His 200 pages of recommendations have since been published (in English as *Sources of Renewal*). In the liberal West, he is often misleadingly represented as right-wing. How far such a judgment is true may become clearer in the next millennium.

Mother Teresa of Calcutta was not trying to solve social problems through her work with the poorest of the poor. She saw Jesus Christ in the abandoned children or the dying to whom she showed practical love

Something beautiful for Jesus

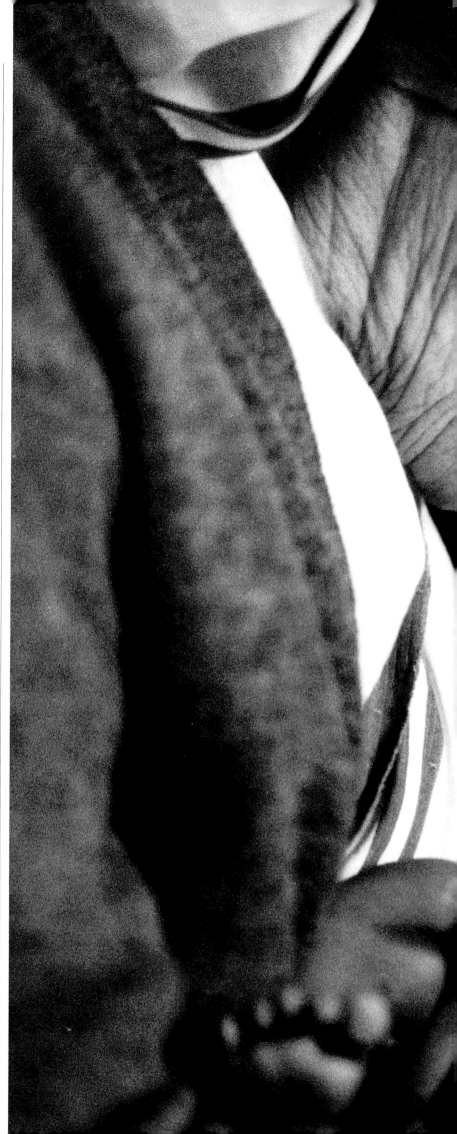

Mother Teresa of Calcutta, the tiny nun in a cotton sari habit, died with a universal reputation for holiness in 1997, aged 87. She stood out as a witness to religious values in a secular age; moreover her work grew in the post-colonial, predominantly non-Christian setting of India.

She made her teaching plain by repeating a few sayings. Her work was to be with "the poorest of the poor" in whom she and her nuns saw Jesus Christ. Do "something beautiful for Jesus" she would ask her helpers; indeed they should "love until it hurts".

In her lifetime she founded 450 centres in 100 countries, treated 90,000 lepers, helped 27,000 friendless people die with dignity, fed 500,000 families a year. But she did not see herself as a solver of social problems. The poor she worked for – lepers, dying street people, babies found on rubbish tips – had already fallen through whatever safety-net the state offered. Nor was she a coercive converter of the heathen – she wanted dying people to be better Hindus, better Muslims. In the meantime she and her Missionaries of Charity would spoonfeed, wash or just hold the hand of a dying woman or old man.

She was born Gonxha ("Rosebud") Agnes Bojaxhiu in Skopje, Macedonia, just south of Kosovo, in 1910. Her father was in sympathy with Albanian patriots; her mother was a Roman Catholic. She became a missionary nun, trained in Ireland, taught in India and was so affected by seeing the poor that in 1948 she started, against great odds, a religious congregation to work for them.

Her nuns have two cotton saris, one of which they wash in a bucket. They get up early, kneel on the ground for their morning prayers, attend Mass, go about tending the poor, take no payment, eat simply. They do not go out without permission, entertain guests or watch films.

Doctrinally Mother Teresa was simply orthodox; but she could see that abortion was bad in any case, for it showed a lack of love. "If you don't want a child," she said, "give it to me." She drew attention to rough sleepers in cardboard boxes when she visited London. She told her nuns to care for people suffering from Aids where they were left unattended and unloved. "Being unwanted is the worst disease any human being can experience." She did not mind talking to monstrous dictators if she thought they would let her work in their countries.

Mother Teresa was given the Nobel Prize for Peace and her canonisation is expected as soon as the regulations allow.

Mother Teresa in 1979 when she was awarded the Nobel Peace Prize. The grant of more than $100,000 has been used to carry out her work

The Polish people had always resisted the Communist regime imposed on them after the Second World War by the neighbouring Soviet Union. The election of Karol Wojtyla as Pope was the catalyst that brought eventual victory for the anti-Communist movement in Poland and throughout the Soviet bloc

The fall of Communism

In the 1970s it seemed inconceivable that the Communist system which controlled the Soviet Union and its subject states in Eastern Europe could be brought down. An experiment in Czechoslovakia of Communism with a human face, known as the Prague Spring, was crushed in 1968 by Soviet tanks. Dissidents within the Soviet Union were picked off one by one; the best known and most consciously prophetic, Alexander Solzhenitsyn, was exiled in 1974 for writing his relentless exposure of the repressive state, *The Gulag Archipelago*.

The Soviet machine was corrupt, but all the less movable for that. It was the enemy of anyone who sought freedom. It was the enemy of the Christian churches, by their very nature. But the crack in the Soviet Empire that was to make it crumble and fall was its most religious vassal state, Poland. And the man who did most to encourage the change was Karol Wojtyla, elected Pope John Paul II in October 1978.

Polish workers had risen against the ruling party before. In 1956, the same year that the Hungarian uprising was crushed, 79 strikers were killed at Poznan, and in 1970 strikers at Gdansk were killed. Wojtyla, as Archbishop of Krakow, had been accustomed to the struggle against the Communist regime, as when he backed the campaign to build a church for the steel town of Nowa Huta outside Krakow.

Ten million see the Pope

In 1979 after Wojtyla had become Pope the authorities delayed a visit to his homeland. But during an eight-day tour in June he was seen in person by 10 million, a third of the nation. Everyone saw him on television (though the regime came up with the feeble expedient of ordering cameras not to show the crowds around him). "Christ cannot be kept out of the history of Man in any part of the globe," the Pope said in a sermon to crowds chanting, "We want God."

A strike by workers at the Lenin shipyard, Gdansk, was led by Lech Walesa. He happened to be a particularly committed Catholic, and the Church was a rallying point for the strikers. Behind the walls of the yard they heard Mass and made their confessions kneeling on the asphalt;

the twin icons tied to the gates were of the black Madonna of Czestochowa (an ancient hilltop shrine linked to Polish nationhood) and the Pope.

Walesa signed the agreement that humiliated the government with an outsize souvenir pen from the Pope's visit. But in 1982 a new Party leader, General Wojciech Jaruzelski, suppressed Solidarity, Walesa's independent trade union, and imposed martial law. Journalists noted references to "solidarity" in the Pope's addresses, and though this was a term that featured innocently in his sociological vocabulary, the Pope made it explicitly clear that the plight of Poland was much in his mind.

"My land is bathed by the blood and sweat of its sons and daughters," he told pilgrims in St Peter's Square. "I put this problem before the conscience of the world."

Glasnost and the Vatican

Solidarity continued underground. The Pope returned for a visit in 1983 (when he paid tribute to those who had died at Poznan in 1956) and in 1987. A wave of strikes in 1988 forced the Party back to the negotiating table. Walesa and his colleagues succeeded in securing democratic elections for 1989. (Walesa was to become President.) In 1988 the Vatican Secretary of State, Cardinal Casaroli, had visited Moscow and talked with Mikhail Gorbachev, the Soviet leader who was announcing new policies of *perestroika* (reform) and *glasnost* (openness in government). Gorbachev learnt of the Vatican's preference for democratic socialism to "real" socialism, according to Gorbachev's later version of their talks.

Mass protests in Czechoslovakia led in November 1989 to the ceding of power there by the Communist Party, and this time Russian tanks did not move in. East Germans began to stream into West Germany and the Berlin Wall, a symbol of the prison mentality of the Soviet bloc, was breached amid scenes of jubilation. On December 1 1989 Gorbachev became the first Soviet leader to make a visit to the Vatican.

Strikers inside the Lenin shipyards in Gdansk put up pictures of Pope John Paul II on the locked gates

Popular religion

The technology that has transformed daily life in the Western world since the Second World War has not made religion wither away. Christian sects thrive as much as they did in the 17th century. Sometimes folk devotion is accommodated in the mainstream churches

Papa Giovanni Paolo II

Some fringe denominations come and go faster than others. The last Muggletonian, for example, is said to have died in 1958. Muggletonians followed Lodowicke Muggleton (1609-98), a London tailor who was the "mouth" of John Reeve, the bringer of a new dispensation that was meant to supersede that of Jesus Christ.

An example of a more showy but less lasting blossoming was Irvingism, founded by Edward Irving (1792-1834). He had fallen in love with Jane Welsh (the future wife of the thinker Thomas Carlyle), but married another. Jane Welsh Carlyle later remarked that there would have been no weird manifestations in his church if he had married her. Irving was an ordained minister of the Church of Scotland but went to London and founded the so-called Catholic Apostolic Church. There was not much either Catholic or Apostolic about it, but he could hold a congregation of 1,000 spellbound for three hours, and had an idea that the end of the world was at hand. In 1833 he was deprived of his Scottish ministry. At this, his London congregation rather surprisingly dropped him, and he died within a year. A fine big church in Bloomsbury, later sold and now used by the University of London, stands as a monument to him and his followers.

It would be a mistake to write off followers of such sects as either stupid or mad. Michael Faraday, one of the greatest scientists, was a Sandemanian, a narrow sect that had developed the teachings of John Glas (1695-1773). Glas was another Scot, among whose ideas was the institution of an *agape* (*see page 22*) on a supposedly biblical model in the form of homely meals with cabbage and potatoes. A phenomenon often found in enthusiastic sects such as Irvingism (though not Sandemanianism) was speaking in tongues (glossolalia). It had struck unpredictably during 18th-century Wesleyan meetings too. Glossolalia has never been so common as it is today, thanks to the popularity of the Pentecostal movement.

The central idea of Pentecostalism is that after baptism there should be another crisis – a baptism of the spirit. In keeping with biblical accounts of the first Pentecost, the gift of the Spirit may be accompanied by signs, such as glossolalia, falling, writhing and weeping.

In the United States and in a growing number of congregations in Britain Penetecostalism has attracted black congregations. Some people have seen in the American experience a survival brought by slaves from African religions. In Britain, Pentecostal churches throve when immigrants from the West Indies found that worship in British Anglican, Baptist or Roman Catholic churches was ▶

An old woman kisses an image of San Campio at the village of Figueiro, Pontevedra, in Spain. Popular customs may be accommodated more of less by mainstream creeds

too bland; the new Pentecostal churches made them "feel at home". It is impossible to generalise about Pentecostalism because it has no head office, no historic shrine, no comprehensive theology and no elaborately trained clergy. Pentecostalism has, however, influenced mainstream churches, though these prefer to accept versions of a "charismatic" revival that place a stress on the work of the Holy Spirit without defying orthodox teaching. Huge congregations are drawn, for example, to a Church

of England parish, Holy Trinity, Brompton, where prosperous and intelligent worshippers accept charismatic manifestations (such as glossolalia and falling down) as gifts of the spirit.

It has always been the case that popular practice has developed in the main churches more or less independently of official teaching. In the touching photograph (above) of an old woman kissing an image of San Campio there are survivals of customs which, if not in

contradiction to Church teaching, have taken on a life of their own. At the foot of the saint's image is a little heap of wax votive offerings. These, fashioned in the shapes of hands, feet, ears, are left in thanks for the saint's healing intercession. On the saint's feastday (July 30), handkerchiefs are passed over his image to be kept as holy reminders of his intercessory power. For some, the ritual may be perfunctory, for others it may express a profound and genuine religious devotion.

There are survivals of customs which, if not in contradiction to Church teaching, have taken on a life of their own; sometimes they express profound devotion

Impact of the masses

People in the Western world tend to judge religious observance by the people they meet or by what they see on television. Large but distant groups are usually undervalued.
But mass gatherings make a memorable impression

Everyone thinks that not so many people go to church as they did. That is true of Britain, but credible statistics of those affiliated to Christian churches in "more developed countries" show a rise between 1970 and 1985 from 698 million to 747 million; for "less developed countries" there was a jump from 443 million to 679 million.

In Britain, most people know Quakers, for example, and are ignorant of Syro-Malabarese Christians; but the world numbers for Quakers in 1985 was 502,000 and for Syro-Malabarese in communion with the Pope 3.2 million.

One way in which Christian denominations consolidate their own identities is by mass gatherings. That is not always the intention, but if Billy Graham comes to town a football stadium is filled. If the Pope visits Ireland, a third of the population crowds into Phoenix Park.

Yet these phenomena can come without central planning by the authorities. There is a theory that Lourdes was encouraged by a papacy keen to enhance its authority by promoting the dogma of the Immaculate Conception (the teaching that Mary, the mother of Jesus, was from the first moment of her existence without sin, even original sin), promulgated in 1854. But this theory is unconvincing.

In 1858 Bernadette Soubirous, aged 14, the daughter of a poor and unfortunate family in the south of France, saw a vision of a young, unknown woman at a cave near the river at Lourdes. Bernadette was beaten by her mother when she told her. Her periodic visions continued. During her 16th vision she asked the young woman who she was; the answer in Provençal was: "*Que soy era Immaculada Councepciou,*" (I am the Immaculate Conception") which the girl did not understand, but reported to her parish priest. The Church authorities forbade any public devotions at the site until 1862. In 1866 Bernadette went off to be a nun at Nevers, far from Lourdes, and she died aged 35.

Bernadette knew nothing of any cures at Lourdes, but pilgrims soon began reporting them. By 1872 a rally attracted 20,000 people to the shrine. In 1958, the centenary of the visions, it attracted six million visitors.

A medical commission sits to scrutinise reports of miraculous cures. To count as a miracle it must be a sud-

Billy Graham, the 'great sinner'

The evangelist Billy Graham comes from a tradition of public commitment and confession alien to the European experience. It has made him the most prominent religious figure in America

The evangelist Billy Graham has preached in person to more people than anyone who has ever lived. What began in country churches and trailer parks in the American south became a world crusade, moving through cathedrals, stadiums and public squares. Altogether Graham has invited 100 million people to "accept Jesus Christ as your personal saviour", of whom nearly three million have "stepped forward" according to his staff. Graham preaches a raucous, muscular Christianity, but the message is simple: Each person is sinful before God, but can be redeemed through faith in Jesus Christ.

Born in 1918, William Franklin Graham Jr grew up on a dairy farm in North Carolina's Great Smokey Mountains, the son of pious parents who believed in clean living, spankings and Bible readings. In 1933 he became teetotal after his father made him drink beer until he was sick. Later he and his followers would sign the "Modesto Manifesto" pledging honest statistics and clean finances and never to be alone with women other than their wives.

Graham's conversion came in 1934 at a revivalist meeting addressed by Mordecai Ham, a travelling preacher famous for his fire and brimstone sermons. Pointing at Graham, Ham declared: "You're a sinner! We have a great sinner here tonight." Graham says: "Right then and there, I made my decision for Christ."

He enrolled at the Florida Bible Institute, where he practised sermons in a shed, and was ordained by the Southern Baptists in 1940. In 1949 he captured the support of William Randolph Hearst with a speech in Los Angeles. "Puff Graham," the press baron instructed his editors.

Graham excites powerful reactions. Strict fundamentalists see him as a traitor for his willingness to work with Catholics. To Harry S. Truman he was a "counterfeit". But to George Bush, he was simply "America's Pastor".

Providing a moral lead to post-war generations of Americans, Billy Graham was a dominant personality of the 1950s and 1960s, preaching to more people than anyone who has ever lived

A candlelight procession at Lourdes. An underground basilica has been built that can hold 10,000 worshippers

den, complete and lasting cure of a serious, organic and objectively proved disease. This year the 66th medical miracle was announced – a Frenchman cured of multiple sclerosis in 1987. The Church authorities are insistent that pilgrims should go to Lourdes not seeking cures of the body but out of devotion, to pray. Volunteers make their own pilgrimages to look after the sick pilgrims. In the domain near the river there are no souvenir sellers. In the town outside the Church's authority, shops sell postcards, umbrellas, plastic rosaries, paper-weights containing a little statue of the Virgin Mary. The hotel and bar owners do well.

To Fatima in Portugal, where three children repeatedly saw Mary in 1917 (she asked them to pray and do penance) throngs of peasants walk barefoot. At Knock in Ireland, 15 villagers spent two hours on August 21 1879 standing in the rain and saying the Rosary while before them on the gable end of the local church they could see a vision of the Virgin Mary; a century later Connaught Regional Airport was built to cater for pilgrim flights. The Spanish Tourist Board marks the road to Santiago prominently on its maps. Some of this is in bad taste. Some Christians think much of it idolatry. But it is undoubtedly popular and spontaneous.

Whatever they get caught out in, American Presidents cannot afford to ignore the body of religious believers. Popular television evangelical churches, with personality preachers and prime-time hype, have yet to recover from their own sex scandals

The American way of belief

Taking the

The snake-handling churches of the Deep South are one of the strangest manifestations of American Christian life in a country with a high level of churchgoing but a multitude of creeds

The congregation in Macedonia, Alabama, handle a poisonous rattlesnake during a service. About 100 have died from bites since the practice began early this century

On stage and on television: a preacher at the Praise the Lord Heritage Village Church, New Charlotte, North Carolina

Although the Constitution expressly forbids any formal link between Church and State, America's public life has a powerful religious dimension. Since 1865 the coinage has been inscribed with "In God We Trust" and the citizen's pledge of allegiance is to "the nation under God", the last two words added as recently as 1960.

No American politician dare ignore the religious voter. Following the retirement of President Reagan in 1988 the Christian Coalition – a right-wing body led by an evangelist, Pat Robertson, who claimed to represent the "moral majority" –was strong enough to attempt to capture the leadership of the Republican Party.

Meetings of the House of Representatives always begin with prayer, conducted by its chaplain, and Presidents call prominent Church leaders to the White House for advice and for the offering of prayer on important occasions.

Since the days of Eisenhower the Prayer Breakfast has been a significant element in American life. Attended mainly by professional people, a substantial breakfast is accompanied by one or more sermons, usually of an evangelical character, and some homespun prayers. Public figures are frequently present and it was at a White House Prayer Breakfast that President Clinton made his first real confession of guilt in the Monica Lewinsky affair.

America's evangelical religions have their biggest audience on television, but they have yet to recover from the

scandals of the 1980s when they were at their height. At nine on Sunday evenings channels provided viewers with hour-long programmes consisting mainly of sermons of a ranting kind given by hell-fire preachers who used highly manipulative techniques – threats, tears, promises – to secure "conversions". The same techniques were used also to extract huge sums of money from viewers. The preachers appealed for funds to finance their heavy broadcasting costs and sometimes charities.

The Rev Jim Bakker's PTL (Praise the Lord) organisation broadcast to 2.6 million viewers on 161 stations and had an income of $150 million a year, of which Bakker was paid $1.6 million plus bonuses. His career ended when a rival tele-evangelist, the Rev Jimmy Swaggart, revealed that Bakker had once spent a night in a hotel with a church secretary. Later he was sent to prison for defrauding his "electronic church" of $158 million.

Swaggart, who headed a $120 million a year organisation broadcasting on 287 channels and enjoyed an affluent life-style, was himself brought down when a former tele-evangelist produced evidence of his frequenting a New Orleans motel with prostitutes. This marked the end of such broadcasts on the main television channels, but tele-evangelism continues on small, local stations.

ible literally: 'They shall take up serpents'

In the United States following a post-war religious boom, fuelled perhaps by the equation of Christianity with patriotism and anti-Communism in the Cold War era, church attendance in 1960 reached 69 per cent.

Large losses of membership were sustained in the changed climate of the 1960s and 1970s. Church attendance is now at about 43 per cent and there are 400,000 places of worship. In places such as Dallas, in the South, many local churches have membership rolls of 5,000 and more. Sunday worship is often followed by Bible study classes.

A marked feature of American church life is its many divisions.

Almost 200 denominations are large enough to have statistical significance on a national level. There is a multitude of other, smaller sects with distinctive names, beliefs and practices.

There can be fewer stranger examples of diversity in American belief than the snake-handling churches of the South. The motive for handling snakes derives from the words of Jesus about his followers recorded in Mark's Gospel: "They shall take up serpents; and if they drink any deadly thing, it shall not hurt them."

In 1998 an Alabama preacher, John Wayne Browne, died of a rattlesnake bite sustained while he was delivering a sermon; his wife had died of snake-bite in 1995. Some 100 snake-handling Christians have died since the habit became established early this century in the region where Tennessee, North Carolina, Georgia and Alabama meet. The services of the Holiness Church, which specialises in this weird form of witness, may last for several hours with energetic music punctuated by cries of praise from men and women draped with rattlesnakes. At the end of the service the snakes are put away in their boxes and accompany their owners home.

Though the majority of North American Christians are Protestant, the largest single denomination is the institutionally undivided Roman

Catholic Church, with about 58 million members and 53,000 priests. Next comes the Southern Baptist Convention with 15 million members and 35,000 ministers. There are another 20 federations of Baptist churches, some of which have large memberships.

The Methodist Church has about 40,000 places of worship and several million members, while the Lutheran and Presbyterian Churches and the Churches of Christ all have large followings. The Anglican Church is relatively small, with 7,000 places of worship and about three million members, many of them in the upper echelons of American society.

The Millennium and

Christians believe that Jesus Christ will come again, that the dead will rise and be judged, that a new Heaven and a new Earth will be wrought. These heady ideas have throughout history attracted the wildest millenarians and false messiahs

The New Testament is full of references to the end of the world. It is foreseen as the second coming of Jesus. "Ye shall hear of wars and rumours of wars: see that ye be not troubled: for all these things must come to pass, but the end is not yet. For nation shall rise against nation, and kingdom against kingdom: and there will be famines, and pestilences, and earthquakes in divers places," Jesus says in the Gospel according to Matthew. "As the lightning cometh out of the east, and shineth even unto the west; so shall also the coming of the Son of man be. For wheresoever the carcase is, there will the eagles be gathered together."

The sentence about the carcase and the eagles is a piece of advice to read the signs of the times. Unfortunately that is something that people have been singularly bad at doing over the past two millennia. There seems little doubt that the early Christian community thought that Jesus would be coming again in power quite soon. St Paul had to explain that those who had died already would not be denied the benefits of Christ's coming in glory.

Ever since, millenarianism has been a favourite bee in the bonnets of heresiarchs. But the term millenarianism has more than one meaning. Just at the moment we tend to connect it with the coming of the millennium. But previous predictions of the end of the world were not limited to the first millennium in AD 1000, or even the 6,000th anniversary of the supposed year of creation. Millenarianism can also mean the same as chiliasm, that is, the ushering in of a thousand-year reign of peace with Christ as king on earth. A good example was that of the Fifth Monarchy Men in 17th-century England. They were no joke. Several of them were MPs in the Barebones Parliament (nominated by the Independent churches) during

> **'Wheresoever the carcase is, there will the eagles be gathered together'**

the interregnum after the beheading of Charles I in 1649. They took their name from the prediction in the second chapter of the Book of Daniel of five great kingdoms; theirs was to be the last, ruled by Jesus· Christ. One of their leaders, Thomas Venner, was said by the Speaker, Thurloe, to be "a fellow of desperate and bloody spirit, and suspected to have designs to blow up the Tower". Nevertheless he was let out of jail and on January 6 (the Epiphany) 1661, in the first year of the reign of the restored Charles II, Venner and 50 supporters burst out from their meeting-house in the City of London intent on establishing the Fifth Monarchy; their watchword was "The King Jesus, and the heads upon the gates". Those not killed were arrested; Venner was hanged drawn and quartered outside their own meeting house 13 days later.

The Fifth Monarchy episode is just one of a rich and surprising history of millenarianism, sometimes mixed up with messianism. In 2nd-century Phrygia the Montanist

The Anastasis, a mural from 1320 in Kariye Camii in Istanbul. Jesus pulls Adam and Eve from their graves at the end of time

heretics expected the New Jerusalem to descend. In Münster in 1534, an Anabaptist New Jerusalem was declared, which turned into a bloody farrago of dictatorship and antinomianism put to an end only by the slaughter of its proponents. In 1993 the American millenarian sect, the Branch Davidians, perished in a fire after a siege by federal agents. It is something that seems to appeal to the human imagination, especially a disturbed one.

But perfectly orthodox Christianity entails a belief in the final coming of the Kingdom of God to complete the work of Jesus. The last book of the Bible, Revelation, ends with "Amen. Even so, come, Lord Jesus."

A pattern in 2,000 years

History is one damned – or blessed – thing after another. Christianity is still here. Both unexpected causes and clear human choices have made it what it is

the end of the world

This book, *AD*, was not intended to be a history of salvation. Christians believe there is such a thing, but it is not entirely available for human study.

In retrospect, there is a pattern of a kind. Look back on the six chapters of *AD*; it is a series of snapshots, of scenes from history. Run through them fast and there emerges a blurred but moving picture, like a child's flick-book.

The survival of Christianity has been a close-run thing. If Paul had not fallen from his horse, his energy might have succeeded in exterminating the nascent Church. If Constantine had been a fierce persecutor, then it might have been the end. If the Muslim invasions had not stopped at Poitiers in 732, why should all Europe not have become an Islamic empire?

Continuity in Christian culture means it is much easier for anyone brought up in England to understand literature, painting, music from its past than if that civilisation had abruptly been extinguished. It is still delightful to look at Matthew Paris's pen and ink pictures from 700 years ago; the music of Hildegard of Bingen from 800 years ago is enjoying a current vogue.

The memorable Christians are thoroughly human, with marked characters: Teresa of Avila, Thomas Becket, Francis of Assisi, Augustine of Hippo, John Wesley. If they are not much like us, we can at least see beneath the surface.

But if Christians trust in Providence, they also read dark words in the Book of Revelation – of times that will sieve believers to the last grain. But Christians also trust with certainty in the one who as Alpha started history and as Omega will end it.

2,000 Years of Christianity

CONTRIBUTORS

Editor and main contributor
Christopher Howse

Consulting contributor
The Very Reverend Trevor Beeson
Dean Emeritus of Winchester

Contributors
Sheridan Gilley
Reader in Theology, University of Durham
Mark Allen
Robert Gray
George Ireland
James Owen
Katharine Ramsay
Bess Twiston-Davies
James Young

Designer
Margaret Donegan
Design adaptation (book)
Sarah Reynolds
Picture research
Suzanne Hodgart
Main Events graphics
Vivian Kent
Maps
Susanna Hickling
Editorial assistant
Nathalie Mohoboob
Production
Roger Williams
Index
Christopher Pipe

𝕿𝖍𝖊 𝕯𝖆𝖎𝖑𝖞 𝕿𝖊𝖑𝖊𝖌𝖗𝖆𝖕𝖍
Creative Director
Clive Crook
Editorial Projects Director
George Darby
Books Publisher
Susannah Charlton

Many of the books listed are out of print, but should be obtainable through libraries. Some have been reissued in new editions.

Chapter One
AD 1-400

Bercot, David W (ed)
A Dictionary of Early Christian Beliefs
(Hendrickson, 1998)

Cholij, Roman
Clerical Celibacy in East and West
(Gracewing, 1988)

Nichols, Aidan
Holy Order
(Veritas, 1990)

Chapter Two
AD 400-800

Augustine of Hippo
The Confessions
(many editions)

Bede
Ecclesiastical History of the English People
(Penguin Classics, 1991)

Boethius
The Consolation of Philosophy
(Penguin, 1969)

Dawson, Christopher
The Making of Europe
(Sheed and Ward, 1932)

Chapter Three
AD 800-1200

Knowles, David
The Evolution of Mediaeval Thought
(Longman, 1962) and
The Monastic Order in England
(Cambridge, 1941)

Runciman, Steven
A *History of the Crusades*
(Cambridge, 3 vols, 1951)

Southern, R W
St Anselm and His Biographer
(Cambridge, 1963)

Chapter Four
AD 1200-1500

Copleston, F C
Aquinas
(Penguin, 1991)

Dante
The Divine Comedy
(Trans Dorothy L Sayers, Penguin, 3 vols, 1962)

Duffy, Eamon
The Stripping of the Altars
(Yale, 1992)

Horrox, Rosemary
The Black Death
(Manchester University Press, 1994)

Julian of Norwich
Revelations of Divine Love
(Trans Clifton Wolters, Penguin, 1966)

ding

Kempe, Margery
The Book of Margery Kempe
(Trans W Bowdon-Butler,
World's Classics, 1954)

Knowles, David
*The Religious Orders
in England*
(Cambridge, 3 vols, 1959)

Lewis, C S
The Discarded Image
(Cambridge, 1994)

Pope-Hennessy, John
Fra Angelico
(Phaidon, 2nd edition, 1974)

Ridolfi, Roberto
*The Life of Girolamo
Savonarola*
(1959)

Southern, R W
*The Making of the
Middle Ages*
(Hutchinson, 1953)

Tugwell, Simon
St Dominic
(Editions du Signe, 1995)

Chapter Five
AD 1500-1800

Ackroyd, Peter
Thomas More
(Chatto & Windus, 1998)

Andrewes, Lancelot
Preces Privatae
(Trans J H Newman, in
Prayers and Devotions,
Ignatius 1989)

Boswell, James
Life of Johnson
(many editions)

Bunyan, John
*Grace Abounding to the
Chief of Sinners*
(Penguin, 1987)
Pilgrim's Progress
(Oxford Paperbacks, 1998)

Fox, George
The Journal
(Penguin Classics, 1998)

Gerard, John
Autobiography
(Trans Philip Caraman,
Longmans Green, 1951)

Herbert, George
Poems
(many editions)

Kamen, Henry
Philip of Spain
(Yale, 1997)

Knox, Ronald
Enthusiasm
(Oxford, 1950)

Law, William
A Serious Call
(Westminster, John Knox
Press, 1968)

Taylor, Jeremy
Holy Living and Holy Dying
(Clarendon Press, 1989)

Teresa of Avila
*The Life of Teresa of Avila
by Herself*
(*Collected Works*, trans
K Kavanaugh and
O Rodriguez, Institute of
Carmelite Studies, 1985)

Wesley, John
Journals
(Epworth Press, 1938)

Woodforde, James
Diary of a Country Parson
(The Canterbury Press,
Norwich, 1999))

Chapter Six
AD 1800-2000

Booth, William
*In Darkest England and
the Way Out*
(Patterson Smith, 1997)

Chadwick, Owen
The Victorian Church
(A&C Black, 2 vols, 1970)

Fothergill, Brian
Wiseman
(Faber, 1963)

Gilley, Sheridan
Newman and His Age
(Darton, Longman and
Todd, 1990)

Ker, Ian
Newman, A Biography
(Oxford, 1988)

Newman, John Henry
Apologia
(Penguin Classics, 1994)

Nichols, Aidan
*Catholic Thought Since
the Enlightenment*
(Gracewing, 1998)

Thompson, Damian
The End of Time
(Vintage, 1999)

General

Attwater, Donald, and
John, Catherine Rachel, (eds)
*The Penguin Dictionary
of Saints*
(Penguin, 1995)

Betjeman, John
English Parish Churches
(Collins, 1958)

Duffy, Eamon,
*Saints and Sinners: A History
of the Popes*
(Yale, 1997)

Jenkins, Simon
Bible Mapbook
(Lion, 1985)

Robinson, John Martin
*Treasures of English
Churches*
(Sinclair Stevenson, 1995)

Thorold, Henry
*Cathedrals, Abbeys
and Priories of England
and Wales*
(Collins, 1986)

Watkin, David
*A History of Western
Architecture*
(Barrie and Jenkins, 1986)

2,000 Years of Christianity

Index

A

Aachen 67

abbots, in medieval Irish Christianity 57; in Benedictine Rule 63-4

Abelard, Peter (1079-1142) 100

Adelard of Bath (12th century) 75

Aelfric (c955-1020) 70

Affre, Denis Auguste (Archbishop of Paris, died 1848) 164-5

Aix-la-Chapelle 67

agape 22, 24, 177

Alaric (c370-410) 46-47

Albigensianism 95, 98-9

Alcuin (c737-804) 68

Alexander II (Pope, reigned 1061-73) 74

Alexander VI (Pope, reigned 1492-1503) 125

Alexandria 23, 42

Alphege (died 1012) 79

Alfred (King, reigned 871-99) 64-5

Ambrose (c340-97) 38-39

anathema 44

Andrewes, Lancelot (1555-1626) 138

Angelico, Fra (artist, c1387-1455) 28-9, 99, 125

angels 53

Anno Domini 16

Anselm (1033-1109) 72-3

Anskar, Apostle of the North (801-65) 82

Anthemius of Tralles (6th century) 50-1

Anthony of Egypt (c250-c356) 34

anti-clericalism in Spain 165

Antioch in Syria 13, 15

B

antipopes 85, 112-3

Apostles 10, 24

Aquinas, Thomas (1225-74) 53, 100-1

architecture *see* church architecture

Arianism 28-9, 35, 48, 62

Aristotle (384-322BC) 23, 75, 100

Athanasius (295-373) 35, 148

Athens 14

Athos, Mount 147

Attila the Hun (reigned 434-453) 47

Augsburg, Council of (1077) 85

Augustine of Canterbury (?-604) 58-9

Augustine of Hippo (354-430) 31, 36-9; and *The City of God* 46; compared with Boethius 49; on music 94

Authorised Version (1611) 41, 134-5

Autun Cathedral 92-3

Averroes (1126-98) 100

Avicenna (980-1037) 74-5, 100-1

Avignon, Popes at 112-3

Axum 148

Bach, Johann Sebastian (1685-1750) 153

Bakker, Jim 182

baptism 22, 26; of Constantine 32; of Clovis 54

Barnabas (1st century) 13, 15

Barnardo, J T (1845-1905) 165

Bartolomeo, Fra (artist, 1472-1517) 125

Basle, Council of (1431-49) 113

C

Becket, Thomas (1118-70) 90-1

Bede (c673-735) 60

Bellini, Giovanni (artist, c1430-1516) 40-1

Benedict of Nursia (c480-c547) 63-4

Benedictines 63-4; in England 71

Berea 14

Bernard of Clairvaux (1090-1153) 87, 95

Bernadette (1844-79) 180

Bible translation 40-1, 112, 128, 134-5

bishops 28-9; Augustine as model 38; Bede's instructions for 60

Bishops' Bible (1568) 135

Bithynia 15, 18

Black Death 110-1

Boethius (475-525) 48-9, 53, 104

Bonhoeffer, Dietrich (1906-45) 170

Boniface (c675-754) 61

books of devotion 115, 138-9

Booth, William (1829-1912) 165

Boris I (King of Bulgaria, reigned 852-889) 84

Borromeo, Charles (1538-84) 142

Botticelli, Sandro (1444-1510) 125

Bradford 160-1

Branch Davidians 184

Bucer, Martin (1491-1551) 130

Bulgaria 78, 84

Bunyan, John (1628-88) 151

Bury St Edmunds 70, 131

Butler, Joseph (1692-1752) 153, 154, 158

Byrd, William (1543-1623) 139

Byzantium *see* Constantinople

Calvin, John (1509-64) 129

Campio, San 178-9

Canterbury, wall painting 13; becomes Augustine's base 58-9; Cathedral 104-5

Canute (King of England, reigned 1017-35) 79-80, 82

Carmelites, and Teresa of Avila 142-3

Carpaccio, Vittore (artist, c1460-c1525) 36-7

Cassino, Monte 63, 101

Castle Acre 130-1

Catherine of Siena (c1347-80) 112-3

Catholic Apostolic Church 177

Catholic Emancipation 164

Celestine I (Pope, reigned 422-432) 44

Celestine V (Pope, reigned 1294-96) 104

Cerularius, Michael (Patriarch of Constantinople 1043-85)

Chalcedon, Council of (451) 47

Challoner, Richard (1691-1781) 152

chant 94

charismatic revival 178

charitable orders 114

Charlemagne (King of the Franks, reigned 768-814) 66-8

Chi-Rho monogram 4, 24, 52

Christ, meaning of the word 10

Christ in Majesty 10-11

Christian Socialist movement 166

Chrysostom *see* John Chrysostom

church architecture, Byzantine

Remigius (died 533) 54-5
Ricci, Matteo (1552-1610) 146
ritualism 161
Robertson, Pat (1930-)182
Roger of Hauteville (King of Sicily, reigned 1072-1101) 88-9
Roger II (King of Sicily, reigned 1130-1154) 88-9
Rome, and Jerusalem 16; St Peter's basilica 17, 66, 67, 172-3; and persecution under Nero 18; and Constantinople 42, 84-5; sacked (410) 46-7; and Ostrogoths 48-9; captured by Henry IV 85; recognised by Clement III (1188) 85
Roman Catholic Church, and mission to England (5th-6th centuries) 58-9; and Church of England 136, 140, 152, 156-8; and Ethiopian church 148
Ross, William (artist, 19th century) 157
Rublev, Andrei (artist, c1360s-c1430) 147
Russia 78, 147; Stalinist persecutions 168

S

sacraments 29; validity 31; see also baptism, Eucharist
sacrifice, certificates of 20; of Melchizedek 23
St Gall monastery plan 64-5
St George in the East, and anti-ritualist riots 161
saints, devotion to 118-19; relics of 108-9
saints' days 25
Saladin (c1137-93) 87
Salvation Army 165-6
Sandemanians 177
Saracens 85
Savonarola, Girolamo (1452-98) 124-5
Scandinavia 82
schools see education
Scotland, and John Knox 135

Shaxton, Nicholas (1485-1556) 108
shepherd, symbolising Christ 26
Sicily 88-9
social work 114
Society of Jesus see Jesuits
Soviet Union 168-9, 176-7
Spain before the Moors 62; medieval period 74-5; under the "Catholic Kings" 122-3; and Latin America 144-5; and 19th-century anti-clericalism 165; Civil War 165
Stalin, Joseph (1879-1953) 168-9
statistics, of church membership 8, 180; of Russian church 168; of United States churches 183
Stead, W T (1849-1912) 165
Stephen (deacon and 1st-century martyr) 17
Stephen (King of Hungary, 975-1038) 78
stigmata 96-7
Sunday, recognised by Constantine 32; enforced by Canute 80
Sunday Schools 153, 161
Sverker (King of Sweden, reigned 1130-55) 82
Swaggart, Jimmy (1935-)182
Sweden 82

T

Tacitus (55-117) 18
Tallis, Thomas (1505-85) 139
Tarsus 12
Taylor, Jeremy (1613-67) 139
tele-evangelists 182
Temple, of Jerusalem 16
Teresa of Avila (1515-82) 142-3
Teresa of Calcutta (1910-97) 174-5
Tertullian (c160-230) 20, 27
Theodosius II (Emperor, 401-50) 44
Theophilus (Archbishop of Alexandria, died 412) 42
Thessalonica 14

Thomas of Celano (died 1255) 94
Thomas Aquinas see Aquinas, Thomas
Thomas Becket see Becket, Thomas
Tibet 146
tithes 80
Toledo 744-5
Tong near Bradford 152
tongues 177-8
Torquemada, Tomas de (1420-98) 123
Tractarians 156
Trajan (Emperor, reigned 98-117) 18
Trent, Council of (1545-53) 140-2
Troas 15
Tyndale, Walter Frederick Roofe (artist, 19th century) 162-3
Tyndale, William (c1492-1536) 134-5

United States of America: Great Awakening 154-5; religious phenomena in 20th century 182-3
Urban II (Pope, reigned 1088-99) 89

Valentinian III (Emperor, reigned 425-55) 47
Valerian (Emperor, reigned 253-60) 20
Vandals 39, 47, 53
van der Weyden, Rogier (artist, 1399-1464) 120-1
Vatican Council (1st, 1870) 158
Vatican Council (2nd, 1962-5) 172-3
Venner, Thomas (died 1661) 184
vestments, of deacons 17, 18
Visigoths 62
Vladimir (Prince of Rus, reigned 980-1015) 78
votive offerings 179
Vulgate Bible 41

Walesa, Lech (1943-) 176
Wesley, Charles (1707-88) 161-2
Wesley, John (1703-91) 154
Westcott, B F (1825-1901) 166
Westminster, Archbishopric of 164
Westminster Abbey 9, 80, 136
Westminster Directory 135, 150
Whitby 57; Synod of (664) 59
Whitefield, George (1714-1770) 155
William of Flete 112, 121
William of Ockham (1285-1349) 100
William of Tyre (1130-85) 87
Winchester, and Alfred 69; Synod of (970) 71
Wiseman, Nicholas (1802-65) 164
women role of 120-1; and Jerome 40; typified as Eve 92, as Virgin Mary 116, 117; exemplified by Catherine of Siena 112, by Teresa of Avila 142
Woodforde, James (1740-1803) 152
Worms, Diet of (1521) 129
Wulfstan (c1008-95) 80
Wyclif, John (1330-84) 112

Xavier, Francis (1506-52) 146
Ximenes de Cisneros, Francisco (1436-1517) 74, 123

York, origins of Archbishopric 59; education 68

Zosimus (Pope, reigned 417-9) 47